NEW DIRECTIONS FOR YOUTH DEVELOPMENT

winter 2004

Professional Development for Youth Workers

Pam Garza
Lynne M. Borden
Kirk A. Astroth

issue editors

JOSSEY-BASS
A Wiley Imprint
www.josseybass.com

PROFESSIONAL DEVELOPMENT FOR YOUTH WORKERS
Pam Garza, Lynne M. Borden, Kirk A. Astroth (eds.)
New Directions for Youth Development, No. 104, Winter 2004
Gil G. Noam, Editor-in-Chief

Microfilm copies of issues and articles are available in 16mm and 35mm, as well as microfiche in 105mm, through University Microfilms Inc., 300 North Zeeb Road, Ann Arbor, Michigan 48106-1346.

NEW DIRECTIONS FOR YOUTH DEVELOPMENT (ISSN 1533-8916, electronic ISSN 1537-5781) is part of The Jossey-Bass Psychology Series and is published quarterly by Wiley Subscription Services, Inc., A Wiley company, at Jossey-Bass, 989 Market Street, San Francisco, California 94103-1741. POSTMASTER: Send address changes to New Directions for Youth Development, Jossey-Bass, 989 Market Street, San Francisco, California 94103-1741.

SUBSCRIPTIONS cost $80.00 for individuals and $170.00 for institutions, agencies, and libraries. Prices subject to change. Refer to the order form at the back of this issue.

EDITORIAL CORRESPONDENCE should be sent to the Editor-in-Chief, Dr. Gil G. Noam, Harvard Graduate School of Education, Larsen Hall 601, Appian Way, Cambridge, MA 02138 or McLean Hospital, 115 Mill Street, Belmont, MA 02478.

Cover photograph © Getty Images.

www.josseybass.com

Contents

1. Professional development in the youth development field:
   Issues, trends, opportunities, and challenges   *13*
   Jane Quinn

   This chapter sets the context for the rest of the volume and provides a brief
   history of professional development in the youth development field.

2. Getting down to business: Defining competencies for entry-level
   youth workers   *25*
   Kirk A. Astroth, Pam Garza, Barbara Taylor

   The authors describe the National Collaboration for Youth's development
   and endorsement of front-line worker competencies and discuss implications for the field.

3. Achieve Boston: A citywide innovation in professional
   development   *39*
   Moacir Barbosa, Ellen S. Gannett, Jude Goldman,
   Samantha Wechsler, Gil G. Noam

   The authors explain how this citywide initiative has been able to coordinate
   intermediaries and training opportunities for youth workers.

4. The intermediary role in youth worker professional
   development: Successes and challenges   *51*
   Elaine Johnson, Fran Rothstein, Jennifer Gajdosik

   The chapter explores the role of youth development training intermediaries
   and their successes and challenges in providing high-quality services.

5. Professional development in national organizations: Insights
   from Girls Incorporated   *65*
   Heather Johnston Nicholson, Susan Houchin, Brenda Stegall

   Girls Incorporated takes a comprehensive approach to professional development for youth development workers.

Issue Editors' Notes

> Youth development is what you'd do for your own kid
> on your best day.
>
> —Hugh Price, president and CEO, National
> Urban League

EDITING A JOURNAL on the professional development of youth workers begs a fundamental series of questions: Is youth development a *profession?* Is it a distinct *field of study*, or in academic terms, a *discipline?* What constitutes a profession? Using Ernest Greenwood's work[1] as their guide, Andrew Hahn, associate dean and professor at Brandeis University, and Gordon Raley, former executive director of the National Collaboration for Youth, discussed the characteristics that distinguish a profession from a nonprofession:

- A profession develops a body of systematic theory that informs its practice.
- A profession develops practitioners who have specialized, unique knowledge and expertise that elevate them over mere dilettantes.
- A profession offers training centers and accreditation, curriculum, admissions, and licensing systems that regulate and control who can be a member of the profession.
- A profession develops a code of ethical conduct that governs professional behavior.
- A profession develops a culture that is promoted and sustained in institutional settings, educational and research centers, and through professional associations.[2]

NEW DIRECTIONS FOR YOUTH DEVELOPMENT, NO. 104, WINTER 2004 © WILEY PERIODICALS, INC.

Youth development has often been perceived as a "fugitive discipline"—scattered among several departments at universities and hard to identify. This is changing (for the better) as the chapters in this issue make clear. The need for a consistent articulation of youth work that is grounded in theory and held to high standards of quality is evident. Professional development is one path along the road to professionalization and the formation of a field.

Our field can best be understood by understanding the role of the youth development professional, which is to enhance the positive development of young people. Youth development professionals are most effective at doing this when all systems, including learning opportunities, policies, and organizations, are informed by basic and applied scholarship derived from sustained collaborations among scholars, practitioners, and communities.[3]

Researchers, practitioners, and others have emphasized that caring adults are necessary for a young person's positive development. Caring adults can be found in families, communities, schools, faith-based organizations, and youth development programs across the nation. Thus, youth workers can be key adults in the lives of young people. Considering the importance of the caring adult's role, professional development opportunities for youth workers should be designed to build their skills and increase their efficacy. A variety of learning opportunities must be available and affordable if they are to ensure that young people have the necessary opportunities and supports.

Since the early 1990s, the youth development field in general and concerned funders specifically have directed more time and resources (as Jane Quinn points out in her chapter) to the professional development of youth development workers. There has been wide recognition that a trained and capable staff is essential in youth development programs, but youth workers' choices remain limited. This volume is designed to present a snapshot of key professional development opportunities available to youth workers in the United States. It is not meant to be a comprehensive study, but rather to describe high-quality examples where systematic, intentional youth worker development is being offered in individual cities or states or nationwide.

In Chapter One, Jane Quinn provides an overview of the history and progress that has been made in professional development in the youth development field over the last few decades, and the lessons learned. The chapter outlines some of the significant investments made in building capacity both nationally and locally. There is much to celebrate, but important work remains to be done. Quinn suggests, for example, that effective professional development involves more than training; it is a legitimate, necessary, and essential cost of doing business; it is inclusive and available at all levels of the organization; and it builds on the emerging consensus on essential knowledge and core competencies of youth work practice.

The next two chapters focus on efforts in the city of Boston and across the nation to formulate necessary competencies and construct the infrastructure that youth workers need to succeed. In Chapter Two, Kirk Astroth, Pam Garza, and Barbara Taylor explain why consistent standards and agreed-upon competencies are needed to move the field forward. In Chapter Three, Moacir Barbosa, Ellen Gannett, Jude Goldman, Samantha Wechsler, and Gil Noam, collaborators in the Achieve Boston initiative, describe their efforts to help youth workers gain the respect, recognition, compensation, and opportunities they deserve. Both chapters describe the process and make further recommendations.

Chapters Four and Five discuss national intermediaries and how they work with local organizations to enhance the capabilities of staff members in thousands of youth-serving agencies across the nation. In Chapter Four, Elaine Johnson, Fran Rothstein, and Jennifer Gajdosik describe the National Training Institute for Community Youth Work. They also shares the lessons learned from this effort to provide training and technical assistance to state and local intermediaries that work across organizational lines to prepare youth workers. In Chapter Five, Heather Johnston Nicholson, Susan Houchin, and Brenda Stegall provide a case study of Girls Incorporated, a national youth-serving organization. Like many national organizations, this one offers its local boards, executives, and staff the training they need to provide high-quality youth development.

In Chapter Six, Lynne Borden, Deborah Craig, and Francisco Villarruel explore the opportunities currently offered youth workers to gain higher education credit in college and university settings. Focusing on two case studies—one at the junior college level and one an online master's or certificate program—this chapter describes some innovative approaches to expanding the professional development opportunities for all youth workers, no matter how little free time they have or where they live.

In Chapter Seven, Karen Pittman explains how youth work is structured in Great Britain, offering this as a model for an enhanced professional development infrastructure in the United States.

The authors included in this volume share a commitment to young people and the people who work with and for them. To create high-quality professional development opportunities for youth workers, we need to take several key steps:

- Use well-researched materials.
- Work collaboratively with those who work with and for youth.
- Engage and support youth development professionals in their work.
- Identify the systems and structures needed to prepare, develop, and retain these individuals.

These chapters present a snapshot of some of the work occurring at this time, but they also reveal the evolution of the youth development field. The field is growing, and efforts to enhance professional development are strengthening our capacity to do better work. The information contained in this volume may be used to further develop and build a comprehensive system that can meet the needs of both youth workers and the young people they come into contact with each day.

Notes

1. Greenwood, E. (1957). Attributes of a profession. *Social Work, 2*(3), 44–55.
2. Hahn, A. B., & Raley, G. A. (1998). Youth development: On the path toward professionalization. *Nonprofit Management and Leadership, 8*(4), 387–401.

3. Lerner, R. M., & Hertzog, S. M. (Summer, 2004). *Creating a community youth development profession: From vision to instantiation.* (Concept paper). Boston: Tufts University; Jacobs, F., Wertlieb, D., & Lerner, R. M. (Eds.). (2003). Enhancing the life chances of youth and families: Public service systems and public policy perspectives. In R. M. Lerner, F. Jacobs, & D. Wertlieb (Eds.), *Handbook of applied developmental science: Vol. 2. Promoting positive child, adolescent, and family development through research, policies, and programs.* Thousand Oaks, CA: Sage.

Pam Garza
Lynne M. Borden
Kirk A. Astroth
Editors

PAM GARZA *is director of the National Youth Development Learning Network at National Human Services Assembly/National Collaboration for Youth. She has been in the youth development field for twenty-six years.*

LYNNE M. BORDEN *is an associate professor and extension specialist in family studies and human development at the University of Arizona.*

KIRK A. ASTROTH *is director of the 4-H Center for Youth Development at Montana State University-Bozeman and past president of the National Association of Extension 4-H Agents.*

Executive Summary

Chapter One: Professional development in the youth development field: Issues, trends, opportunities, and challenges

Jane Quinn

The youth development field has made significant progress over the past fifteen years in clarifying the knowledge and skills that are central to effective youth work practice. Once considered "nice but not necessary," professional development is now generally regarded as a necessary cost of doing business. Building on early efforts such as the National Youth Worker Education Project, funded by the Lilly Endowment some three decades ago, private foundations have provided important leadership as well as financial support that has contributed to progress at both the national and local levels. These investments have revolved around three strategies: (1) a national strategy that has enabled twenty-one national organizations to build their professional development systems and to create new models; (2) a local strategy through which fourteen intermediary organizations have provided professional development for youth workers in their areas; and (3) a field-building strategy that has supported cross-cutting studies, concept papers, and clearinghouses. Based on these and other efforts, several important points have been made: professional development involves more than training; professional development is a legitimate, essential cost of doing business; an effective system of professional development occurs at multiple levels; and

NEW DIRECTIONS FOR YOUTH DEVELOPMENT, NO. 104, WINTER 2004 © WILEY PERIODICALS, INC.

an effective system of professional development builds on the emerging consensus on the essential knowledge and core competencies of youth work practice.

Chapter Two: Getting down to business: Defining competencies for entry-level youth workers

Kirk A. Astroth, Pam Garza, Barbara Taylor

An organization's ability to make a difference in the lives of young people depends on the quality of its staff. Those working in the field of youth development require knowledge, skills, and personal attributes that will allow them to create positive youth development settings. Recently, the National Collaboration for Youth attempted to define core competencies needed by entry-level youth workers. A set of commonly agreed-upon competencies can guide youth development organizations in staff recruitment, staff assessment, and design of professional development plans and training. It can also help ensure portability of skills between organizations and influence higher education curriculum design in youth development. This chapter describes how this set of competencies was developed, gives examples of how the competencies have influenced youth development organizations, and makes recommendations and outlines the opportunities that still lie ahead.

Chapter Three: Achieve Boston: A citywide innovation in professional development

Moacir Barbosa, Ellen S. Gannett, Jude Goldman, Samantha Wechsler, Gil G. Noam

Achieve Boston is a collaborative effort to create a professional development infrastructure for those who work with young people ages five to twenty-two during the out-of-school-time hours.

According to Achieve Boston, a professional development infrastructure has five key components: a list of core competencies;
coordinated, accessible training opportunities; a system to ensure
the quality of training; a registry for documenting practitioners'
professional accomplishments; and a career lattice or pathway that
links professional roles, competencies, and salary ranges. This
chapter chronicles the story of Achieve Boston, beginning with a
broad vision for change; a two-year planning, consensus-building,
and pilot phase; and its current status as it begins its three- to five-
year plan for implementation. The chapter also describes Achieve
Boston's next steps and underlines the importance of collaboration
in creating a system that will fundamentally change the way higher
education, the community, and intermediaries support out-of-
school-time workers, and consequently, radically improve the
opportunities and services available for young people and their
communities.

*Chapter Four: The intermediary role in youth worker
professional development: Successes and challenges*

Elaine Johnson, Fran Rothstein, Jennifer Gajdosik

Since it began seven years ago, the BEST network has grown to
include twenty-three local and three regional systems of youth
worker professional development. Using a nationally recognized
curriculum, Advancing Youth Development, as the starting point,
BEST has built a comprehensive professional development system
that has trained more than nine thousand local youth development
workers and 130 training facilitators and provided consultation to
youth-serving agencies. As youth development workers and their
organizations identified the need for additional professional development products and services, NTI responded by creating new
resources or disseminating locally developed products and strategies through the intermediary network. Providing a case study of
the successes, challenges, and lessons learned by this national

intermediary, this chapter addresses the basic concerns of most youth development organizations and networks.

Chapter Five: *Professional development in national organizations: Insights from Girls Incorporated*

Heather Johnston Nicholson, Susan Houchin, Brenda Stegall

The fundamental skills of the youth workers and their dedication to youth development are similar from one national organization to the next, yet each professional development system takes on the values and character of the particular organization. The volunteers and paid staff who work at the thousands of local agencies affiliated with a national youth organization are often able to tap into its education and support system to increase their knowledge and skills. This chapter offers a case study of the large-scale and comprehensive professional development efforts of one national organization: Girls Incorporated.

Chapter Six: *Professionalizing youth development: The role of higher education*

Lynne M. Borden, Deborah L. Craig, Francisco A. Villarruel

The increasing number and diversity of those in the youth development field who are seeking advanced educational opportunities has motivated higher education institutions to offer a variety of programs to meet their demands. Formal coursework for youth workers is now available that is relevant, useful, and designed to meet the needs of both front-line workers and the managers and directors of youth development programs. Courses can be taken to gain certificates, credentials, or advanced degrees. However, although the availability of educational opportunities in higher education has increased, there are still many challenges. This chapter assesses the educational opportunities now available to youth workers and focuses specifically on two case studies: a community college degree that uses the Advancing Youth Development Curriculum as its core coursework and the Great Plains Initiative, an online master's and certificate degree program offered by collaborating colleges and universities.

Chapter Seven: Reflections on the road not (yet) taken: How a centralized public strategy can help youth work focus on youth

Karen J. Pittman

Public systems designed to serve children and youth in the United States continue to fall short in delivering equitable supports to all youth. As a result, there is a growing need for enhanced professional development that can improve supports available to our young people and their families. Advocates should consider the field-building efforts of the United Kingdom in particular. In 2002, the British government established the National Occupational Standards for Youth Work to reaffirm the level of public support required to facilitate youth-centered policies that promote learning, social development, youth engagement, and civic responsibility. This chapter explores how the definition of *youth work* in the United Kingdom goes far beyond traditional assumptions of program provision to embody a core set of values, leveraged interactions, diversity in services, comprehensive training, and appropriate qualifications to ensure that youth workers and youth-serving organizations provide an exceptional level of service to every young person who uses and depends on them. By examining characteristics that make the British system successful, we can better assess our potential in the United States.

This chapter reviews key issues in professional development in the youth development field, describing important work done over the past two decades and lessons learned from major philanthropic investments in capacity building both nationally and locally.

1

Professional development in the youth development field: Issues, trends, opportunities, and challenges

Jane Quinn

MY ENTRY INTO THE YOUTH WORK FIELD over three decades ago was launched by a graduate school course on the psychopathology of adolescence. In fact, I had wanted to deepen my understanding of *normal* adolescent development, but no such course was offered.

In many ways, this snapshot from my career encapsulates the history of youth work. It is a field that has moved from a sole focus on the treatment of youth problems to their prevention, and more recently, the promotion of normal, healthy development. Concurrent with this trend to a more comprehensive approach to youth services (one that serves a continuum from promotion to prevention to short- and long-term treatment) has been the growth of professional development strategies that prepare and support workers in the "shallow end" of the services continuum—that is, in their role as youth development specialists.

NEW DIRECTIONS FOR YOUTH DEVELOPMENT, NO. 104, WINTER 2004 © WILEY PERIODICALS, INC.

This chapter provides an overview of the main issues involved in professional development in the youth development field today and examines accomplishments and challenges from a national perspective, while also discussing local practice that exemplifies many of the principles of best practice in youth development.

A brief history

Professional development efforts have existed for several decades in the youth development field, especially among national youth organizations that have paid significant attention to training for youth work executives and to program support, such as handbooks and short training courses, for volunteers.

Early efforts had limited scope

For example, when I became the national program director at Girls Clubs of America (now Girls Incorporated) in 1981, I learned that this organization conducted a well-established weeklong management seminar for new club executives each year. Similarly, I learned that several other youth-serving agencies provided support for new and more seasoned leaders, and organizations such as the Scouts, Camp Fire, and 4-H had a long tradition of providing guidance and support to their volunteer troop and group leaders.

As worthy as these early efforts were, several levels of these organizations were all but ignored in the professional development offerings, and much of the guidance and support for volunteer leaders had a limited focus. For example, these programs suggested an array of possible activities for use in group meetings but offered little or no guidance on developmental stages of youth, group work techniques, or how to deal with behavioral issues.

A landmark initiative

Professional development among national youth organizations took a giant leap forward in the mid-1970s when the Lilly Endowment made a multiyear grant to support the National Youthworker Education Project. Under the leadership of professor Gisela Konopka at the University of Minnesota, this initiative linked theory to practice in a meaningful way by offering a rigorous and extended course of study to carefully selected emerging leaders in the youth work field. The ten-day course included classes on such varied topics as "adolescenthood" (youth development), cultural diversity, adolescent sexuality, special challenges of youth in the juvenile justice system, working with youth in crisis situations, and program planning. A follow-up evaluation by researcher Judith Erickson indicated that the project was successful on several fronts, particularly in creating a cohort of youth work leaders in several national organizations who stayed in the field and made significant contributions to their respective (and other) organizations.[1] Despite this positive evaluation, professional development in youth organizations garnered precious little foundation interest or support for at least a decade, until the DeWitt Wallace-Reader's Digest Fund (now named the Wallace Foundation) made a multiyear investment of $55 million at both national and local levels.

Recent accomplishments

Over the past ten to fifteen years, as the field of youth development has matured and come into its own, professional development programs have proliferated, along with an increased consensus about the competencies needed for effective youth work practice. Other chapters in this volume will explore the competency issues in depth, and will describe specific national and local delivery systems. My purpose here is to offer a brief overview of several key accomplishments and to outline a set of findings on principles of best practice that have emerged from these initiatives.

The $55-million-dollar question

Early in my nine-year tenure as national program director at Girls Clubs of America, I observed that most of our professional development work focused on local club directors. Although I understood the rationale for this approach, I grew increasingly worried about the obvious gaps in these professional development offerings, particularly at the direct service and program development levels. Whenever I raised this need with potential funders, I would find the conversation shifting quickly to "And what are your other priorities?" It was clear to me that the professional development of program staff, including front-line workers, was simply too basic, too bedrock, too unsexy to generate philanthropic interest. Or so I thought, until I met Donna Dunlop, who served as program director of the DeWitt Wallace-Reader's Digest Fund from 1987 to 1992. In what might be best characterized as a wide-ranging discussion (by now I knew to come into such meetings with my list of categorical program priorities), Donna listened carefully and then asked me a question that no foundation staffer had ever posed: "What is the single greatest need your organization is facing right now?" Without hesitation, I replied that we needed to create an ongoing professional development system for the program staff at our local clubs. Instead of changing the subject as I expected her to do, Donna responded that she had heard similar thoughts from other youth organization executives and that she was open to pursuing the idea. Under her leadership (and later, mine and Pam Stevens'), the Wallace fund invested $55 million in professional development at youth organizations over a ten-year period. Three strategies drove these investments: (1) a national strategy, through which twenty-one national youth organizations[2] received grants to build their professional development infrastructure and systems and to create new approaches targeted at multiple levels, including direct service workers, program directors, and board members; (2) a local strategy through which fourteen local intermediary organizations[3] provided professional development to youth workers in their areas, revolving around the Advancing Youth Development youth work training curriculum[4] and coordinated by the National Training Institute of the Academy for Educational Development (see Chapter Four for additional information); and (3) a field-building strategy through which cross-cutting studies (for example, on youth worker hiring and compensation patterns), concept papers, and clearinghouses resulted.[5]

In 1995, the Wallace fund commissioned an external analysis of these investments, conducted by the Chapin Hall Center for Children.[6] The following year, the fund itself published a monograph based on this and its own assessment of its investments.[7] This report concluded that there had been many positive outcomes:

These grants strengthened individual youth-serving organizations by allowing them to concentrate resources on the professional development of their workers; they also strengthened the field of youth work by providing intermediary organizations [the] funding necessary to begin developing a theoretical framework to support youth work as a distinct profession. This commitment has been pivotal to the advancement of the field and has made the fund a leader in this effort.[8]

An emerging consensus

Concurrent with this expansion of national and citywide professional development initiatives, a consensus is emerging in our field on several critical issues, including that we need basic definitions of youth development, an underlying research base, and agreement on essential competencies for youth work practice. For example, Karen Pittman and Michele Cahill made important conceptual contributions through a set of papers and monographs that outlined basic definitions in the field.[9] The Carnegie Council on Adolescent Development drew on this work and added substantially to it by commissioning twelve papers on various aspects of youth work practice, convening two national meetings on key youth work topics (evaluation and professional development), and publishing and widely disseminating a book-length report on American youth organizations.[10] Subsequently, the National Research Council established a definitive research base for the youth development field.[11] During these fifteen years of progress, another contribution came from the Youth Development Institute of the Fund for the City of New York, which convened experienced youth workers over a multiyear period to define the core competencies of effective youth work practice. The resulting document[12] has influenced the youth development field in many ways both in New York City and nationally—for example, informing the content of the Advancing Youth Development curriculum and the National Collaboration for Youth's youth workers competency project (described in Chapter Two of this volume). The sidebar shown here outlines these competencies.

Working together with experienced youth work staff from nine of New York City's leading youth development organizations, the Youth Development Institute of the Fund for the City of New York created a publication entitled *Core Competencies for Youth Work*. This consensus document outlines the following knowledge and skills as essential to effective youth work practice:

Program Development
- Knowledge of youth development framework
- Knowledge of agency mission
- Knowledge of organizational policies and procedures in regard to youth
- Knowledge of adolescent developmental stages
- Ability to foster youth empowerment

Communication
- Ability to develop and maintain a relationship of trust with young people
- Ability to convey information so it is received in the manner intended
- Ability to communicate effectively (including ability to convey and interpret information in dominant language and in language of the community)

Program Implementation
- Knowledge of group work
- Ability to facilitate groups
- Knowledge of planning activities
- Ability to plan and implement activities
- Ability to motivate and engage young people
- Ability to recognize and respond to youth needs and interests

Advocacy-Networking
- Knowledge of youth rights (for all youth, regardless of legal status)
- Ability to network with a variety of external systems

- Knowledge of school and career options
- Knowledge of social context of youth

Assessment
- Ability to reflect on one's practice and performance
- Ability to organize and manage workload

Community and Family Engagement
- Ability to understand and respect culture of youth and families
- Knowledge of community, especially in regard to youth and family
- Knowledge of family structures

Intervention
- Ability to recognize need for intervention
- Ability to deal with conflicts
- Knowledge of intervention strategies

The state of our art: Lessons learned and principles of best practice

A clear set of lessons and principles emerges from these multiple efforts of the past fifteen years:

- Professional development involves more than training.
- The cost of professional development is legitimate, necessary, and essential to doing business.
- An effective system of professional development encompasses multiple levels, including administration and program levels; board members and staff members; paid and unpaid workers (volunteers).
- An effective system of professional development builds on the emerging consensus on essential knowledge and core competencies of youth work practice

Professional development involves more than training

Although training is certainly an essential component of it, an effective system of professional development pays attention to a much broader set of issues, including recruitment, hiring, orientation, supervision, coaching, and assessment—in addition to pre- and in-service training. Our experience at the Children's Aid Society in New York City can serve to illustrate this point. We have made significant progress over the past several years in effecting such a system through several concrete steps:

- Hiring a director of human resources who has a graduate degree and considerable experience in the human resource field
- Offering regularly scheduled orientations that introduce new staff to the history, mission, and culture of our organization (supplemented by departmental orientations)
- Offering daylong training workshops for all direct service workers in our afterschool programs on a biannual basis (and paying part-time staff for their participation in these events)
- Centralizing our employee recruitment functions through Internet postings and job banks
- Instituting an agency-wide performance management system
- Offering on-site observation and coaching directed toward program improvement

This system is far from perfect and is never complete but the elements currently in place represent solid cornerstones of deliberate agency-wide efforts and investment—which leads to the next point.

The cost of professional development is legitimate and necessary

In my view, our field has come a long way in recognizing the necessity and value of investing in professional development. Fortunately, this recognition on the part of practitioners is increasingly supported by funders. For example, in our own practice in New York City, the After-School Corporation (TASC; an intermediary organization founded and funded by philanthropist George Soros) encourages its grantees to include a line item for professional development in their proposals and annually publishes a catalogue of professional development trainings that

TASC sites can purchase in order to strengthen their programs. (See also issue 94 of *New Directions for Youth Development*, Gil G. Noam and Beth M. Miller, eds.)

Effective professional development occurs at multiple levels

It is becoming the rule, rather than the exception, that youth development organizations offer a variety of professional development opportunities geared to the multiple levels of their work— development of board leadership around policy setting and fundraising, development of staff leadership around management and administration, and development of program staff around program planning, delivery, assessment, and continuous improvement. Many organizations take account of the fact that their program staff consist of two very important groups: permanent, full-time staff (such as program directors), and part-time, often seasonal, group leaders who constitute some or all of their direct service staff. Many have experimented with innovative approaches to developing part-time staff, including online courses and train-the-trainer courses that are often combined with content-specific program curricula and other user-friendly materials.

Effective professional development builds on the emerging consensus on knowledge and core competencies

Although it is probably true that some in the youth work field continue to "reinvent the wheel" because of their isolation from the growing knowledge bases and networks, more and more organizations are following the emerging consensus on what youth workers need to know and be able to do. Clear statements from such groups as the National Research Council, Forum for Youth Investment, Chapin Hall Center for Children, Academy for Educational Development, National Collaboration for Youth, and Youth Development Institute represent both a consensus and a set of guidelines for busy practitioners. Building on models like 4-H and the National Youth Worker Education Project, our field is beginning to embrace models of professional development that link institutions of higher education to youth work practice (see Chapter Six in this volume).

The road ahead

The road ahead surely holds both bumps and smooth spots, challenges and opportunities. Key among the challenges are ongoing issues of high staff turnover (particularly at the direct service level) and funding uncertainties brought about by budget deficits at the state and federal levels and fluctuations in the stock market and broader economy. These macroeconomic issues, of course, affect youth development organizations in all areas, not just professional development. In my view, the opportunities outweigh the challenges, however daunting they may appear at the moment. Consider how far we have come in just fifteen short years. Remember, for example, that youth development language has found its way into important federal and state legislation. Recall too that a substantial portion of the $1 billion in 21st Century Community Learning Centers funds is designated for training and technical assistance. And do not forget that the Younger Americans Act, if passed, will help to build additional professional development infrastructure in the youth development field.[13] Finally, the introduction of the Federal Youth Coordination Act in June 2004 signals that the importance of professional development will only increase. This legislation, if eventually signed into law, will seek to bring greater accountability for outcomes in the youth development field. Professional development will play a key role in helping federally funded programs meet these accountability standards.

To make a reality check, I contacted my graduate school to see if it had caught up with the times. Had the youth development messages permeated the walls of academia? The answer was a resounding *yes*—three of six separate courses on working with adolescents were now focused on promotion of healthy adolescent development. Even a pessimist would have to admit that we have come a long way and that the landscape ahead is looking fairly sunny.

Notes

1. Erickson, J. B. (1986). *A follow-up study of the national youthworker education project, 1975–1980.* St. Paul: Center for Youth Development and Research, University of Minnesota.

2. These groups included the Academy for Educational Development (Center for Youth Development and Policy Research/National Training Institute for Community Youth Work), Big Brothers/Big Sisters of America, Boy Scouts of America, Boys and Girls Clubs of America, Camp Fire Boys and Girls, Center for Population Options (now Advocates for Youth), Child Welfare League of America, Congress of National Black Churches, Girl Scouts of the USA, Girls Incorporated, Jewish Community Centers of North America, Junior Achievement, Inc., Milton S. Eisenhower Foundation, National 4-H Council, the National Network of Runaway and Youth Services (now National Network for Youth), Search Institute, United Neighborhood Houses, WAVE, Inc., YMCA of the USA, and YWCA of the USA.

3. These groups included a wide variety of local intermediaries, such as YouthNet in Kansas City (Missouri), the Pinellas County (Florida) Juvenile Welfare Board, the Youth Development Institute of the Fund for the City of New York, and Community Network for Youth Development in San Francisco. See Chapters Four and Five for additional information about these organizations and their work funded under this initiative.

4. Center for Youth Development and Policy Research/National Training Institute for Community Youth Work. (1996). *Advancing youth development: A curriculum for training youth workers.* Washington, DC: Academy for Educational Development.

5. One of several examples of this funding was the establishment of a Youth Development Information System, a national clearinghouse created by the National Collaboration for Youth (National Assembly). This organization also received a grant to conduct a youth worker compensation study.

6. Ogletree, R., Garg, S., Robb, S., & Brown, P. (1995). *Strategic analysis of the DeWitt Wallace-Reader's Digest Fund's grantmaking in support of the recruitment and development of youth workers.* Chicago: Chapin Hall Center for Children at the University of Chicago.

7. DeWitt Wallace-Reader's Digest Fund. (1996). *Strengthening the youth work profession: An analysis of and lessons learned from grantmaking by the DeWitt Wallace-Reader's Digest Fund.* New York: DeWitt Wallace-Reader's Digest Fund.

8. DeWitt Wallace-Reader's Digest Fund, p. 12.

9. Pittman, K. J., & Cahill, M. (1991). *A new vision: Promoting youth development.* Washington, DC: Academy for Education Development.

10. Carnegie Corporation of New York. (1992). *A matter of time: Risk and opportunity in the nonschool hours.* New York: Carnegie Council on Adolescent Development.

11. Eccles, J., & Appleton Gootman, J. (Eds.). (2002). *Community programs to promote youth development.* Washington, DC: National Research Council, 2002.

12. Pitts, L. (n.d.). *Core competencies for youth work.* New York: Networks for Youth Development, Youth Development Institute, Fund for the City of New York.

13. The Younger Americans Act was introduced as proposed federal legislation in 2001. Known as H.R. 17 in the House of Representatives, the bill has seventy-nine cosponsors. Its stated purpose is "to provide assistance to mobilize and support United States communities in carrying out youth

development programs that assure that all youth have access to programs and services that build the competencies and character development needed to fully prepare the youth to become adults and effective citizens." On the Senate side, the bill is called S. 1005 and has nine cosponsors.

JANE QUINN *is assistant executive director of the Children's Aid Society in New York City.*

In January 2004, the National Collaboration for Youth approved a list of core competencies needed by entry-level youth development workers for effective youth development practice. This chapter provides an overview of these competencies, explaining why and how the list was created, outcomes, and recommendations for next steps.

2

Getting down to business: Defining competencies for entry-level youth workers

Kirk A. Astroth, Pam Garza, Barbara Taylor

Through its extensive experience in the field, the Casey Foundation has found that a stable, prepared, and motivated human services workforce yields real reform and better results for children and families.
—Annie E. Casey Foundation, Human Services Workforce Initiative

OVER THE PAST DECADE, those involved in education have concluded what many parents have known all along: a caring adult can have a profound impact on a young person's life.[1] Evidence in formal education shows that teacher quality "accounts for the lion's share of variance in student scores."[2] Yet at the same time, there is little consensus around what makes for a high-quality teacher.[3]

NEW DIRECTIONS FOR YOUTH DEVELOPMENT, NO. 104, WINTER 2004 © WILEY PERIODICALS, INC.

Some see teaching as a complex endeavor that requires professionals with formal, guided, and specialized training. Others view it as simple, routine work that any reasonably intelligent person can do. According to this view, specialized training is not needed and "street sense" is more valuable.[4]

Those working in youth development are split along the same philosophical divide. There is agreement that staff characteristics are critical to high-quality youth development, but there is no consensus around what those characteristics are or how a youth worker should best acquire them. There is little research showing the connection between professionally trained youth workers and positive youth outcomes. Even the National Research Council report *Community Programs to Promote Youth Development* is notable in its omission of such a discussion.[5] The report focuses on features of positive youth development settings, although various characteristics of staff—such as their ability to provide supportive relationships, meaningful roles, and physical and psychological safety—are discussed.

The debate over appropriate preparation and training for youth workers has also recently surfaced in the media, most notably in the pages of *Youth Today*.[6] Although some advocate professionalizing the field of youth development through college education, others argue just as vehemently for experience-based training and preparation. According to some, there is tension in the field between those who have proven experience on the front lines of youth development but meager educational credentials and those who have a degree but little practical field experience. As Pam Stevens, former program officer for the Wallace Foundation, observed, "There is a feeling that if one prevails over the other, creativity will be lost."[7]

Nonetheless, the field of youth development seems to be moving toward a more formal level of professionalism requiring some educational credentials. Organizations like the Metropolitan Milwaukee YMCA have found a correlation between degreed workers and reduced turnover—professional staff turnover is down by 2 percent. Still, others wonder if a higher retention rate of 2 percent is worth the higher cost for degreed workers. An organization's ability to make a difference in a young person's life ultimately depends on the people in that organization. Regardless of the programs and services offered, competent, trusted staff is essential to nurturing positive life outcomes. In fact, the three main reasons for the failure of youth organizations are the absence of a leader, lack of commitment, and lack of leader support.[8] Success often depends on dedicated, skilled, and creative people—people who can manage and implement high-quality programs—to lead organizations.[9] Whether paid or unpaid, leadership "is consistently named as a central issue, perhaps the central issue, in strengthening programs for adolescents."[10] As an evolving profession, the youth development field needs to define and describe the core competencies necessary for staff that lead to positive outcomes for young people.

So what exactly are competencies? In the youth development profession they are the knowledge, skills, and personal attributes workers need to create and support positive youth development settings. Core competencies are the "demonstrated capacities" that form a foundation for high-quality performance in the workplace, contribute to the mission of the organization, and allow youth development workers to be resources for young people, organizations, and communities.

Early efforts to define youth development competencies

In the early 1990s, the Center for Youth Development and Policy Research/National Training Institute for Community Youth Work at the Academy for Educational Development (the center) began work on the Stronger Staff, Stronger Youth project. This project was designed to identify and help implement strategies to strengthen youth worker staff development opportunities and build the field of youth development. The center worked with twenty-five national youth-serving organizations to gain an understanding of their staff development efforts. The National Network for Youth conducted extensive interviews and surveys with over five hundred youth workers and held discussions to determine the staff development needs of the field. Based on this work, the center developed a listing of youth worker core competencies that could be used to develop recruitment, retention, training, supervision, and compensation strategies.[11]

This work was based on several assumptions:

- Core competencies can provide a concrete way to distinguish youth development workers from the many other persons who provide service to young people.
- Core competencies can provide a framework for designing staff development strategies, including training, supervision, and personnel evaluation.
- Core competencies can provide a framework for designing performance and credentialing standards for youth development workers.

The center and others have continued to develop and provide professional development to youth workers across the nation. For example, the Youth Development Practitioner Apprenticeship program (YDPA) funded by the U.S. Department of Labor, targets entry-level youth workers. Participants attend training, workshops, and college courses and get on-the-job training based on YDPA-defined core competencies. The YDPA's core competencies were developed using feedback from professionals in the youth development field.

In spite of all of the activity on developing a commonly accepted set of core competencies, none as yet permeates the field. There is fragmentation, even among the largest youth-serving organizations. To capitalize on the last decade of work, a greater attempt needs to be made to provide a more consistent set of core competencies in youth development. This kind of consistency will lead to a recognized field of study with an agreed-upon knowledge base and ensure high-quality interactions between youth development staff and young people. Although many organizations are already working with a set of competencies, there is a need to simplify the language for front-line staff and to recognize and take advantage of the knowledge of the collective field.

The National Collaboration for Youth begins work

"Many youth workers come to this work with energy and good intentions but little training or knowledge of child and youth development. As a result, staff turnover can be high, as high as 100 percent a year. By establishing . . . baseline competencies, we hope to encourage more youth workers to stay in the field and to advance in it," says Shay Bilcheck, executive director of the Child Welfare League of America and National Collaboration for Youth chair.[12]

In June 2003, the program group of the National Collaboration for Youth (NCY), which is based in Washington, D.C., began exploring ways to support, develop, and professionalize youth workers. After discussing both the need for training and communication networks, career paths and options, and higher education opportunities, the group appointed a task force to review existing youth worker competency guidelines and make recommendations to peers to establish a basic set of guidelines, or expectations, for staff. Included on the task force were representatives from a range of youth development organizations, including Boys and Girls Club of America, Camp Fire USA, 4-H, and the YMCA of the USA.

The NCY task force committed to: (a) developing a set of competencies that could be used and adapted by a variety of organizations; (b) keeping the language and concepts simple so anyone could understand them; (c) adding key indicators to amplify the meaning of each competency; and (d) designing competencies that could serve as starting points. Organizations would be free to add or modify competencies or insert additional indicators to make them agency-specific.

To accomplish these goals, the NCY task force reviewed competencies developed in the early 1990s by the Center for Youth Development and Policy Research/National Training Institute for Community Youth Work that had included input from the survey and interviews conducted by the National Network for Youth. In addition, the task force examined the more contemporary models from the YDPA that had been developed with direct input from front-line workers at both the YMCA and 4-H and the North American Certification Project for Child Care providers. The team also reviewed descriptions of competencies developed by the organizations the NCY represented (for example, the professional and research taxonomy of the National Association of Extension 4-H Agents, Girl Scouts, Boys & Girls Clubs of America).

This comprehensive review of existing listings of competencies provided both a historical perspective—competencies that were developed with input from thousands of youth workers across the nation and used for over a decade—and newer ones developed with front-line workers in mind. Considering the diversity of organizations, missions, and types of positions in organizations, the task force decided there was a need to focus on a common denominator: the front-line youth worker. As a result, the group created a simple set of competencies that entry-level workers, including part-time and full-time staff and volunteers, should possess when they begin a job or should acquire during the first few years to be effective when working with youth.

This list of ten basic competencies for front-line staff and volunteers who work with youth are based on task force members' knowledge and professional experiences, and documents in use throughout the field. Each competency is accompanied by indicators that serve as examples to clarify it and illustrate how it might be assessed. The list is neither comprehensive nor all-inclusive but rather designed to enable each organization, based on its unique membership, mission, and program objectives, to edit them to make them relevant for the youth workers they employ.

The first draft of this list of competencies was sent to NCY members for review and input later in 2003. Members were asked to circulate the draft to national staff and staff at their local affiliates to allow for broad participation. This targeted solicitation of both individuals and organizations was designed to create a stronger, more usable, more acceptable document that could be approved and used across organizational lines.

After several modifications, the NCY approved the list in January 2004 and began the task of disseminating it to organizations and urging implementation.

National Collaboration for Youth: Youth Development Worker Competencies

1. Understands and applies basic child and adolescent development principles.
   - Understands ages and stages of child development.
   - Applies fundamentals of positive youth development.
   - Takes into consideration trends and issues that affect children and youth.
2. Communicates and develops positive relationships with youth.
   - Listens in a nonjudgmental way.
   - Uses the language of respect.
   - Exhibits concern for the well-being of others and interest in the feelings and experiences of others.
3. Adapts, facilitates, and evaluates age-appropriate activities with and for the group.
   - Relates to and engages the group.
   - Initiates, sustains, and nurtures group interactions and relationships through completion of an ongoing project or activity.
   - Teaches and models effective problem solving and conflict negotiation.
   - Guides group behavior in an age-appropriate manner.
4. Respects and honors cultural and human diversity.
   - Exhibits an awareness of commonalities and differences (such as gender, race, age, culture, ethnicity, class, religion, disability) among youth of diverse backgrounds and shows respect for those of different talents, abilities, sexual orientation, and faith.
   - Builds on diversity among and between individuals to strengthen the program community, and the community at large.
   - Serves as a role model for the principles of inclusion and tolerance.
5. Involves and empowers youth.
   - Actively consults and involves youth to encourage them to contribute to programs and to the communities in which they live.
   - Organizes and facilitates youth leadership development activities.
6. Identifies potential risk factors (in a program environment) and takes measures to reduce those risks.
   - Identifies basic risk and protective factors in youth development.
   - Designs and monitors emotionally and physically safe program environments, interactions, and activities for youth and intervenes when safety demands it.

- Identifies potential issues (and possible signs and symptoms) with youth who require intervention or referral (for example, suicidal tendencies, substance abuse, child abuse, violent tendencies, eating disorders, obesity, and sexually transmitted diseases).

7. Cares for, involves, and works with families and community.
   - Understands and cares about youth and their families.
   - Actively engages family members in program and community initiatives.
   - Understands the greater community context in which youth and families live.
   - Communicates effectively with youth and their families—in one-to-one communications as well as in group settings.

8. Works as part of a team and shows professionalism.
   - Articulates a personal "vision" of youth development work (to coworkers, volunteers, and participants) and expresses current and potential contributions to that vision.
   - Adheres to ethical conduct and professionalism at all times (maintaining confidentiality, honoring appropriate boundaries).
   - Acts in a timely, appropriate, and responsible manner.
   - Is accountable, through work in teams and independently, by accepting and delegating responsibility.
   - Displays commitment to the mission of the agency.

9. Demonstrates the attributes and qualities of a positive role model.
   - Models, demonstrates, and teaches positive values, such as caring, honesty, respect, and responsibility.
   - Incorporates wellness practices into personal lifestyle.
   - Practices stress management and stress reduction.

10. Interacts with and relates to youth in ways that support asset building.
   - Challenges and develops values and attitudes of youth in a supportive manner.
   - Designs program activities, structure, and collaborations that show evidence of asset building.

A foundational piece of professional development

"The competencies will be used by agencies in recruitment, job descriptions, interviews, supervision, training, and professional development of youth workers. We identified those elements around which there is wide consensus. The result is a set of competencies that apply to front-line youth workers in almost any setting," says Judith Pickens, senior vice president, Program Services, Boys & Girls Clubs of America, and NCY committee chair.[13]

However, before these lists of youth worker competencies can be widely accepted in the field, directors and administrators must understand how to use them.. There are several ways that they can be used in a program, a community, and the youth development field generally.

- Selection, interviewing. *The list of competencies provides a foundation on which to build interview questions that assess each candidate's existing strengths and competencies and anticipated training needs.*
- Staff assessment. *Assessment tools based on the competency framework tie evaluation back to expectations, training, and on-the-job coaching.*
- Staff development plan. *Once hired, supervisors can assess new employees' competencies and identify their development needs. Staff can craft a targeted development plan that provides specific work experiences, coursework, training, mentoring, and coaching opportunities to increase each employee's competence level.*
- Training. *Curricula based on the competencies can be matched to training objectives to deliver high-quality programs and produce positive outcomes for youth.*
- Staff mobility. *If consistent competencies are recognized across the field, youth workers will have a portability of expertise that has not existed in the past.*
- College and university youth development curricula. *Consensus in the youth development field is useful to higher education as a framework on which to build certificate and degree programs.*

Dissemination and implementation

As already noted, the National Collaboration for Youth has begun circulating the list of competencies throughout the youth development field. They are posted on its Web site at http://www.nydic.org and were published in *Youth Today.* Other organizations have posted them on their own Web sites. There is still much to be done to get as many youth organizations as possible to accept and integrate these guidelines into their work more completely.

There are already some examples of this type of implementation, although, given the potential, they barely scratch the surface:

- The YMCA of the USA has embraced this list of competencies and used them in several ways: It included them in the program design presented to the Department of Labor for the YDPA program. It saw them as impetus for revising its own basic-level training program—*Working with Youth Five to Twelve and Working with Teens Twelve to Seventeen.* And it incorporated them into the revised *Principles of YMCA Youth Work*, a manual designed for all staff working with youth in YMCAs across the country.
- The 4-H Professional Research and Knowledge Base (4-hprk) has been seen as the foundation for competency guidelines in the 4-H youth development profession since it was created in 1985. The national 4-H professional development task force recently conducted a study to update this list of the knowledge, skills, and behaviors that 4-H youth workers need to be effective in working with young people. The NCY's ten competencies identified for entry-level youth workers were a critical and valuable resource, and they were incorporated into the revised version, the 4-H Professional Research, Knowledge, and Competency (4-hprkc 2004) model. Thus, the value of both efforts was reinforced.
- The National Youth Employment Coalition is "cross-walking" the competencies with the work they are doing to identify the knowledge, skills, and attitudes necessary for youth workers doing youth employment work.
- The National Mentoring Partnership has asked to use the competencies as a part of its *Elements of Effective Practice* toolkit that will soon be published.
- The National Youth Sports Corporation requested approval to distribute the list of competencies throughout its network.

To professionalize the field and improve youth development outcomes, dissemination of these competency guidelines is just the beginning. As the ancient Chinese proverb puts its: "A journey of a thousand miles begins with a single step." Next, these competencies must form the basis for recruiting, selecting, training, and assessing youth workers across the entire field, as described in the preceding section.

Eventually, research will also need to be conducted on the relationship between staff possessing these competencies and youth development outcomes.

Recommendations

Although progress has been significant over a year's time and the feedback on the NCY's list of competencies has been positive, there remains much to do to address these issues.

- Continue to work across communities and organizational lines to break down barriers and achieve universal awareness, support, and adoption of the NCY's competencies.
- Continue to explore how youth development organizations and agencies that have already developed or adopted worker competencies of their own might use the new NCY list and integrate it into their own; explore the advantages of using these in place of their current systems; and determine if they might lose something if they chose to switch to the new guidelines.
- Determine what part of overall quality is solely dependent on the competencies of youth workers. Current program evaluations, assessments, and quality measurement tools are often program-specific—that is, they address program environments, program policies, program curricula, program infrastructure, and administrative practices. New research is needed to find out if an effective youth worker in a substandard program can still produce positive outcomes, and if an ineffective youth worker in a high-quality program undermines positive outcomes and to what degree.
- Decide what more might be needed to measure whether a worker has mastered the competencies.

- Develop additional competencies for second- and third-tier youth development professionals—one for program coordinators who have additional responsibility for programming, and another for directors and administrators of youth development agencies and organizations.

Moving forward

Those who work with youth can easily articulate the importance of what they do and the impact they make on the youth they serve. Many feel a sense of pride and believe strongly that they have unique skills that contribute to their effectiveness. To have the greatest impact on the youth of today, all those in the field need to develop specific skills, feel valued for the work they do, and be empowered to grow and develop. They need a vision of what the next job up the career ladder might look like. Outcomes, standards, competencies, worker preparedness, and career advances—these are the opportunities a profession provides.

We still have a great deal of work to do to professionalize the youth development field, but progress is occurring. In just under a year, members of the National Collaboration for Youth have reaffirmed a set of competencies, reached consensus, and disseminated them far and wide in the field. The initial work has been done, but now we must embrace these competencies as a part of our everyday fabric.

Notes

1. Astroth, K. A. (1996, December). Leadership in nonformal youth groups: Does style affect youth outcomes? *Journal of Extension, 34,* 6; Pittman, K. (2002). Community, youth, development: Three goals in search of connection. In J. Terry (Ed.), *CYD Anthology* (pp. 38–42). Sudbury, MA: Institute for Just Communities; Search Institute/America's Promise. (1997). *Five promises for children and youth*. Minneapolis: Search Institute.

2. Berry, B., Hoke, M., & Hirsch, E. (2004, May). The search for highly qualified teachers. *Phi Delta Kappan, 85*(9), 684–689.

3. Archer, J. (2002, April 3). Research: Focusing in on teachers. *Education Week*, pp. 36–39.

4. Cochran-Smith, M., & Fries, M. K. (2001, November). Sticks, stones, and ideology: The discourse of reform in teacher education. *Educational Researcher, 30*(8), 3–13.

5. Eccles, J., & Gootman, J. A. (Eds.). (2002). *Community programs to promote youth development.* Washington, DC: National Academy Press.

6. Alexander, B. (2002, July/August). Agencies say college-educated staff show results. *Youth Today.* Retrieved September 28, 2004, from http://www.youthtoday.org/youthtoday/aaJuly2002/storyone.html.

7. Alexander, B. (2002, May/June). College-linked training spreads, but does it improve youth work? *Youth Today.* Retrieved September 28, 2004, from http://www.youthtoday.org/youthtoday/aaMay2002/storyone.html.

8. Erickson, J. B. (1983). *Directory of American youth organizations.* Boys Town, NE: Father Flanagan's Boys Home, Communications and Public Service; Stephens, W. (1983). *Explanations for failures of youth organizations.* Cited in Scott, D. H., & Reagan, S. (1990). Helping participants complete what they start: Factors affecting 4-H project completion. *Journal of Extension, 28*(3). (ED 228440). Retrieved October 7, 2004, from http://www.joe.org/joe/1990fall/a6.html.

9. Astroth, K. A. (1996). *Welcome to the club: Education where the bell never rings.* Unpublished doctoral dissertation, Montana State University, Bozeman.

10. Hechinger, F. M. (1992). *Fateful choices: Healthy youth for the 21st century* (p. 204). New York: Hill and Wang.

11. *Stronger staff, stronger youth: Conference summary report.* (1993, October 27). Washington, DC: Center for Youth Development and Policy Research/National Training Institute for Community Youth Work.

12. National Collaboration for Youth press release, (2004, March 15).

13. National Collaboration for Youth press release, (2004, March 15).

KIRK A. ASTROTH *is director of the 4-H Center for Youth Development at Montana State University-Bozeman and past president of the National Association of Extension 4-H Agents.*

PAM GARZA *is director of the National Youth Development Learning Network at the National Human Services Assembly/National Collaboration for Youth.*

BARBARA TAYLOR *is senior consultant for program development for the YMCA of the USA.*

Achieve Boston is a broad-based collaborative effort to improve the overall quality of programs for children and youth by establishing a professional development infrastructure that supports those who work with young people during the out-of-school-time hours.

3

Achieve Boston: A citywide innovation in professional development

Moacir Barbosa, Ellen S. Gannett, Jude Goldman, Samantha Wechsler, Gil G. Noam

IMAGINE THAT YOU are an out-of-school-time worker in Boston. Like many others in this field, you started working with youth out-of-school time because, although you were interested in helping children learn, you could not see yourself in a classroom; you were drawn to the more nontraditional setting of an out-of-school program. The first year was especially challenging. You were never sure if you were doing things "right" with the kids, your program constantly struggled with too few resources, and your supervisor was too busy to provide you with much direction. But you developed strong and rewarding relationships with the youth, and through trial and error, discovered what worked well and what did not.

You started your second year on the job with a lot of energy, and having developed more of a rhythm, you felt ready to take some

NEW DIRECTIONS FOR YOUTH DEVELOPMENT, NO. 104, WINTER 2004 © WILEY PERIODICALS, INC.

initiative to participate in professional development workshops. You received information from a variety of organizations about different training programs and conferences, and you went to as many as you could. The topic did not really matter—your decision to attend depended primarily on the location, date, time, and cost. Sometimes the programs were excellent, with relevant, substantive content offered by knowledgeable, dynamic, and skilled trainers who had direct experience in the field. Sometimes they were not useful, but there was no way to tell in advance. Often, they were onetime, two- to three-hour workshops. And usually, you were the only person from your program who was able to find the time to attend; your coworkers had other part-time jobs, and several of them had children of their own, making it difficult for them to attend workshops.

Now approaching the close of your second year, you are frustrated by the low wages and you want health insurance. The training programs you have attended have generally been helpful, and you have been ambitious in trying to apply what you learned on the job. But because the training sessions were not based on an assessment of your professional development needs, because they were so scattershot, and because your coworkers usually did not attend, they have not helped you to make a lasting impact on your program. You also know that this training will not, in any clear and direct way, translate into higher pay for you or more responsibility. You hate the thought of leaving the field, but you are beginning to think about it.

Now imagine this. . . .

Those who work in afterschool and youth work are considered professionals, getting the same respect and recognition as those who work in elementary and secondary education. The courses and degrees specializing in afterschool and youth work are widespread throughout the higher education system. The degree you earn translates into a salary and benefit structure that is commensurate with that of classroom teachers. And a career lattice offers you a wide variety of pathways, roles, and opportunities in any of the converging fields of youth work, afterschool work, and education.

As an out-of-school-time worker, you have opportunities to develop the skills you need to work with elementary-school-age children, adolescents, and young adults in community-based organizations, public schools, residential treatment settings, and municipal agencies such as parks and recreation departments.

Advocates have successfully influenced public policy by making a strong case for sustainable funding for a range of high-quality, out-of-school-time opportunities. Public polls show that the great majority of Americans understand that high-quality afterschool programs make a difference in the development of young people, and that dedicated public funding is not only warranted but also necessary to support the professionals who work in these programs.

This work is considered an attractive career, not just a pass-through option onto another, more lucrative position. The future of the profession holds the promise of a skilled and stable workforce, highly qualified to lead and inspire our young people to become contributing members of their community.

Achieve Boston's achievements to date

Some despair that there is an impossible abyss between the preceding two versions of reality. Yet groups of practitioners, policymakers, and intermediaries have begun to bridge this gap. One such collaboration, Achieve Boston, is creating a path from the former to the latter. As with any journey, its story may best be told in sequence: from its beginning to the place it has reached so far to the road ahead.

Several years ago intermediaries in Boston were challenged to build a continuum of training around a shared set of competencies for those who work with young people ages five to twenty-two during the out-of-school-time hours. After receiving a few small planning grants, local intermediaries teamed up with large youth-serving organizations to develop a process for determining the needs of the workforce, identifying professional development resources, and connecting practitioners. The new team was named

Achieve Boston. An initial review of the research confirmed what these partners already knew: that the out-of-school-time workforce faced myriad challenges, including low wages, few or no benefits, and limited opportunities for professional development. Not surprisingly, the turnover among these workers was high; in this city, it ran up to 49 percent.[1]

Few organizations could provide access to outside professional development for their staff because of time and fiscal constraints; furthermore, information about training was not easily accessible and the training that was available did not for the most part lead to long-term program improvement or individual career advancement.

The Achieve Boston collaborative engaged various constituencies to gain input about training topics, accessibility, challenges, and system development. Focus groups included direct service program staff, school administrators, parents, children, youth, and program directors. Input, particularly from practitioners, helped shape its early ideas for a comprehensive training system:

- It would provide a one-stop shop for training information.
- It would develop one set of competencies for the entire field.
- It would gain support to overcome fiscal and organizational barriers.

The collaborative also saw clearly that a comprehensive professional development infrastructure was needed to support a diverse workforce. According to national research, a well-coordinated professional development infrastructure includes the following key components:

- Core competencies or a core knowledge base
- A system of widely accessible professional development opportunities
- A system to ensure the quality of professional development opportunities

- A registry for tracking and documenting one's professional accomplishments
- A career lattice connecting professional roles, competencies, and salary ranges

Building on earlier work by other organizations, Achieve Boston integrated the core competencies for two traditionally separate fields—afterschool and youth work—to create a set of eleven competency areas that are important to both. They are as follows:

1. Activities, curriculum, and programming
2. Guidance; building caring relationships
3. Child and youth development
4. Safety, health, and nutrition
5. Cultural competence
6. Environment
7. Families, communities, and schools
8. Professionalism
9. Program management
10. Workers as community resources
11. Building leadership and advocacy

Next, a scan of training providers captured the available professional development opportunities. Sixty-four training providers, whose training topics were consistent with one or more of the eleven competency areas, submitted information about their offerings. Achieve Boston then published those offerings, organized by the eleven competency areas, in its *Catalogue of Professional Development Opportunities.*[2] A self-assessment, to help practitioners determine their professional development needs, was included in the catalogue, as well as a set of guiding questions to facilitate reflection and conversation about career development. Achieve Boston also launched a Web site—http://www.achieveboston.org—where people could go for current information on training and other opportunities.

Meanwhile, the collaborative added the support for access that is crucial to the success of the system. Initially, 84 practitioners were selected to receive six $50 scholarship vouchers each to be used with any opportunities listed on the Web site or in the catalogue. By the following year, more than 230 practitioners had been selected.

To inform the creation of a professional development system for out-of-school-time workers, Achieve Boston's managing partners[3] held the first Summit on Building a Citywide Professional Development Infrastructure in the summer of 2003. The summit was attended by local, state, and national program and policy leaders who were creating unique partnerships between child- and youth-serving organizations to build professional development systems in other cities, states, or nationally. There were presentations from six other cities so that everyone could share best practices and lessons learned around the country.

Generous contributions from multiple funders[4] acknowledged the benefits of collaborative work: partnerships form across formerly segmented parts of the field and the willingness to work together makes a big difference in an initiative. The Achieve Boston collaborative grew to include a higher education institution and an organization with connections to state-level professional development work. And its impact began to be felt in many corners.

Achieve Boston convened working groups to develop recommendations for establishing the infrastructure components, brought together training providers to discuss how to work together and to sequence training more efficiently, and reached out to those practitioners who had received the $50 vouchers and others with updates, reminders, and a monthly calendar of professional development opportunities. Meanwhile, the managing partners continued to meet as a team to address broader issues of positioning and sustainability.

Input from various constituencies, including focus groups, individual interviews, agency and program meetings, and a practitioner forum, resulted in a comprehensive set of recommendations for establishing a full-fledged professional development infrastructure titled *A Blueprint for a Professional Development System.*

Key elements of success

Clarity of vision, belief in the possibilities, and a willingness to work toward a goal collaboratively have been at the heart of this effort. In reflecting on the work completed to date, Achieve Boston has identified four key elements of its success, divided into four phases. These may be useful for others in their efforts to create professional development systems.

Partner toward a common goal

Achieve Boston brought together a diverse set of organizations and institutions with often competing self-interests, and successfully moved beyond the boundaries that usually limit efforts to develop comprehensive professional development programs. In Boston, known nationally for the competitiveness of its organizations, institutions, and neighborhoods (Boston has been described as having organizational "fiefdoms"), this is no small feat. In Achieve Boston's case, the mayor was a champion of the effort from the beginning, helping significantly to propel it forward. The goal of the partners has been not to divide resources and operate separately, but rather to work together to create an infrastructure of training that will benefit all out-of-school-time workers, afterschool programs, and children themselves. A collaborative process that builds trust and encourages creative problem solving has been crucial to developing and accomplishing a larger vision for the field.

Commit to building on existing work and assets and to inclusiveness

Achieve Boston has demonstrated its commitment to building on existing assets. It began its work by looking at core competencies that had already been developed, then conducting an inventory of existing training resources that it could bring together into one framework. Achieve Boston also has worked to involve a diverse range of youth-serving agencies and encouraged shared leadership. The partners have engaged various constituencies and stakeholders at different times and in different ways. People have been brought together for focus groups, working meetings, advisory sessions, orientations, and feedback and evaluation meetings—not simply to give the impression of an inclusive process but authentically to inform and drive the work. As a result, Achieve Boston has earned broad-based respect and support.

Create tangible, useful products

Even during its planning phase, Achieve Boston created tangible products, including its Web site, its catalogue of professional development opportunities, and the national summit it hosted. Tangible products show that something has been achieved with the work and money invested, encourage feedback (and involvement) from stakeholders, and help create a public identity or "brand" for the effort.

Lay out a specific, long-range plan for accomplishing goals

Achieve Boston's long-range plan, the blueprint, is a comprehensive document with very specific recommendations for developing an infrastructure. It has been billed as a "living, breathing document" that requires continuous input from stakeholders. Implementing the ambitious goals of the blueprint will ultimately depend on successful coalition building and resource development.

Where does it go from here?

A great deal has been accomplished, yet a tremendous amount remains to be done to achieve the vision that Achieve Boston has articulated. Over the next three to five years, it will complete the system components, including the following:

- A joint set of core competencies and indicators for the after-school and youth work fields
- A training system that includes a recognized "youth development associate" credential
- A training and trainer approval system that ensures that professional development opportunities are of the highest quality
- A professional registry that allows all out-of-school-time professionals to track their skills, experience, training, and movement along their career path
- A career lattice or pathway that links knowledge, experience, skills, and recommended levels of compensation, promoting competence, career advancement, and retention

This is a unique and comprehensive system that will work for the benefit of all out-of-school-time professionals in Boston, and ultimately for all of its children, youth, and families. Reaching out beyond the city's limits, Achieve Boston is integrally connected to state efforts; it has worked to ensure that city initiatives and state initiatives are aligned and complementary, recognizing that some components of the system (such as the competencies, the registry, and the lattice) must be developed and implemented at the state level to be effective for a mobile workforce. It is also connected to national work; a key objective of Achieve Boston is to develop a national youth development associate credential that will be piloted in Boston.

Lessons learned

Every group has to develop its own meaningful approach to professional development in the youth worker and afterschool fields. Collaborative efforts have reached different maturity levels and the leadership can be quite diverse across the country, but there are some generalized themes that emerge from Achieve Boston's experience.

Private-public collaborations

Professional development and training require private and public collaborations because the creation of a system is expensive and time consuming. This collaboration is primarily between government and not-for-profit youth-serving organizations, although there is certainly a place for for-profit companies.

A focus on funding and sustainability

Any effort to create an infrastructure needs funding from the beginning. The effort is very time-intensive, and assigned staff as well as a full-time or half-time coordinator are needed to complete the work.

Incorporation of existing training

Cataloguing all existing training programs and offering stipends (the vouchers) are essential to ensuring that people can access the training.

Engagement of higher education and development of training pathways

An underutilized yet essential resource in every city is its higher education community. Colleges and universities usually offer courses on child and adolescent development, education, nonprofit management, and so on. They can also develop credit-bearing training courses and pathways of training that lead to certification or even degrees. Achieve Boston has begun to convene the higher education community in the area and to define training needs and career pathways for practitioners in different roles.

Connecting city with statewide work

Any city effort needs to build in collaboration with the state in which it is located. This work needs to be managed carefully, because cities have their own local needs and organization. Who is in charge of which aspects of professional development? Is it a collaboration, a division of labor, or the creation of separate systems? Achieve Boston has found it useful to include a statewide organization—the Massachusetts School-Age Coalition—as a member to avoid duplication and share knowledge, infrastructure, and funding.

Achieve Boston has been and will continue to be committed to engaging and maintaining strong involvement by a broad range of stakeholders. The Achieve Boston partners involve those who will be directly affected by the creation and implementation of a professional development system. Through numerous focus groups, advisory and working group meetings, presentations, and phone surveys, Achieve Boston has involved a diverse range of youth-serving agencies from a variety of programs and practitioners concerned with youth and the staff who serve them. This is an enormous undertaking that requires the commitment of the whole field.

When Achieve Boston realizes its vision, what will be different for that second-year staff member described in the opening paragraphs of this chapter? Achieve Boston is creating and supporting a workforce that is well trained, credentialed, and has clearly articulated and broad career options. Second-year staffers will be able to continue to do the work they love and create a stable and progressive career serving children, youth, families, and the community.

Notes

1. *Boston EQUIP school-age survey.* (2001). Boston: Associated Day Care Services.

2. *Catalogue of Professional Development Opportunities, 2003–2004.* (2003, March). Boston: Achieve Boston. Achieve Boston did not use restrictive criteria to determine whether a training program or provider would be included in the catalogue; training needed to be consistent with one or more of the competency areas and training topics, and it needed to be offered in Boston. The group made this decision because it did not feel that it was "authorized" or prepared to judge the quality of training curricula or training providers. The training approval system, for which Achieve Boston has developed recommendations, will, when established, serve that purpose.

3. Achieve Boston's managing partners include Boston 2:00-to-6:00 After-School Initiative; BEST Initiative/the Medical Foundation; Boys & Girls Clubs of Boston; Massachusetts School-Age Coalition; the National Institute on Out-of-School Time; Parents United for Child Care; Program in After-school Education and Research, Harvard University School of Education; YMCA of Greater Boston.

4. Achieve Boston's funders include the Barr Foundation; Boston 2:00-to-6:00 After-School Initiative, formerly of Boston Centers for Youth & Families; the Boston Foundation; the Charles Stewart Mott Foundation; Harvard University; Massachusetts 2020; Massachusetts Department of Education; Robert Wood Johnson Foundation; U.S. Department of Education; Verizon.

MOACIR BARBOSA *is assistant director of training and capacity building and project coordinator of Boston's BEST Initiative at the Medical Foundation, a partner in Achieve Boston.*

ELLEN S. GANNETT *is codirector of the National Institute on Out-of-School Time at the Center for Research on Women at Wellesley College.*

JUDE GOLDMAN *is executive director of the Massachusetts School-Age Coalition, a managing partner of Achieve Boston and a leader in statewide work.*

SAMANTHA WECHSLER *is acting director of the Boston 2:00-to-6:00 After-School Initiative, which was established by Mayor Thomas M. Menino in 1998.*

GIL G. NOAM *is a clinical and developmental psychologist and a professor at Harvard University and McLean Hospital. He is director of the Program in Afterschool Education and Research at Harvard University.*

This chapter examines the role of a national net-work of local and regional intermediary organiza-tions in initiating and sustaining community-based youth worker professional development systems. This approach is instructive for other intermedi-aries in establishing training standards, assessing impact, providing organizational supports for youth development workers, and going to scale.

4

The intermediary role in youth worker professional development: Successes and challenges

Elaine Johnson, Fran Rothstein, Jennifer Gajdosik

IN LESS THAN A DECADE, intermediary organizations have trans-formed youth worker professional development in many places across the nation, with the result being a national network of local, community-based systems of training and support for youth devel-opment workers. Working collaboratively, national and local inter-mediary organizations have supported local capacity to deliver high-quality training and have begun to institutionalize youth worker professional development as a core element of an effective youth-serving sector.

What is an intermediary organization? It is a staffed organiza-tion that promotes and sustains a professional development system

NEW DIRECTIONS FOR YOUTH DEVELOPMENT, NO. 104, WINTER 2004 © WILEY PERIODICALS, INC.

that (a) connects youth development workers and youth-serving agencies to community-based training and technical assistance resources; (b) advances youth development workers' skills and competencies; (c) embeds youth development principles and practices in the day-to-day operations of youth-serving agencies; and (d) enhances the status of youth work as a recognized and valued profession.[1]

The National Training Institute for Community Youth Work (NTI) is a national intermediary organization leading an effort to promote youth worker professional development. In 1997, NTI launched a national collaboration known as the BEST network (*B*uilding *E*xemplary *S*ystems for *T*raining Youth Workers), with start-up funding from the DeWitt-Wallace Reader's Digest Fund (now the Wallace Foundation). BEST was one of the first national efforts to build local systems of training, education, and certification for youth development workers. As the national intermediary and program manager for the BEST network, NTI supported and built capacity in a group of seven carefully selected local intermediary organizations, forming a nucleus that now supports a total of twenty-three local and three regional systems of youth worker professional development.

NTI performs all its functions with two goals in mind. First, it *builds the capacity of local intermediaries* to offer systems of training, education, and professional development for youth workers and youth-serving organizations. Second, in partnership with its affiliated local and regional intermediaries, it *builds the knowledge base of the youth development field* by documenting and disseminating processes, strategies, and innovations, and by sharing lessons learned locally, across sites, and in national policy arenas.

As this intermediary-led community-based system of youth worker professional development evolved, several objectives became paramount: developing standards for training programs and for trainers (including core knowledge, common language, and concepts), assessing the impact of the training on youth development workers, creating additional supports for workers (beyond just the training), and growing the strategy to scale by expanding to new communities.

Not surprisingly, NTI's work in addressing these objectives is inextricably linked with the work undertaken by the local intermediary organizations that make up the BEST network. The local organizations share a commitment to promote youth development principles, deliver training, and collaborate with community leaders—including executives of youth-serving organizations, youth development workers, higher education institutions, and funding organizations from the public and private sectors—in order to institutionalize a community-based, cross-agency, professional development system for youth workers.

The national intermediary's role

National intermediaries connect local intermediaries to one another and enhance their capacity to do their work. Local intermediaries connect individuals, organizations, and resources in their own communities.

Both the national and local organizations must carry out the four functions of an effective intermediary—that is, convening leadership, brokering and providing services, ensuring quality and impact, and promoting policies to sustain effective practices—but in different contexts. NTI does it on a national basis as follows.

Convening leadership

NTI assembles leaders from the local BEST intermediaries to share their experiences, innovations, and challenges. These gatherings also provide forums for collective thinking to advance the work nationally and locally. In addition to executives and trainers, conference attendees have occasionally included partners such as community college leaders, United Way executives, and foundation staff, as well as innovators from higher education, national youth-serving organizations, and federal and state agencies. Virtual convening opportunities have included conference calls, listserv discussions, the NTI Web site, and the e-newsletter *The Connector.*

Brokering and providing services

NTI provides ongoing technical assistance services (on-site as well as by phone and e-mail) at both the staff and the community stakeholder levels, facilitates peer technical assistance meetings for sites facing similar challenges, and arranges consultations with experienced local intermediary staff for new site staff. Equally important, NTI has raised funds from national foundations and federal agencies (for local intermediary subgrants as well as for national research and evaluation) and opened doors to local funding opportunities. These efforts have yielded results ranging from local partnerships with higher education to local site participation in national research and demonstration initiatives, such as the U.S. Department of Labor's Youth Development Practitioner Apprenticeship (YDPA) program.

Ensuring quality and impact

National intermediaries ensure the quality and impact of local youth worker professional development systems by undertaking national evaluations, local performance reviews, national facilitator trainings, and new product development. For example, NTI contracted with the Academy for Educational Development's Center for School and Community Services to determine the impact of BEST professional development on those workers, the impact on local youth-serving organizations involved in local BEST systems, and the BEST initiative's overall successes and barriers to implementation and sustainability.[2] NTI also examined the status and potential of partnerships between youth worker professional development systems and higher education institutions.[3] These studies helped identify promising and effective practices and set directions for subsequent work of both the national and the local intermediaries, thus improving youth work practice as well as strengthening the institutional relationships that surround the work.

Promoting policies to sustain effective practices

National intermediaries contribute to policy development. As a nationally recognized innovator in establishing sustainable youth worker professional development systems, NTI seeks opportunities to share the knowledge gained through the national BEST initiative with numerous policy groups and participates in forums as an advocate for policies that support effective professional development. Through its dual involvement as a national grantee and a partner in the national YDPA clearinghouse, NTI integrated policy recommendations from BEST into the YDPA program.

The local intermediary's role

Local intermediaries "operate in a position between the youth-serving organizations they assist and a body of knowledge, skills, contacts, and other resources. They take a deliberate position as brokers and facilitators, functioning both as representatives and agents of change."[4] National intermediaries work with local intermediaries to help them acquire the knowledge, skills, contacts, and other resources they need to do this work.

This means that local intermediaries organize, promote, sustain, and maintain the quality of local youth worker professional development systems. They work directly with youth-serving organizations to increase the numbers of young people they serve and to improve the quality of service. Each local intermediary offers an array of training programs and opportunities for youth development workers and youth-serving organizations, helping to define youth outcomes, identifying best practices, setting standards for staff competencies, and arranging for delivery of the professional development services that will expand knowledge and use of youth development principles and practices. They "provide training directly, enter alliances with colleges and local training organizations to create training opportunities, and refer youth organizations to existing sources of training and technical assistance."[5] Significantly, especially in advancing the youth work field locally, they broker relationships among youth-serving sectors (for example, community-based youth-serving organizations, schools, libraries, social service agencies, juvenile justice departments) and work across agencies to coalesce, unify, and raise the profile of the youth work field.

The national intermediary's role in new product development

At the heart of any professional development system is a decision about the core knowledge that must be mastered. BEST sites use as their core training the Advancing Youth Development (AYD) curriculum.[6] This foundational training for youth development practice was produced through a partnership between the Academy for Educational Development and the National Network for Youth, with funding from the U.S. Department of Justice. It introduces youth development workers to youth development concepts, principles, and practices.

Although decisions about curriculum content and delivery are critical, youth worker professional development involves more than curriculum. The national evaluation of BEST showed that youth development workers benefit most when they have networks for peer learning, opportunities to discuss their new knowledge in their organizational context, and ongoing supervisory relationships that support BEST practices.[7] Local intermediaries provide this kind of support in different ways. For example, BEST sites have convened AYD graduates for "booster" sessions, retreats, brown bag workshops, and citywide conferences. In addition to reinforcing what youth development workers learn from AYD, these gatherings provide forums for determining unmet professional development needs.

From identifying the need for new professional resources and conceptualizing content for training products to pilot-testing new training programs and providing feedback on draft materials, local BEST intermediaries have been instrumental in creating new products. For example, in response to local demand, NTI collaborated with the New Haven BEST site to develop a supervisors' training course: *Supervising Youth Development Practice: A Curriculum for Training Supervisors of Youth Workers.* This fifteen-hour course balances the supervisor's need to understand youth development concepts and to master specific strategies for supervising youth development practice. It introduces principles and practices of youth development as well as BEST practices in supervising youth development work. It directly supports youth development workers by improving supervision and encouraging supervisors to promote youth development policies in their organizations.

The local intermediary's role in capacity building

Training is only one part of a comprehensive professional development system. Despite its national acclaim, AYD is no more than a training curriculum. However, in the hands of a capable intermediary that can connect youth development workers and their employers to an array of professional development resources, AYD can become the foundation for a sustainable local or regional delivery system for youth worker professional development.

The national evaluation of the BEST network[8] found that local intermediary organizations helped youth-serving organizations to strengthen the system of support available to their workers in three ways:

- They provided increased supports for professional development (for example, mentoring, training, release time for youth development workers to attend conferences and workshops).
- They collaborated more and fostered more networking within the youth-serving sector.

- They increased their commitment to youth development, including aligning their policies and practices to support the youth development approach.

These changes resulted directly from capacity building undertaken by local intermediaries, and they directly reinforced the long-term impact of training. The lesson here is that neither youth worker training nor organizational change alone is sufficient to improve youth development practice. Both must occur on an ongoing basis.

Certain initial capacity-building activities were necessary to lay the groundwork for a sustainable professional development system. Intermediary organizations had to ensure buy-in and participation at all levels through a coordinated marketing campaign, targeting a broad cross section of youth-serving organizations, youth development workers, and other stakeholders (particularly agency executives, supervisors, and potential funders). They had to establish a training track record by delivering the full curriculum to youth development workers and documenting the results. Convening youth development workers enabled intermediaries to reinforce mastery of the curriculum, create peer networks, and solicit youth development workers' input. By launching these initial activities, local intermediary organizations were able to increase the capacity of the youth-serving sector to adopt a common language and a common approach to working with youth, create leadership opportunities for youth development workers and youth to help build the system, and forge interagency partnerships to sustain the system.

Accomplishments to date

The national BEST network has achieved valuable outcomes for the youth development field.

Expanded professional development outside urban communities

Establishing professional development systems in new communities is essential for building a national system of youth worker professional development that is grounded in a set of core beliefs and practices and accessible to independent community-based youth-serving organizations. To increase the number and diversity of communities engaged in BEST, NTI created a new regional delivery system (RDS). With funding from the Ewing J. Kaufmann Foundation, it provided technical assistance and seed grants to launch three regional BEST intermediaries in Philadelphia, Kansas City, and Hampton–Newport News, Virginia. NTI provided technical assistance to support the selection of communities in each region, establish the training delivery system, convene community leaders, and conduct facilitator training programs. These regional BEST intermediaries have established BEST programs in thirteen new smaller and less urban communities, with the capacity to train over one thousand youth development workers and supervisors annually.

Established standards for BEST trainers and training programs

Few trainers have experience in facilitating a training program that relies on their own knowledge of and experience in implementing best practices in youth development. Recruiting sufficient numbers of skilled trainers was a great challenge at BEST sites—not surprising since this training was new to the field. Evaluation of the first year of AYD training found that graduates gave high marks to training that was delivered by experienced youth development workers who could connect concepts to practice. In addition, they appreciated training processes that acknowledged the diversity of learning styles. Based on these findings, NTI established standards for AYD facilitators that describe the knowledge and experience they need to be accepted into its national facilitators training program. NTI also developed training program standards to ensure that the materials and training logistics support an optimal learning environment for participants.

Assessed the impact of the training on participants

To market the training, gain stakeholder support, and secure long-term funding, NTI had to demonstrate that AYD improved youth development workers' practice, and by extension, youth outcomes. Although more research is needed, NTI learned from pre- and posttraining surveys that 75 percent of AYD graduates found that the training helped them increase youth involvement in program development and shift from an adult-centered orientation to a youth-centered perspective. Supervisors of AYD graduates reported that the training helped youth development workers value activities that contribute to youth outcomes.

Provided additional organizational supports for youth development workers

Youth development workers alone cannot transform their organizations. Although most AYD graduates gain new knowledge and practices from their training, more than half reported that they were unable to implement these practices in their programs. In response to a need for increased organizational support, NTI developed the supervisory training program and the YDPA program described earlier.

Challenges ahead

We remain far from our goal of an America in which youth work professionals gain credentials that are grounded in youth development research, are accessible through multiple local entry points, are fortified by trainer certification and institutional accreditation, are recognized by employers and funders through youth development worker compensation, adequate program funding, and supportive human resource policies, and are portable across communities and states.

To move toward that goal, local, regional, and national intermediaries need to work in tandem with research, policy, youth, and youth development worker organizations to establish the following.

National standards for core competency training

Establishing national standards for foundational training, and for the trainers who deliver that training, is a necessary step in establishing youth development work as a profession. Every youth development worker entering the field needs to start with the same set of core competencies—regardless of the setting in which he or she engages with young people. Nationally accepted standards for entry-level knowledge, skills, and abilities are the first step in coming to agreement on prerequisites for entering the field, salary ranges, and career paths across agencies, settings, and systems.

Support for increased human resource capability in youth-serving organizations

Intermediaries are positioned to provide leadership in communities to work toward institutionalizing human resource development as a policy and budget priority. Some national youth-serving organizations have built a professional development infrastructure (for example, YMCA, Boys & Girls Clubs), but independent community-based organizations need to offer the same kinds of training opportunities and career paths. In addition to strengthening the profession, this would expand the role of intermediaries; they would both offer youth worker professional development and serve as advocates and resources for organizational capacity building. In most communities today, only individual workers who want to learn more seek professional development programs, rather than agencies requiring that training as a condition for employment, retention, and advancement. Human resource management of activities such as recruitment, performance evaluations, and promotions are critical to supporting the institutionalization of youth worker professional development.

Widespread availability of youth worker professional development

Once agencies in a community commit to youth worker professional development, they need intermediaries to make it happen. Many communities, however, lack a youth-oriented intermediary that can create and sustain a coordinated, comprehensive system of professional development. Even once a local intermediary emerges and builds a local system, that organization needs several years of experience before acquiring the capacity to expand beyond its own community to serve smaller, less urban areas without their own intermediaries. Moreover, once a local intermediary has gained sufficient experience to expand to new communities in a region, the necessary funding can be difficult to secure because most local donors want their funds to be spent locally. In addition, the intermediary has to be able to sustain and build the local work at the same time it is trying to expand beyond its local boundaries; these are complex and often competing goals that may be difficult for a single agency to achieve.

Assessment of professional development impact on youth outcomes and organizational practices

Research has documented that professional development improves youth worker practice. Even more critical is determining the relationship between improvements in youth worker practice and improvements in youth experiences and outcomes. More clarity is also needed in understanding how youth worker professional development affects agency infrastructure (policies, priorities, budgets). Government agencies and large foundations need to work with universities and other research entities to design, fund, and conduct annual youth surveys, longitudinal studies, and agency analyses that can answer these important questions.

Alignment of core competencies across youth-serving sectors

Intermediaries fill the same role vis-à-vis community-based youth-serving agencies as do the training departments of national youth-serving organizations vis-à-vis their local affiliates. Youth development work as a profession requires alignment of core competencies across publicly funded systems, nationally affiliated youth-serving organizations, and independent youth-serving organizations.

Conclusions

NTI experiences affirm that youth development workers not only desire training but also step forward to lead and expand the current training system. Local intermediaries have embraced their efforts and incorporated this work as a core element of their organizations.

The national BEST evaluation demonstrates that youth development workers' day-to-day practices improve as a direct result of professional development programs led and coordinated by local intermediaries. We also know that youth-serving organizations lack the funding to pay the full costs of these programs. To move the work forward and take youth worker professional development systems to scale, new policies and creative funding strategies are needed.

Community-based, intermediary-led youth worker professional development systems add value to youth programs through program and staff quality enhancements, yet funding for this necessary intermediary infrastructure continues to decrease. Federal coordination of youth programs and national research to advance the youth development knowledge base are necessary, but not sufficient. Youth development workers need access to a continuum of knowledge and skills. Knowledge and skill gains must be tied to increased status and compensation, so that youth development workers can make a long-term career commitment to the field.

We Americans can invest in our young people by investing in the youth work profession. Public agencies and private foundations responsible for supporting America's young people must do more than fund programs and research. They need to sustain and expand the intermediary-led systems that provide youth development workers and supervisors with the knowledge and skills they need.

Notes

1. *The intermediary guidebook: Making and managing the community connections for youth.* (2001). San Francisco: Intermediary Network.

2. Academy for Educational Development. (2002). *BEST strengthens youth worker practice: An evaluation of Building Exemplary Systems for Training Youth Workers (BEST).* New York: Academy for Educational Development, Center for School and Community Services.

3. Center for Youth Development and Policy Research/National Training Institute for Community Youth Work. (2000). *Building sustainable local systems for youth worker professional development: The status and potential of partnerships between youth development worker training programs and higher education.* Unpublished report from the Edna McConnell Clark Foundation, Washington, DC.

4. Wynn, J. R. *The role of local intermediary organizations in the youth development field.* (Discussion paper SC-03, p. 11). Chicago: Chapin Hall Center for Children, 2000. See also Gil G. Noam (Ed.). (2004). *New Directions for Youth Development*, 101.

5. Wynn (2000), p. 11.

6. Center for Youth Development and Policy Research/National Training Institute for Community Youth Work. (1996). *Advancing youth development: A curriculum for training youth workers.* Washington, DC: Academy for Educational Development.

7. Center for Youth Development and Policy Research/National Training Institute for Community Youth Work (1996).

8. Center for Youth Development and Policy Research/National Training Institute for Community Youth Work (1996).

ELAINE JOHNSON *is vice president of the Academy for Educational Development and director of the Center for Youth Development and Policy Research/National Training Institute for Community Youth Work, which manages the BEST network.*

FRAN ROTHSTEIN, *of Rothstein Consulting, is senior consultant to the Center for Youth Development and Policy Research/National Training Institute for Community Youth Work.*

JENNIFER GAJDOSIK *is a consultant to the Center for Youth Development and Policy Research/National Training Institute for Community Youth Work.*

*The largest national youth organizations have tar-
geted, comprehensive professional development systems. For one of them, Girls Incorporated, its
mission "to inspire all girls to be strong, smart, and
bold"SM drives sophisticated, evaluated professional
development for affiliate staff and trustees.*

5

Professional development in national organizations: Insights from Girls Incorporated

*Heather Johnston Nicholson, Susan Houchin,
Brenda Stegall*

WHETHER STAFF MEMBERS are working in urban, rural, or suburban branches, for many years national organizations have been committed to preparing them to work effectively with young people. Over the past couple of decades, national organizations have sought and received strong funding to develop targeted, comprehensive professional development systems to support all levels of their local organizations: boards, executives, program administrators, frontline staff, and volunteers. These national organizations—including the YMCA and YWCA, Girl Scouts and Boy Scouts, 4-H, and Camp Fire USA—provide professional development opportunities to youth workers so they can best meet the needs of young people and enhance their capacities in communities. Like all youth development organizations, these groups grapple with preparing and

NEW DIRECTIONS FOR YOUTH DEVELOPMENT, NO. 104, WINTER 2004 © WILEY PERIODICALS, INC.

developing youth workers to work with *all* youth—rural and urban, conservative and liberal, low-income and wealthy, from immigrant families and from families with a long-standing history in this country, privileged and disenfranchised. This chapter provides some insights into the lessons learned by one of these national organizations, Girls Incorporated.

Youth development professionals as informal educators

Girls Incorporated believes that girls and young women are entitled to out-of-school programs that are both *intentional* and *compensatory*. Intentional programs focus on the strengths and needs, interests and opinions of young people as they are today. Intentional programming goes beyond dropping in and hanging out, beyond pick-up sports, one-day art projects, or recreation. They have goals and objectives attuned to the age and stage of development of the participants. They build from day to day or week to week so that participants and adult facilitators bond as a group to achieve the identified goals. Girls Incorporated program staff are informal educators as well as youth development specialists.

Girls are also entitled to programming that is compensatory. Young people grow up in an inequitable world. They are often put into boxes based on their age, gender, race, culture, national origin, home language, sexuality, ability and disability, immigrant status, body size and shape, family composition and income, and more—factors that often lead to discrimination against them and lower expectations of them. In an inequitable society, youth development programs and organizations must compensate young people for the opportunities and encouragement many of them are not getting from other institutions in their lives. We do not fix young people. Rather, we establish the expectation that girls and young women of every description can excel in every field of endeavor. Our job is to see that their options remain open, by building familiarity, skills, and experience. Girls and young women deserve to be significant actors building a more equitable society. As a result, Girls

Incorporated and our affiliates annually invest significant resources in the training, preparation, opportunities, and tools our staff need to implement intentional and compensatory programming for today's girls. We support adults who work with girls, as well as the girls themselves, to be change agents toward a more promising tomorrow.

Mission-based professional development

Drawing on forty years of regular workshops for managers and volunteers and intensive training for program implementation staff, Girls Incorporated currently implements a national system of training and professional development that makes the mission come alive and ensures program authenticity and effectiveness.

At the heart of our professional development for program managers is the five-day Program Directors Institute (PDI), offered annually to some thirty participants from across our network of affiliates. We train these individuals to become change agents, thus helping our affiliates to become even more effective at positive youth development with a pro-girl focus. We began in the mid-1990s to develop the system, but an independent three-year longitudinal study involving three Girls Incorporated affiliates affirmed for us that our goals were being realized, and it has helped us continually to refine the system.[1]

The following are some of the strategies and techniques we have developed and refined over the years. We believe these techniques are best practices, and we welcome others charged with creating professional development systems to borrow or adapt them.

- Registering a program manager or facilitator for training sets up an expected relationship between the participant, her supervisor, and the executive director.
- Using self-assessment forms provided with the registration materials, the participant assesses her (or his) own skills and styles, discusses these with her supervisor, and submits the results to the trainer prior to the training.

- Again prior to the training, the participant conducts an environmental audit of his or her center to determine the extent that it is girl-centered, nonsexist, inclusive, resourceful, accessible, inviting, challenging, democratic, and equitable—in short, whether the center, and indeed the whole organization, fosters positive youth development for girls.
- Ideally, the participant conducts the environmental audit with a team involving administrative and program staff, girls, parents, and board members, all of whom are then primed to improve the physical, social, and emotional environment upon the participant's return from the training.
- Training teams are diverse in background and experience and include national staff, key consultants, and affiliate staff members who have completed a train-the-trainers program.
- The training teams establish a positive environment with high expectations for individual performance and organizational change. For example, they craft the training environment and agenda to create a safe space in which participants can entertain new ideas and gather new energy. They specifically use the field and the language of youth development and treat participants with the respect due them.
- Participants examine their own beliefs about young people, compare them through engaging activities with the national organization's knowledge and beliefs, and begin a discussion that lasts throughout the training and beyond. During the session, they bond with one another and with the trainers by engaging in hands-on mutual learning.
- Training activities use interactive learning in small groups; they begin with goals, involve practice, and end with reflection—modeling, rehearsing, discussing, and reinforcing the way we expect participants to interact with staff they supervise as well as with girls back in their local organizations.
- Toward the end of the workshop each participant develops a plan for using the knowledge and experience back home, both to improve job performance and to increase the effectiveness of the organization.

- The participant's supervisor receives the plan of action directly, to encourage the participant and supervisor, or the environmental audit team, to adapt and implement the plan.
- On a self-addressed postcard sent three to six months after the workshop, participants are asked how the plan of action is going.
- Participants from the same workshop keep in touch with each other, their trainers, and Girls Incorporated national staff through various means: at regional meetings, on optional listservs, and at training events on other topics or more advanced levels.
- Whenever feasible, participants in the Program Directors Institute participate in a reunion training session that focuses on successes and challenges to renew their energy and teach the national staff what works and why.

Experiential learning cycle

A hallmark of Girls Incorporated training is the experiential approach: getting participants actively involved in their learning. This approach recognizes the knowledge and experience that participants bring to the training.

Participants engage in role-play, brainstorming, and other small group activities to draw their own conclusions, examine their own attitudes, get excited about a new idea, see a skill in action, learn from other participants, and practice new ways of behaving. They reflect on their experience, discussing how they felt, making connections to the real world, and planning how to apply the experience in their lives and work. By the end of the training session and the follow-up activities, the participants own the content and values and have incorporated these into the ways they think and act. They then deliberately plan to transfer the knowledge, skills, styles, and ways of acting and interacting in their roles as youth development professionals.

The system of professional development for program staff thus is deliberately designed to see that girls, too, participate in their own learning, according to best practices of youth development.

We continue to expand training and professional development opportunities for program staff and managers. We offer intensive workshops for program implementers at each of three regional conferences and whenever we release new programs. In addition, the research, program development, and communication departments regularly conduct workshops targeted to program facilitators and managers. On average, about 68 percent of our affiliates send at least one person for training each year and many affiliates send three or more. An energetic team of national and affiliate staff members are designing a new Middle Management Institute to follow up on PDI. PDI is regularly oversubscribed, as affiliates send the second, third, or tenth participant. The Girls Incorporated affiliates whose executives and boards consistently invest in professional development for program staff are growing and thriving. Professional development for youth development professionals is fun for the participants and cost-effective for their organizations.

Managing through the mission: Preparing executive directors and trustees

The evaluators of PDI found that affiliates were more likely to benefit from sending a participant if those organizations had the following qualities:

- Were ready for change
- Had a sound infrastructure
- Were relatively stable
- Accepted the goals of organizational change
- Invested in training for more than one person and at more than one level of the organization[2]

As a result, we provide management and trustee education to enhance the knowledge and skills of these youth development professionals and to increase organizational capacity. The national services department provides most of the training and technical assistance for managers and trustees, amounting to dozens of offerings, hundreds of hours of education, and hundreds of participants each year.

Training staff members and volunteers to understand the mission of Girls Incorporated is important throughout our network. When Girls Incorporated began training the paid staff leaders of its affiliates in the early 1950s, many of the executive directors had not been professionally trained in nonprofit administration but rather had been promoted from the ranks of the direct service staff. To ensure that its affiliate agencies were effectively managed, the national organization committed training resources to preparing those women (and a few men) in their new duties. Over the years the training continued, and it is now called the Executive Leadership and Management Seminar. Through the needs assessment, seminar leaders found that many executive leaders came to their jobs with professional degrees and years of experience as managers. What they needed was mission-based education. Today's seminar builds on the management skills and experience that new executives already bring, and emphasizes the knowledge, culture, and values that our leaders need to contribute to the community.

Preparing board members to hold the mission in trust

In 1992, Girls Incorporated initiated its Trustee Education for Excellence Program, designed to educate board members of affiliates about both their board responsibilities and their role as the guardians of the agency mission. Building on eight years of trustee education work, we utilize an entire educational system for boards—including two guides, a group of trained trustee educators, and a track of board workshops offered at every national and regional conference. The long-term effect of this effort is that today, Girls Incorporated boards are mission-based, committed to youth development in pro-girl environments, and fully prepared to carry out their stewardship responsibilities on behalf of girls. Trustees recognize and value the youth development professionals.

It takes a knowledgeable and committed board to recognize the differences in education, talent, and experience (and thus in salaries and benefits) between babysitters, on the one hand, and youth development professionals and informal educators, on the other. Trustees visit centers and learn the responsibilities of program staff for planning, implementing, and evaluating research-based programs—activities that necessarily extend beyond the time they are interacting directly with girls and young women.

Technology as grease and glue for professional development

Since 1996, Girls Incorporated has actively been incorporating information technology into the expansion of organizational capacity. The internal Web site, *Affiliate Central*, posts masses of resources, from training schedules and application forms to program curricula, logic models and pre- and posttraining questionnaires for evaluation, and a sophisticated set of tools for planning and management. *Training Central* is developing rapidly and will include scripts for in-service training, examples of outstanding programming techniques, and conversations with peer groups of trainees. To help affiliates see if their implementation of national identity programs works for girls, facilitators will be able to sign up girls on another internal site to complete pre- and posttraining surveys, have the results analyzed by research staff, and obtain outcomes for each girl and the group.

Program staff already use nationally developed listservs to give advice to one another and to find Web links that girls use avidly to explore the world.

New directions in pro-girl professional development

At Girls Incorporated, we invest in outcome and impact evaluation of programs. This evaluation tells us a great deal about the training and preparation, skills and styles of the staff who implement programs and create environments that inspire girls to be strong, smart, and bold. We are turning our attention to girls as trainers and evaluators, and have developed a comprehensive quality assurance system that ties girls and family members together with program and executive staff, trustees, and community leaders. Among the goals is increasing the interaction of affiliates with families and others in the community. Important mechanisms for greater community involvement include girls as evaluators of their own experience in a Girls Incorporated community. What effect has it had on them, their families, and their communities? We wish to improve the whole local organization toward better performance for girls and young women in the community context. We see a greater role for technology as we knit together cost-effective systems for getting training opportunities to part-time and short-term program staff. Once again, the goal is a coherent and flexible system of professional development for adults, dedicated to the optimal development of today's girls. We believe, and work to ensure, that today's girls make up at least half of all the leaders and change agents of today and tomorrow.

Notes

1. Girls Incorporated. (1996). *Becoming strong, smart, and bold: Girls Incorporated program directors as change agents: Executive summary.* Indianapolis: Girls Incorporated. Principal investigator Paula Schmidt-Lewis of PSL & Associates concluded that participants from the case study sites reported important personal gains, including increases in self-confidence and enthusiasm for their work, and that the mission and values of the organization were used as forces for inducing and guiding organizational change toward greater importance of the mission, values, and national programming.

2. Girls Incorporated. (1996).

HEATHER JOHNSTON NICHOLSON *has led research and evaluation for Girls Incorporated for twenty-two years.*

SUSAN HOUCHIN *is in charge of affiliate services for Girls Incorporated.*

BRENDA STEGALL *is director of training for Girls Incorporated and has been with the organization for thirty-eight years.*

Certificates, credentials, and degrees offered through institutions of higher education allow youth development professionals to acquire educational experiences that are recognized in a formal manner.

6

Professionalizing youth development: The role of higher education

Lynne M. Borden, Deborah L. Craig, Francisco A. Villarruel

THE FIELD OF YOUTH DEVELOPMENT is evolving, with growing attention being paid to the professional development opportunities afforded those who work with and on behalf of young people. Formal coursework for youth workers must be relevant and useful and meet the needs of diverse audiences, including both front-line workers and the managers and directors of youth development programs.

When certificates, credentials, and degrees are offered through institutions of higher education, youth development professionals can acquire learning that is formally recognized. The emergence of these higher education programs could lead to a more formal educational structure for youth development workers, similar to that for public school teachers. Such programs often help participants understand the needs of young people, work effectively as partners with youth, work with families and in the context of community, and reach all youth, including underserved populations. They also teach program development, implementation, management, and evaluation. Although the availability of educational

NEW DIRECTIONS FOR YOUTH DEVELOPMENT, NO. 104, WINTER 2004 © WILEY PERIODICALS, INC.

opportunities in higher education has increased, the field still faces many challenges—critical issues such as low wages, a scarcity of full-time jobs, and a lack of a comprehensive career path.

Educational opportunities for youth development workers

The field of youth development continues to evolve with all the opportunities, challenges, and obstacles that accompany the evolution of a new discipline. Over the past fifteen years, there has been increased public and private investment in community-based programs for youth to provide opportunities that support the positive development of young people. Youth development is a broad field with many constituencies in grassroots community organizations, in state and national youth-serving organizations, and at colleges and universities. The National Collaboration for Youth has estimated that approximately six hundred thousand full- and part-time staff work for private, nonprofit, or nationally affiliated youth organizations.

Recent research indicates that these programs have a positive influence on the development of young people.[1] Researchers, practitioners, policymakers, and funders have all begun to recognize the need for multilevel, comprehensive educational offerings for workers in the field, including periodic trainings and workshops, preservice educational programs, and certificate and degree programs at all levels.[2]

Youth development experts (for example Peter Benson, Jacquelynne Eccles, Robert Granger, Reed Larson, Richard Lerner, Milbrey McLaughlin, Gil Noam, and Karen Pittman) further assert that the skills and professionalism of youth development workers can be enhanced through educational coursework and the cultivation of a practical set of skills that prepare them to design and deliver high-quality programs for young people in communities. Educational programs should teach a wide range of skills, including how to identify the needs of young people, design and implement effective programs, and work with broad-based community efforts.[3] The field of youth development must identify and support multiple pathways for youth development professionals to access a comprehensive and systematic range of educational opportunities to prepare them to meet the needs of young people successfully.

Comprehensive educational opportunities help move youth development workers to the point where they are acknowledged as experts and recognized as professionals. Lerner and Herzog have described the youth development professional as "a community builder [working] on behalf of youth development."[4] The goal of the youth development professional is to create positive adults who can contribute to their families, communities, and society. Such a lofty vision deserves equally high-quality training.

As the youth development field evolves, degree programs are beginning to focus strictly on this field. Traditionally, those who wanted to work in this field had to take courses in numerous departments. For example, they would take child development courses in the psychology department, management courses at the business school, and evaluation courses at the school of education. Moreover, existing degrees (such as nonprofit management, adolescent development, parks and recreation, social work, human development) were often not specific to the work of the youth development professional. Recently, however, a few community colleges as well as colleges and universities have started offering specific knowledge- and skill-based programs for youth development professionals. An overview of the current status of some of these recently developed programs follows.

Community colleges

Community colleges are becoming more actively involved in providing educational opportunities to those in the field of youth development. Their programs are often modeled on successful programs offered by community colleges for child care workers. Not unlike the early childhood education programs that were a partnership between Head Start and local community colleges, today's youth development programs are often partnerships between youth-serving organizations and community colleges. Courses cover topics such as building relationships, understanding youth development, improving communication skills, and creating positive environments for youth.

One example of a partnership between a community college and a local youth-serving organization is the Seattle Making the Most of Out-of-School Time (MOST) program. This agency has developed a partnership with Seattle Central Community College that offers a Child and Family Certificate with a specialization in youth and families. The total program consists of forty-five credit hours and qualifies students for the Child Development Associate (CDA) credential.

The United States Department of Labor recently recognized "youth development practitioner" as an occupation that can be apprenticed and has developed a Youth Development Practitioner Apprenticeship (YDPA) program. The program includes both job-related experiences and educational opportunities. In response, community colleges have developed programs to meet the educational needs of those who participate in the apprenticeship program. Two examples are the Youth Development Practitioner Apprenticeship Program Certificate program at Maui Community College in Hawaii and the Youth Work Certificate at the Community College of Philadelphia in Pennsylvania. It is clear that there is growing interest among community colleges to provide educational opportunities for youth development workers.

Case study: YouthNet and community colleges

As the coordinating body for a collaboration of youth-serving agencies working in Kansas City's urban core, YouthNet[5] had seven years of experience working with outreach workers employed by affiliate agencies. Every Friday, all youth workers funded through the collaboration met together with an outreach coordinator to share ideas and resources as they recruited young people into their agency programs. What became apparent through those weekly meetings was that a great majority of those youth workers had little or no college education. Their only point of reference for making decisions about how to engage young people in their programs was how they themselves had been raised. They had no access to a body of knowledge that could help guide their work. Furthermore, a small number of youth workers were burned out from performing front-line work but could not move into other jobs in their agency or the field because they lacked college degrees.

These concerns were amplified by another one as YouthNet went about defining a training system for youth workers. Youth-Net could not promise participants any type of recognition by their employing agency for their participation in in-service training or any rewards in the form of pay increases or promotions. What would motivate youth workers to participate in training—beyond altruism and wanting to do a good job? The answer was to create a system that was flexible and carried its own reward: college credit.

YouthNet was fortunate to have a strong working relationship with the Coalition for Positive Family Relationships, a large group of nonprofits and government agencies serving families in the metro area. Having experience working with the University of Missouri system to create a master's in social work degree program at the Kansas City campus, the coalition advised against both a long, difficult, and politically charged master's program and an overly expensive degree from a private, four-year institution. Instead, it advised YouthNet to look to community colleges that were responsive to community needs, accessible, affordable, and able to address the academic deficits that confronted some youth workers. The coalition had a close relationship with the Metropolitan Community College (MCC) system and brought both parties to the table to design and implement a college-accredited certificate program. A plan was soon developed to provide service training tracks and a college-accredited certificate.

In the fall of 1997, a youth development worker certificate program requiring twelve hours of college credit was launched at Penn Valley Community College, the branch of the Metropolitan Community College system that was most accessible to urban youth workers. The certificate program was housed in the Department of Human Services, which already offered an associate degree with an emphasis on human services. Two concentrated courses were developed specifically for the certificate and were combined with four existing classes, one of which included a practicum experience.

To ensure that the newly developed courses were true to a positive youth development philosophy, YouthNet negotiated to have YouthNet staff help develop and teach the courses. This was a real challenge, because in 1997 there were no textbooks for youth work and very limited academic work of any kind to serve as a basis for coursework.

Youth workers frequently do not self-identify as youth workers. In addition, multiple funding streams employ a variety of job titles, such as *outreach worker, prevention specialist,* and *youth leader.* There are no local publications in which to advertise and no hangouts for youth workers where posters can be displayed. YouthNet relied on its relationships with local youth-serving agencies to market the program initially and has remained very active in marketing ever since.

The prospect of effective recruitment for the nascent certificate program was given a significant boost in 1997 when the Ewing Marion Kauffman Foundation set up a $200,000 scholarship fund for youth workers at the Metropolitan Community Colleges Foundation (MCC). YouthNet could then offer the enticement of college credit without the financial barriers to enrollment.

Today, YouthNet provides extensive support to certificate students to help ensure their academic success. New recruits are enrolled in classes by YouthNet staff at the YouthNet office. In addition, YouthNet staff members facilitate an extensive orientation to campus and college life for each new cohort, and the scholarship fund pays for any remedial classes.

As students began completing the twelve-hour certificate, many also began to inquire about working toward a college degree. Based on that interest, YouthNet and MCC defined a thirty-three-hour youth work certificate program that was offered beginning in the year 2000. This certificate incorporates additional courses that assist in developing the skills of the youth worker while getting them closer to the sixty-two-hour associate degree in human services. General education courses, with titles such as Technology and Information Management, Introduction to American National Politics, and General Psychology, are included, as is a specialized course in adolescent psychology. YouthNet has also worked with the MCC foundation to identify other scholarships to help students earn the associate degree.

Youth-serving agencies are accustomed to relying on volunteers and part-time staffers in order to cut costs. Low pay scales constantly push those who are attracted to youth work and who are good at it into management or the field of education. Furthermore, there is no formal way of entering the field of youth work. Many "stumble" into it because they happen to apply for a job at a youth-serving agency and discover that they enjoy it. In response, YouthNet has become a local sponsor of the federal YDPA program. It uses its youth work certificate programs to fulfill related instruction requirements and negotiates with its affiliate agencies to hire apprentices. The desire to professionalize the field further also pushes YouthNet to continue to explore the development of a four-year degree program for youth workers in the state of Missouri.

Colleges and universities

Colleges and universities have also begun to design programs to respond to the educational needs of youth development workers. They offer certificate programs and degrees at all levels—B.A., M.A., and Ph.D. Moreover, programs are being offered on an increasing number of campuses across the United States, including Clemson

University, Michigan State University, the Pennsylvania State University, Tufts University, University of Minnesota, and others.

College and university programs are often designed to offer the youth development worker the chance to receive a certificate without completing a degree (for example, Cornell University, Concordia University, Case Western University, and others). One example of this blending of educational opportunities is located at Harvard University. Harvard has designed two programs in one framework. A student can choose to take the youth development program with emphasis on adolescence from age eleven through nineteen and receive a certificate of advanced study—a one-year program designed for midcareer professionals—or they can choose to work toward a master's of education, which is a thirty-two-credit program.

University and college programs not only vary in type but in focus. Programs may prepare youth development workers to work directly with young people, to manage programs, to work on behalf of young people in the policy arena, to work in governmental positions, or to occupy other positions. There are several universities offering programs degrees in youth development—for example, Columbia University, Brandeis University, and Portland State University.

Universities and colleges also deliver these educational programs in varying manners. Often these programs are offered in the evening, on weekends, in intensive one- or two-week courses, or online. A growing number of certificate and degree programs are available to individuals whose schedules will not permit them to attend classes in person or who live too far away to do so (for example, Concordia University in St. Paul, Minnesota).

Case study: The Great Plains initiative

The Great Plains Interactive Distance Education Alliance (Great Plains IDEA, or GPI) is a consortium of human science colleges at ten universities that offer multi-institutional post-baccalaureate degree programs in three programmatic areas: family financial planning, gerontology, and youth development. Although not all ten institutions are necessarily involved in the development and delivery of all programs, the Great Plains IDEA operates on the premise that degree programs are developed and driven by faculty strengths and processes that optimize learning for students across the nation.

The youth development program, established in 2004, offers a thirty-six-credit master's degree as well as two certificates for individuals who do not wish to pursue a master's degree: specialist certificates in youth development or youth program management and evaluation. Twenty-eight credits for this program are offered through the consortium, with the remaining eight credits offered through the student's "residential institution."[6] These last eight credits permit faculty and degree candidates to take courses furthering their specialization or negotiate practicum experiences, where they can work with their faculty adviser to enhance and apply the skills that they have acquired.

Based on seven educational objectives,[7] teaching faculty have constructed a series of asynchronous courses that are designed to maximize participant engagement through cooperative learning and critical analysis. One component of this curriculum permits students to discuss local issues with their cohorts. Because the learning environment is asynchronous, the students can solicit input from other participants around the nation who are working with youth in an array of programs and contexts.

Online programs offer many advantages. Many youth professionals, for example, already hold a degree in other professions, have families, and are employed. Although asynchronous learning environments may be foreign to many, they permit individuals to minimize making changes in their lives. Stated somewhat differently, the youth development program developed by the GPI member institutions assumes that prospective students will not need to relocate to an institution of higher education that is involved in delivering the program. Moreover, students from throughout the United States, and possibly other nations, can enroll in this program. Thus, the program makes geographical and professional diversity a cornerstone of the online learning community. This virtual community may create an informal network of youth professionals who have a similar sense of identity and similar perspectives on the professionalization and standards of youth work.

Educational challenges

Although a growing number of programs are being offered at community colleges, colleges, and universities, there is no coordinated effort to bring these programs together into some type of career ladder. This lack of a nationally agreed-upon curriculum for youth development workers and the lack of an accrediting body leaves youth development workers unable to take their educational experience with them from one place to another. What was valued by one organization may not be valued by the next, which then requires the individual to take its own training and educational courses.[8] The case studies presented here offer two options currently available to youth workers. But those involved in the YouthNet program are bound by the place. Although it provides an excellent model for other communities, if people do not live in that area they will not have access to this program. Great Plains offers greater flexibility in that enrollees can live anywhere; however, they do not build on a physical network of youth workers as they engage in this work because it is strictly virtual.

The development of college and university career tracks for youth workers will not resolve the issues facing the field. Youth development continues to be heavily reliant on a part-time workforce and volunteer support. The current pay levels will continue to force individuals who are adept at working with youth out of direct service work and into management positions or alternate fields such as education. Increasing the availability of higher education courses is only the first step in addressing the challenges faced by those in the field who work with and on behalf of young people. The next step is to develop a comprehensive career ladder or lattice and a system that offers youth development workers the opportunity to take advantage of their educational experiences in subsequent positions.

Notes

1. Quinn, J. (1995). Positive effects of participation in youth organizations. In M. Rutter (Ed.), *Psychological disturbances in young people: Challenges for prevention* (pp. 274–304). Cambridge: Cambridge University Press; Eccles, J. S., & Gootman, J. A. (Eds.). (2002). *Community programs to promote youth development: Committee on community-level programs for youth.* Board on Children, Youth, and Families, Division of Behavioral and Social Sciences and Education. National Research Council and Institute of Medicine. Washington, DC: National Academy Press; McLaughlin, M. (2000). *Community counts: How youth organizations matter for youth development.* Washington, DC: Public Education Network; Perkins, D. F., & Borden, L. M. (2003). Key elements of community youth development programs. In F. A. Villarruel, D. F. Perkins, L. M. Borden, & J. G. Keith (Eds.), *Community youth development: Practice, policy, and research* (pp. 327–340). Thousand Oaks, CA: Sage.

2. Hahn, A., & Raley, G. (1998). Youth development: On the path toward professionalization. *Nonprofit Management & Leadership, 8*(4), 387–401.

3. McLaughlin, M. W., Irby, M. A., & Langman, J. (1994). *Urban sanctuaries: Neighborhood organizations in the lives and futures of inner-city youth.* San Francisco: Jossey-Bass.

4. Lerner, R. M., & Hertzog, S. M. (2004, June). *Creating a community youth development profession: From vision to instantiation.* (Concept paper; p. 1). Boston: Tufts University.

5. In 1995 YouthNet, a youth development nonprofit organization, received a planning grant from what was then called the DeWitt Wallace-Reader's Digest Fund through an initiative called BEST, Building Exemplary Systems for Training Youth Workers. (For more on BEST, see Chapter Four in this volume.)

6. A residential institution is an institution at which young people have the opportunity to live on-campus. Further, it is a place where students attend classes in person with an instructor.

7. For more specific information on these objectives, visit http://www.gpidea.org/prospective/ydedobjects.htm.

8. Borden, L. M. (2002). *Educating youth development professionals: Current realities, future potential.* Tucson: Institute for Children, Youth and Families, University of Arizona.

LYNNE M. BORDEN *is an associate professor and extension specialist in family studies and human development at the University of Arizona.*

DEBORAH L. CRAIG *is the president of YouthNet of Greater Kansas City.*

FRANCISCO A. VILLARRUEL *is a university outreach and engagement fellow and a professor of family and child ecology at Michigan State University.*

Karen Pittman calls for innovation and systemic change in the U.S. youth work by examining the key values of the United Kingdom's national youth work system.

7

Reflections on the road not (yet) taken: How a centralized public strategy can help youth work focus on youth

Karen J. Pittman

AS A FORMAL OBSERVER of youth development work for the last fifteen years, I am pleased to say that the field in the United States has made great progress in creating and institutionalizing the basic elements of a mature professional development system and in becoming purpose-driven. Topics such as youth worker competencies, links to higher education, professional support networks, adequate recognition and compensation for skills, and career ladders for growth have not only been debated but, as documented in the other chapters in this volume, addressed at state and local levels across the country. There have even been promising glimpses of action at the national level as these issues have been taken up by policy researchers, national intermediaries, and government agencies.

Recently, however, I have been increasingly concerned that the field may be gaining momentum but losing its focus. Efforts to refine definitions of the youth development field and youth worker

NEW DIRECTIONS FOR YOUTH DEVELOPMENT, NO. 104, WINTER 2004 © WILEY PERIODICALS, INC.

competencies appear to be more centrally focused on where and when than on what and how. Yet the latter, for me, lead directly to the elements of youth work that distinguish it from the related professions of teaching, counseling, or social work. I am convinced, there is not a more elegant statement of the purpose of youth work than that offered by the British government as articulated in the National Occupational Standards for Youth Work (NOS):[1] "The key purpose of youth work is to work with young people to facilitate their personal, social, and educational development, and enable them to gain a voice, influence, and place in society in a period of transitions from dependence to independence." This definition does not bother with where or when the work is done, but only with why and (in subsequent paragraphs) how.

I am not in any way suggesting that those who see themselves as youth workers would disagree with this definition of their goals. I do not believe they would disagree. My concern is that, as a profession, youth workers were just beginning to gain their "purpose-driven" voice when they were forced to align their efforts with a very powerful place- and time-driven movement: the afterschool movement. Early professional development efforts focused on establishing youth work as a distinct profession that admittedly works with young people primarily in the out-of-school hours, but also works toward goals with strategies that complement rather than copy those of formal educators or compensate for them. The primary lines for distinguishing youth work from teaching and youth programs and organizations from classrooms and schools were not time and place but outcomes and strategies.

In short, my concern is that the emerging youth work field has succumbed to market pressures created by the rapidly growing afterschool movement. This movement, as its name implies, has members who are defined more by their relationship to formal education than by their adherence to a coherent set of youth-centered principles.

Over the past five years, the U.S. afterschool movement has easily eclipsed the youth work, or youth development movement in its capacity to spark public demand, generate public dollars, and institutionalize public or public-private infrastructures that address professional development issues. But the afterschool field is struggling to find politically acceptable middle-ground definitions of purpose *(how much focus on academic achievement?)*, practice *(how much focus on specific content and participation guidelines?)*, place *(how much preference for school-based or school-linked programs?)*, personnel *(what proportion of staff should be credentialed, and what credential?)*, and population *(how much of a press to engage teens, especially high school students?)*. In contrast, youth work, or at least the version of it practiced in the U.K. and Commonwealth countries, has already answered these questions.

For this reason I have chosen to ground my reflections on the state of the field's professional development in the United States in an examination of the United Kingdom's youth work structure. An important beginning of a dialogue between these countries occurred last year at the annual "Learning with Excitement" conference at Harvard University. During this conference, organized by the Harvard Program in Afterschool Education and Research (PAER), Ian Fordham presented the impressive British perspective.[2] I hope that a comparative analysis will jump-start a discussion about what may be missing in current efforts to strengthen the field here.

After more than a decade of field-building work in the United States, I believe that what is lacking is the external validation and broad-based, cross-sector demand for high-quality youth work that can only come from a clear public understanding of the value of the work and a national commitment to compensate the workers adequately. My sense is that although it may seem expedient to win this validation by appealing to concerns and fears about the challenges of "unused time," it is wiser to take the time to engage the public, policymakers, and practitioners in richer discussions of the challenges of "untapped potential."

Looking across "the pond"

Many of the youth development seeds I had a hand in planting have now gone through three, even four generations. Some, however, seem to have withered rather than bear fruit. Most notable among these are those brought over from Great Britain and other European and Commonwealth countries, including South Africa. They affirm that youth work is as Johnston Nicholson, Houchin, and Stegall suggest in Chapter Five, an "intentional and compensatory" movement to support young people's full transition into work and community.

In 2002, the British government reaffirmed its long-standing commitment to youth work, and after a comprehensive consultative process with the field, developed the National Occupational Standards for Youth Work, articulating the key aspects of the field—the anchor points for the development of detailed standards—similar to those developed in the United States, including things like building positive relationships, facilitating learning and social development, enabling youth to take responsibility, and so on. The six underlying values and structures of the British youth work system that I summarize in the following paragraphs are worth noting.

Equity and justice are core values

The values that underpin youth work derive from a clear understanding of and commitment to learning and development, equal opportunity, social inclusion, and the educational and social importance of choice, freedom, responsibility, and justice.

"Informed by youth work values, the role of the youth workers is therefore to work with young people in ways that are:

- Educative
- Participative
- Empowering
- Promote equality of opportunity and social inclusion"[3]

These values and goals are embedded in the language of competencies used by many U.S. organizations and networks. But there is something very powerful about seeing them stark, stripped of all conditional phrases, in the opening pages of a 160-page document that outlines "an agreed set of aspects, units, and elements that can be used to inform the design of qualifications and awards for Youth Work practitioners"[4] for youth work across England, Northern Ireland, Scotland, and Wales. And there is something equally powerful about the clarity of the principles that flow directly from these values.

The youth work profession is clearly defined

The youth work profession is clearly defined as distinct from, but equal to, teaching, counseling, social work, and "play work"—work with children primarily eleven and under.

Building on a 1996 summation of the defining characteristics of youth work, the report asserts that youth work can be distinguished from other professions "at the point of encounter with young people" because:

- Young people choose to be involved.
- The work starts where young people are.
- The work seeks to go beyond where they start, encouraging them to be critical and creative in their responses to their experience and the world.
- It takes place because young people are young people, not just because they have been labeled.
- It focuses on the young person as a whole person with particular experiences, interests, and perspectives.
- It recognizes, respects, and is actively responsive to the wider networks of peer community and culture that are important to young people.
- Through these networks it seeks to help young people achieve stronger collective identities (for example, as blacks, as women, as gays).
- It is concerned with how young people feel and not just with what they know and can do.
- It works with other agencies that contribute to young people and social and personal development.
- It complements school and college-based education by encouraging and providing opportunities for young people to achieve and fulfill their potential.[5]

Interaction is the defining feature

Leveraged interactions, not places and activities, are the defining feature of the work. Youth work in the U.K. is not defined by programs and activities but is embodied in the nuanced skills of youth workers regardless of whether they do "buildings-based work," detached work (that is, with young people who cannot or choose not to use centers), outreach work, work in mobile units taken to particular locations, work in schools and colleges, work in government training programs, cross-community and international work, or focused project work (for example, youth councils, group counseling, arts or youth action projects).[6]

"Youth Work takes place where youth workers and young people meet to engage in activities that are in line with its key purposes and reflect its key principles. It takes place indoors and outdoors, in the community and away from the community, in places set aside for young people and places where the community meets and goes about its business."[7]

In the U.K., the most visible differences between instances of youth programming occur in the type of activities offered: drama, music, or outdoor recreation, for example. These differences, however, are considered superficial. The "programme of activities is . . . merely the medium through which [the] experience which leads to personal and social development is offered."[8]

The goal is an integrated youth service

The goal is an integrated youth service that utilizes a diverse base of organizations and programs. The youth service in the U.K. is "a complex network of providers, community groups, voluntary organizations, and local authorities"[9] that share a set of youth work values. The local authorities (of which there are about 150 in England) are responsible for ensuring that there is a youth service for their area, and for working with the voluntary sector and other partners to ensure that an adequate youth service is available.

In 1999, in response to concerns about the extent of local variations in the quality of the youth service, the government began a review process that resulted in the Transforming Youth Work initiative, which "set out the government's view of the youth service in England and outlined a program of modernization to ensure that youth services deliver a consistently high standard of youth work."[10] These standards were developed through comprehensive research.

The national Transforming Youth Work initiative requires local youth service authorities to develop annual youth service action plans that must include information on key priorities and target groups, strategies for achieving the outlined goals and objectives, involvement of young people in developing the service, and partnerships with the voluntary sector and government programs.[11] "Youth services must also have a clear statement about their youth work curriculum (that is, their approaches and methods) which shows how it complements formal education in promoting and assessing the development of young people. . . . The quality of youth work in individual local authorities and national voluntary youth organizations is monitored and evaluated through inspections by Her Majesty's Inspectorate."[12]

The preceding quotation is the equivalent of a mandate that every jurisdiction (for example, every county) have a youth service plan for coordinating public *and* private efforts to support the personal, social, and civic development of all youth (with targeted supports for marginalized youth) and ensure their inclusion in the community and economy.

What makes these standards significant is that, from their inception, they have represented a mutual agreement between government agencies and community organizations with the primary intention of creating more opportunities for young people through practical application and youth-centered insight. In 1989, a series of ministerial conferences were held to determine the infrastructure of what the country now defines as its youth service. In each of these sessions, youth workers operated collaboratively with the prime minister to create a system that promoted empowerment, accessibility, and equality.

It would be naïve to propose that the United States could implement such an initiative in one fell swoop. But this kind of approach could be called for at the state level, or proposed as a way to monitor and upgrade youth services across neighborhoods or communities in a city or county. Controlling definitions of quality and sustaining them in communities will undoubtedly require a balanced method for examining these systems. This is also the most direct method for developing sufficient incentives for professional development, stair-stepped compensation, and career growth within the youth work field.

New York State, which has a state youth bureau in every county, is currently the only state in the country with a purpose-built infrastructure in place that is similar to England's local youth authorities.[13,14] But there are many similar structures in place—for example, workforce investment boards; the national, state, and county-based 4-H system; new intermediaries like Achieve Boston or the After-School Corporation; local youth development intermediaries like Kansas City YouthNet; state-level intermediaries like the Indiana Youth Institute. All of these structures have the potential to perform this function if called upon to do so.

Part of the challenge in this country is the lack of consistent infrastructure across jurisdictions. But the main challenge is a lack of clarity, lack of vision, and most importantly, lack of external demand for this kind of alignment. Creative systems are being created, but no public or government is actually calling for them, supporting their development, or monitoring their performance.

Well-trained workers are at the core

At the core of the system is a cadre of well-trained, visibly deployed youth workers. The Transforming Youth Work initiative did not stop with a set of mandates for local authorities. The government charged the National Youth Agency with developing specific standards of youth work that must be achieved by all local authorities. "The standards provide detailed underpinning of a youth pledge— telling young people what they can expect from their local youth services—which each local authority is expected to develop. . . . For the first time, the government has powers to intervene if it considers that a local authority is not carrying out its duties properly, by giving direction and, if necessary, requiring the service in a locality to be operated by a body other than the local authority."[15]

The standards referred to here are not licensing standards for programs (although those do exist) but rather professional standards that guide what an integrated team of youth workers does to support youth across a range of programs, systems, and settings. The National Youth Agency is a quasi-governmental body set up expressly for the purpose of bridging the gap between providers, government, and youth workers. The mandates for local authorities are being pushed by the NYA and the Community and Youth Workers Union. Under their direction, local authorities are the equivalent of youth councils that are government-sanctioned and charged with responsibilities that go far beyond reallocating federal funding, to include creating a youth plan (in conjunction with and implemented by nongovernmental organizations and others) and securing sufficient funds for youth programming.

Transforming Youth Work defines key components of a good youth service "which young people would want to use" as follows:

- Offers quality support to young people that helps them achieve and progress.
- Enables young people to have their voice heard and influence decision making at various levels.
- Provides a diverse range of personal and social development opportunities.
- Helps prevent disaffection and social exclusion.
- Focuses on achieving outcomes that meet young people's needs and priorities.[16]

All youth workers need appropriate qualifications

Youth workers—full-time, part-time, and volunteer—are expected to hold appropriate qualifications achieved through multiple pathways, linked to definable positions. National standards are only as useful as the professional development and accreditation systems that support them and the compensation and recognition systems connected to them. In the U.K., youth workers can acquire credentials through certified training programs offered by employers (sometimes in conjunction with a community college) or through institutions of higher education. In the same tradition of a system that promotes opportunities being made available to all youth, the structure and diversity of certification paths in the youth service offer opportunities to all types of workers, including those who lack high school degrees or are not interested in attending college. The vocational degrees are for front-line workers and those doing a combination of front-line and program management work. University programs (full- and part-time) vary in length and focus and require the completion of substantial field work placements; graduates are then eligible for higher management or expert youth worker positions. Students with relevant youth work experience but who lack academic experience are welcome to apply.

Training programs are developed by a range of employers, colleges, and universities, but they are centrally certified by the National Youth Agency. This means that vocationally and academically trained youth workers hold equally "portable" degrees that are recognized across the region, and pegged to a "single spine" of employment positions with different levels of responsibility and pay. The conditions for pay and job responsibilities are determined by the Joint Negotiating Committee for Youth and Community Workers (JNC), a committee comprising employers and members of the Community and Youth Workers Union.

The youth service is visible, but not sizable. There are approximately 11 million young people ages eleven to twenty-five in England. The National Youth Agency estimates that there are about twenty-five thousand full-time and part-time youth workers and managers in England and about five hundred thousand volunteers. Quick calculations suggest a ratio of one certified youth worker for every 450 young people, and one volunteer for every 22 young people. The agency estimates that about 60 percent of youth use the youth service at some point in their adolescent or young adult years.[17]

Conclusions

Public systems designed to serve children and youth in the United States are converging on a crisis point. It is clear that they are not and in all likelihood cannot deliver equitable supports to young people.

I do not mean equitable outcomes, I mean equitable supports. Low-income young people and young people of color have different life options than those in the majority population and are achieving less because of the quality and quantity of the supports available to them. Central to these inequities are serious disconnects between these young people and many of the professionals they encounter—teachers, counselors, probation officers, police officers, health care professionals.

I believe that the future holds real opportunities for youth workers—whatever their specific occupational title or compensation arrangement—who have at the core of their training a professional commitment to the development, empowerment, and social inclusion of young people and especially those in marginalized circumstances.

These workers will be found in schools, courts, homes, malls, health clinics, employment programs, drop-in centers, and faith-based institutions. Their primary reasons for being there will be that (a) young people will choose or be required to be there, and (b) society recognizes the need for young people to have advocates, enablers, and advisers as well as parents, teachers, and service providers.

Observers from other countries are usually amazed by the sophistication of our youth programs but stunned by our lack of infrastructure and policies to support those programs. From my perspective, this problem plagues our professional development work as well. There is a subtle but important distinction between the way professional development systems are justified and developed in the United States and how they have grown up in the U.K. For me, the distinction comes down to a focus on place versus purpose. I vote for the latter.

Clearly, staff quality is a critical issue in the field, and professionalizing the workforce remains a laudable goal. But as we tackle this challenge, I recommend that we fight against the implicit but pervasive assumption in this country that the essence of youth work happens inside of programs rather than between people and in communities. Young people do not grow up in programs; they grow up in communities. Therefore, youth work should not just be practiced in programs but be present in communities. There is a growing need to define a common core approach to professional development that crosses territorial and structural barriers. An approach such as this would not only need to be informed by the full range of organizations that employ (or could employ) youth workers, but can and should be delivered in ways that are as diverse as the young people it intends to serve.

Clearly, organizations hire youth workers. But good youth workers use their organizations as bases for outreach to young people, families, schools, businesses, other community organizations, and public institutions. We must move beyond training youth workers to run programs inside the confines of an organization to training youth workers to find, meet, and work with teens where they live and spend their time. Good youth-serving organizations support this by seeing themselves as a part of a whole informal support network—or youth service, to use the British term.

Clearly, youth workers and organizations need to have a say in the shape and structure of standards and systems. However, it is not only possible but also necessary that youth worker training, like any other professional development system, make the commitment to bringing the full set of government agencies, employers (including schools and juvenile justice agencies), workers (full-time and part-time), and trainers-educators (campus- and field-based) to the table at the local, regional, and national levels to engage in ongoing and specific dialogues about competencies, compensation, and core goals.

Notes

1. PAULO. (2002). *National occupational standards for youth work*. Leicester, UK: PAULO, p. x. Retrieved August 10, 2004, from: http://www.paulo. org.uk/pages/nos/nos_youth.pdf.

2. The conference proceedings, including Ian Fordham's contribution, has been published in Gil G. Noam (Ed.). (2004). *New Directions for Youth Development*, 101.

3. PAULO (2002), p. iv.

4. PAULO (2002), p. i.

5. PAULO (2002), p. ii.

6. National Youth Agency. (n.d.). *The NYA guide to youth work and youth services*. Leicester, UK: National Youth Agency. Retrieved August 10, 2004, from: http://www.nya.org.uk/Templates/internal.asp?NodeID=90356&ParentNodeID=89721.

7. PAULO (2002), p. ii.

8. Department of Education and Science. (1987). *Effective youth work. A report by HM inspectors* (p. 4). London, UK: Department of Education and Science. Retrieved August 10, 2004, from: http://www.infed.org/archives/gov_uk/effective_youth_work.htm.

9. Department of Education and Skills (2002). *Transforming youth work: Resourcing excellent youth services* (p. 6). London, UK: Department of Education and Skills/Connexions. Retrieved August 10, 2004, from http://www.connexions.gov.uk/partnerships/publications/uploads/cp/TransYouth.pdf.

10. National Youth Agency (n.d.), p. 2.

11. One of the primary new programs is Connexions, a government support service for thirteen- to nineteen-year-olds that links services and supports designed to ensure that young people are engaged in education, training, or employment and provides all eligible young people with a personal adviser. See http://www.connexions.gov.uk.

12. National Youth Agency (n.d.), p. 3.

13. See the Association of New York State Youth Bureaus' Web site at: http://www.anysyb.com.

14. New York State Office of Youth Development. (2001, December). Taking the lead in institutionalizing youth development. *Forum for Youth Investment Newsletter, 1*(2). Retrieved August 10, 2004, from: http://www.forumfor youthinvestment.org/fyi/nyyouthdev.pdf.

15. National Youth Agency (n.d.), p. 3.

16. National Youth Agency (n.d.), p. 3.

17. National Youth Agency (n.d.), p. 2.

KAREN J. PITTMAN, *a youth development advocate for more than two decades, is executive director of the Forum for Youth Investment and president of Impact Strategies, both located in Washington, D.C.*

Index

Notes for Contributors

New Directions for Youth Development: Theory, Practice, and Research is a quarterly publication focusing on current contemporary issues challenging the field of youth development. A defining focus of the journal is the relationship among theory, research, and practice. In particular, *NDYD* is dedicated to recognizing resilience as well as risk, and healthy development of our youth as well as the difficulties of adolescence. The journal is intended as a forum for provocative discussion that reaches across the worlds of academia, service, philanthropy, and policy.

In the tradition of the New Directions series, each volume of the journal addresses a single, timely topic, although special issues covering a variety of topics are occasionally commissioned. We welcome submissions of both volume topics and individual articles. All articles should specifically address the implications of theory for practice and research directions, and how these arenas can better inform one another. Articles may focus on any aspect of youth development; all theoretical and methodological orientations are welcome.

If you would like to be an *issue editor*, please submit an outline of no more than four pages (single spaced, 12 point type) that includes a brief description of your proposed topic and its significance along with a brief synopsis of individual articles (including tentative authors and a working title for each chapter).

If you would like to be an *author*, please submit first a draft of an abstract of no more than 1,500 words, including a two-sentence synopsis of the article; send this to the managing editor.

For all prospective issue editors or authors:

- Please make sure to keep accessibility in mind, by illustrating theoretical ideas with specific examples and explaining technical terms in nontechnical language. A busy practitioner who may not have an extensive research background should be well served by our work.

- Please keep in mind that references should be limited to twenty-five to thirty. Authors should make use of case examples to illustrate their ideas, rather than citing exhaustive research references. You may want to recommend two or three key articles, books, or Websites that are influential in the field, to be featured on a resource page. This can be used by readers who want to delve more deeply into a particular topic.
- All reference information should be listed as endnotes, rather than including author names in the body of the article or footnotes at the bottom of the page.

Please visit http://ndyd.org for more information.

Back Issue/Subscription Order Form

Copy or detach and send to:
Jossey-Bass, A Wiley Company, 989 Market Street, San Francisco, CA 94103-1741

Call or fax toll-free: Phone 888-378-2537 6:30AM – 3PM PST; Fax 888-481-2665

Back Issues: Please send me the following issues at $29 each
(Important: please include series initials and issue number, such as YD100.)

_____

_____

_____

$ _____   Total for single issues

$ _____   SHIPPING CHARGES: SURFACE   Domestic   Canadian

		Domestic	Canadian
First Item		$5.00	$6.00
Each Add'l Item		$3.00	$1.50

For next-day and second-day delivery rates, call the number listed above.

Subscriptions: Please __start __renew my subscription to *New Directions for Youth Development* for the year 2____ at the following rate:

U.S.	__Individual $80	__Institutional $170
Canada	__Individual $80	__Institutional $210
All Others	__Individual $104	__Institutional $244

**For more information about online subscriptions visit
www.interscience.wiley.com**

$ _____   Total single issues and subscriptions (Add appropriate sales tax for your state for single issue orders. No sales tax for U.S. subscriptions. Canadian residents, add GST for subscriptions and single issues.)

__Payment enclosed (U.S. check or money order only)
__VISA __MC __AmEx #_____ Exp. Date _____

Signature _____ Day Phone _____
__ Bill Me (U.S. institutional orders only. Purchase order required.)

Purchase order # _____
           Federal Tax ID13559302   **GST 89102 8052**

Name _____

Address _____

_____

Phone _____ E-mail _____

For more information about Jossey-Bass, visit our Web site at **www.josseybass.com**

Other Titles Available

push to preserve the character of afterschool as an intermediary space, and the need to create and further programs that are grounded in reliable research and that demonstrate success.
ISBN 0-7879-7304-1

YD100 **Understanding the Social Worlds of Immigrant Youth**
Carola Suárez-Orozco, Irina L. G. Todorova
This issue seeks to deepen understanding of the major social influences that shape immigrant youths' paths in their transition to the United States. The authors delve into a number of social worlds that can contribute to the positive development of immigrant youth. They also provide insight into sources of information about identity pathway options available to those youth. The chapters offer new data regarding the developmental opportunities that family roles and responsibilities, school contexts, community organizations, religious involvement and beliefs, gendered expectations, and media influences present.
ISBN 0-7879-7267-3

YD99 **Deconstructing the School-to-Prison Pipeline**
Johanna Wald, Daniel J. Losen
This issue describes how school policies can have the effect, if not the intent, of setting youths on the "prison track." It also identifies programs and policies that can help schools maintain safety and order while simultaneously reaching out to those students most in need of structure, education, and guidance. Offering a balanced perspective, this issue begins to point the way toward less punitive, more effective, hopeful directions.
ISBN 0-7879-7227-4

YD98 **Youth Facing Threat and Terror: Supporting Preparedness and Resilience**
Robert D. Macy, Susanna Barry, Gil G. Noam
Intended to help clinicians, youth and community workers, teachers, and parents to support resolution and recovery, this volume examines the effects of threat, stress, and traumatic events, including acts of terror, on children and youth. It addresses not only the individual repercussions of threat but also a collective approach to threat. It also illustrates important ways to prevent traumatic situations from having lifelong, negative impacts. These methods involve providing immediate intervention and fostering safety as soon as a threatening incident has occurred as well as preparing children for future threats in ways that enhance feelings of safety rather than raise anxiety.
ISBN 0-7879-7075-1

YD97 **When, Where, What, and How Youth Learn**
Karen J. Pittman, Nicole Yohalem, Joel Tolman
Acknowledging that young people learn throughout their waking hours, in a range of settings, and through a variety of means, this volume presents practical advancements, theory development, and new

research in policies and infrastructures that support expanded definitions of learning. Representing the perspectives of a broad range of scholars and practitioners, chapters explore ways to connect learning experiences that happen inside and outside school buildings and during and after the school day. The contributors offer a compelling argument that communitywide commitments to learning are necessary if our nation's young people are to become problem free, fully prepared, and fully engaged.
ISBN 0-7879-6848-X

YD96   **Youth Participation: Improving Institutions and Communities**
Benjamin Kirshner, Jennifer L. O'Donoghue, Milbrey McLaughlin
Explores the growing effort in youth organizations, community development, and schools and other public institutions to foster meaningful activities that empower adolescents to participate in decision making that affects their lives and to take action on issues they care about. Pushing against long-held, culturally specific ideas about adolescence as well as institutional barriers to youth involvement, the efforts of these organizations engaged in youth participation programs deserve careful analysis and support. This volume offers an assessment of the field, as well as specific chapters that chronicle efforts to achieve youth participation across a variety of settings and dimensions.
ISBN 0-7879-6339-9

YD95   **Pathways to Positive Development Among Diverse Youth**
Richard M. Lerner, Carl S. Taylor, Alexander von Eye
Positive youth development represents an emerging emphasis in developmental thinking that is focused on the incredible potential of adolescents to maintain healthy trajectories and develop resilience, even in the face of myriad negative influences. This volume discusses the theory, research, policy, and programs that take this strength-based, positive development approach to diverse youth. Examines theoretical ideas about the nature of positive youth development, and about the related concepts of thriving and well-being, as well as current and needed policy strategies, "best practice" in youth-serving programs, and promising community-based efforts to marshal the developmental assets of individuals and communities to enhance thriving among youth.
ISBN 0-7879-6338-0

YD94   **Youth Development and After-School Time: A Tale of Many Cities**
Gil G. Noam, Beth Miller
This issue looks at exciting citywide and cross-city initiatives in after-school time. It presents case studies of youth-related work that combines large-scale policy, developmental thinking, and innovative programming, as well as research and evaluation. Chapters discuss efforts of community-based organizations, museums, universities,

schools, and clinics who are joining forces, sharing funding and other resources, and jointly creating a system of after-school care and education.
ISBN 0-7879-6337-2

YD93   **A Critical View of Youth Mentoring**
        Jean E. Rhodes
        Mentoring has become an almost essential aspect of youth development and is expanding beyond the traditional one-to-one, volunteer, community-based mentoring. This volume provides evidence of the benefits of enduring high-quality mentoring programs, as well as apprenticeships, advisories, and other relationship-based programs that show considerable promise. Authors examine mentoring in the workplace, teacher-student interaction, and the mentoring potential of student advising programs. They also take a critical look at the importance of youth-adult relationships and how a deeper understanding of these relationships can benefit youth mentoring. This issue raises important questions about relationship-based interventions and generates new perspectives on the role of adults in the lives of youth.
        ISBN 0-7879-6294-5

YD92   **Zero Tolerance: Can Suspension and Expulsion Keep Schools Safe?**
        Russell J. Skiba, Gil G. Noam
        Addressing the problem of school violence and disruption requires thoughtful understanding of the complexity of the personal and systemic factors that increase the probability of violence, and designing interventions based on that understanding. This inaugural issue explores the effectiveness of zero tolerance as a tool for promoting school safety and improving student behavior and offers alternative strategies that work.
        ISBN 0-7879-1441-X

AIRLINE COMPETITION: DEREGULATION'S MIXED LEGACY

Dedicated to the memory of my father,
William George Williams

Airline Competition:
Deregulation's Mixed Legacy

GEORGE WILLIAMS

Ashgate

Published by
Ashgate Publishing Limited
Gower House
Croft Road
Aldershot
Hants GU11 3HR
England

Ashgate Publishing Company
131 Main Street
Burlington, VT 05401-5600 USA

Ashgate website: http://www.ashgate.com

British Library Cataloguing in Publication Data
Williams, George, 1948-
    Airline competition : deregulation's mixed legacy. - (Ashgate
    studies in aviation economics and management)
    1.Aeronautics, Commercial - Deregulation 2.Competition
    3.Airlines - Management
    I.Title
    387.7'1

Library of Congress Control Number: 2001099945

ISBN 0 7546 1355 0

Printed and bound in Great Britain by MPG Books Ltd, Bodmin, Cornwall

Contents

List of Figures

List of Tables

Acknowledgements

I should like to pay particular thanks to Ian Stockman, Dr Romano Pagliari and Andy Foster, who were of great help to me during the preparation of this book. My gratitude is also extended to those who have encouraged me to write this second book.

Introduction

It is clear that deregulation has radically altered the way in which airlines are operated and managed. The cosy world of the past in which carriers were protected from the onslaught of competition by the actions of regulators has been replaced by one in which each party has to ensure its own wellbeing. The ways in which airline markets are supplied and services offered have altered dramatically. Substantial barriers to market entry have been devised and existing ones exploited by incumbent airlines, but have not proved so effective as to prevent the aspirations of every new entrant being realised. An amazing mixture now exists in which certain types of city-pair market exhibit high degrees of competition, whilst with others it is difficult to discern any real change on pre-liberalisation days when rivalry was near non-existent. How regulators should respond, if at all, to this seemingly contradictory mix is a perplexing question.

That there is no certain link between the number of firms supplying a market and the degree of competition likely to be experienced has long been apparent. This feature of the economic behaviour of firms is as observable in the provision of air transport services as it is in other industries. In airline markets significant variations are apparent between the volume of passenger traffic on a route and the number of operating carriers. Some of the differences, of course, arise as a result of different route characteristics and regulatory conditions, but by no means all. For example, it is possible to find many examples of routes supplied by two competing airlines where the number of passengers carried annually is less than a few thousand. In other instances however, routes with only one carrier exist on which passenger demand exceeds more than a million annually.

Some of these apparent anomalies arise where demand is seasonal and consists predominantly of holiday traffic, and, as such, services are often concentrated at weekends. For example, between Edinburgh and Jersey during summer weekends British Midland and British European (formerly Jersey European) provide competing services, while during weekdays a British Airways franchise partner maintains a link with two en-route stops.[1]

1

Another situation in which low traffic levels can sustain two or more competing operators occurs with third level services to remote locations. Many such routes are served with very small aircraft, typically equipped with fewer than 40 seats. Brazil is one country with routes that have exhibited such characteristics.[2] Providing a plausible justification for routes with high volumes of traffic that are supplied on a monopolistic basis is less easy.

It would be an interesting exercise to provide a comprehensive assessment of the degree of competition that exists and has existed in the various airline markets around the world. To undertake such a task, however, would be way beyond the scope of a single book. It is possible though by examining how competition has evolved in a number of different types of market across the globe to gain an overall impression. The aim of this text is to examine the response of carriers to liberalisation in a number of representative air transport markets and to provide an explanation for the wide variation in the level of competition apparent across city-pair markets. How this situation is likely to alter as the sector is freed from the remaining restrictions placed upon it will also be discussed.

Notes

1. There were nine UK regional towns and cities provided with non-stop scheduled services to the island of Jersey during the winter of 1999, but over the summer months the number increases to sixteen.
2. Two competing carriers currently serve Cuiaba – Sinop daily, a route on which annual passenger demand is fewer than 15,000.

1 Extent and impact of deregulation

Much of the focus of air transport has concerned the provision of international services, on which with relatively few exceptions regulatory controls continue to have a major impact. Interestingly however, the ten city pair markets with the largest numbers of passengers are with one exception domestic routes as Table 1.1, reveals. (The data shown refers to the number of seats provided in one week in June 2000.)

Table 1.1 World's ten busiest routes in 2000

Seats supplied	Route	HHI	Market share by Carrier (%)
210,820	Tokyo - Sapporo	0.31	All Nippon 34 Japan Airlines 35 Japan Air System 25 Hokkaido 6
202,345	Taipei - Kaohsuing	0.23	Far Eastern 34 Transasia 22 Mandarin 19 Uni 17 U-Land 8
185,148	Tokyo - Fukuoka	0.30	All Nippon 34 Japan Airlines 31 Japan Air System 28 Skymark 7
146,318	Rio de Janeiro - Sao Paulo	0.24	Varig 36 TAR 25 Vasp 20 Transbrasil 8 Rio-Sul 6 TAM 4*
143,426	Sydney - Melbourne	0.50	Qantas 58 Ansett 42
141,500	New York - Chicago	0.32	United 41 American 36 Continental 13 American Transair 8 Delta 1
133,120	Tokyo - Osaka	0.36	All Nippon 41 Japan Airlines 38 Japan Air System 21
132,715	New York - Washington	0.23	Delta 31 US Airways 27 United 20 Continental 15 American 4 TWA 3
129,000	Taipei - Hong Kong	0.34	Cathay 44 China Airlines 36 Thai 8 EVA Air 7 Japan Asia 3*
126,764	Huston - Dallas	0.38	Southwest 54 American 23 Continental 20 Delta 3

Source: OAG. (*2 other carriers serve the route each providing < 1% of the available seats.)
HHI, the Hirschman Herfindahl Index, measures market concentration. It is calculated by summing the squares of the market shares of the individual carriers. The lower the HHI value, the less concentrated the market. The inverse of the HHI provides a measure of the number of carriers operating a particular route having taken account of the differing capacities provided by each of them.

1.1 Deregulation of domestic markets

Since the US Administration deregulated its domestic air transport sector, many other countries around the world have followed suit. Table 1.2 provides a listing of 30 representative countries from around the world showing both the date each began to deregulate their domestic air transport markets and whether or not the process is now complete.

Table 1.2 Domestic deregulation

Country	From	Status now	Country	From	Status now
USA	1978	Full	Argentina	1994	Full
Japan	2000	Full	Sweden	1992	Full
Canada	1988	Full*	Malaysia	1994	Partial
Brazil	1996	Full	Thailand	1995	Full
China	1987	Partial	South Africa	1991	Full
Australia	1990	Full	Turkey	1994	Full
Spain	1994	Full	New Zealand	1984	Full
Italy	1993	Full	Venezuela	1990	Full
France	1994	Full	Chile	1982	Full
Mexico	1993	Full	Peru	1990	Full
Germany	1993	Full	Portugal	1993	Full
UK	1993	Full	Egypt	2000	Partial
Taiwan	1987	Partial	Morocco	2000	Full
India	1990	Partial	Ireland	1993	Full
Norway	1993	Full	Kenya	1995	Full

(*Air transport services within northern Canada remain a closed market.)

To give an idea of the relative size of each country's domestic market, Table 1.3 ranks the number of seats supplied weekly by scheduled operators during the summer of 2000. As may be seen, when measured in this way the US has by far and away the largest domestic air transport market, some eight times the size of the second biggest, Japan. China, the third largest, has seen spectacular growth in the size of its domestic market since deregulation. Between June 1989 and June 2000, the number of seats supplied in its domestic market has been subject to a 538% increase, representing the largest change of all of the 30 countries analysed. (Further details about the impact of deregulation in China are given in Chapter 3.) Table 1.4 shows that other countries (Taiwan, Chile, Turkey and Thailand) have also experienced spectacular growth in their domestic markets, as a result of liberalisation.

Table 1.3   Seats supplied per week in domestic markets

USA	19,694,178	Argentina	297,193
Japan	2,427,504	Sweden	265,034
China	1,759,184	Malaysia	248,005
Brazil	1,166,708	Thailand	230,483
Canada	890,340	South Africa	215,971
Australia	849,397	Turkey	210,169
Spain	776,435	New Zealand	186,267
Italy	742,074	Venezuela	145,855
France	733,479	Chile	129,155
Mexico	659,011	Peru	99,470
Germany	652,241	Portugal	97,121
UK	564,961	Egypt	52,522
Taiwan	525,119	Morocco	31,853
India	484,393	Ireland	30,171
Norway	412,040	Kenya	20,257

Source: OAG.

Not all countries however, have experienced such a large increase in capacity. For example, Canada and Venezuela witnessed a reduction in the number of seats supplied in their domestic markets between 1989 and 2000. In the case of Canada the demise of Wardair and the subsequent merger of Air Canada and Canadian were key contributors to this contraction. The failure of flag carrier VIASA and the country's weak economy were major factors with respect to Venezuela's supply situation. Over the same period the number of seats supplied in the US market increased by a modest 19%, reflecting its maturity following a decade of deregulation.

In terms of numbers of domestic routes operated, Turkey and China have experienced the greatest percentage increase since 1989 and Morocco the largest reduction, as Table 1.5 reveals. To show the evolution of these changes, Table 1.6 shows the number of routes operated in June of 1989, 1992, 1996 and 2000 in each of the 30 sampled countries.

Table 1.4   Number of seats supplied weekly 1989 and 2000

	1989	2000	% change
China	275,582	1,759,184	538
Taiwan	96,141	525,119	446
Chile	33,528	129,155	285
Turkey	72,712	210,169	189
Thailand	79,774	230,483	189
Mexico	344,034	659,011	92
Malaysia	133,723	248,005	86
Brazil	639,961	1,166,708	82
Portugal	54,779	97,121	77
Spain	441,119	776,435	76
Peru	56,729	99,470	75
Argentina	170,036	297,193	75
Japan	1,395,783	2,427,504	74
Norway	245,189	412040	68
Italy	446,307	742,074	66
Australia	530,672	849,397	60
Egypt	34,032	52,522	54
UK	370,244	564,961	53
India	332,840	484,393	46
South Africa	152,449	215,971	42
Sweden	191,412	265,034	39
Germany	476,694	652,241	37
Ireland	23,660	30,171	28
France	577,009	733,479	27
Kenya	16,964	20,257	19
USA	16,514,699	19,694,178	19
Morocco	31,359	31,853	0
New Zealand	188,679	186,267	0
Canada	1,045,256	890,340	-15
Venezuela	201,014	145,855	-27

Source: OAG.

Table 1.5   Change in the number of routes operated

	1989	2000	% change
Turkey	40	100	150
China	483	1,203	149
Mexico	203	380	87
Sweden	73	117	60
Thailand	58	86	48
Germany	165	237	44
Japan	309	443	43
Taiwan	40	55	38
Italy	218	262	20
Spain	200	236	18
Brazil	449	499	11
USA	5,583	5,617	6
Chile	55	57	4
UK	308	301	-2
France	340	320	-6
Egypt	35	32	-9
Portugal	67	58	-13
Norway	246	212	-14
Kenya	34	29	-15
Canada	1,072	908	-15
Malaysia	147	116	-21
Australia	878	656	-25
New Zealand	146	106	-27
Venezuela	101	71	-30
Argentina	269	183	-32
India	384	260	-32
Ireland	20	12	-40
South Africa	142	84	-41
Peru	77	44	-43
Morocco	62	26	-58

Source: OAG.

Table 1.6   Number of routes operated between 1989 and 2000

	1989	1992	1996	2000
USA	5,583	5,595	5,542	5,617
Canada	1,072	1,035	978	908
China	483	554	1,115	1,203
Australia	878	714	669	656
Brazil	449	415	615	499
Japan	309	352	441	443
Mexico	203	313	341	380
France	340	331	382	320
UK	308	311	316	301
Italy	218	195	180	262
India	384	303	266	260
Germany	165	239	223	237
Spain	200	182	247	236
Norway	246	253	254	212
Argentina	269	178	149	183
Sweden	73	124	132	117
Malaysia	147	161	176	116
New Zealand	146	119	120	106
Turkey	40	62	74	100
Thailand	58	88	78	86
South Africa	142	136	85	84
Venezuela	101	102	76	71
Portugal	67	43	47	58
Chile	55	49	49	57
Taiwan	40	36	38	55
Peru	77	57	103	44
Egypt	35	22	38	32
Kenya	34	35	27	29
Morocco	62	57	38	26
Ireland	20	16	14	12

Source: OAG.

1.2 Deregulation of international markets

International airline markets have also been subject to liberalisation of the economic rules controlling them. However, only one region to date has been able to achieve the full deregulation of its air transport services.

Within Europe the arcane system of exchanging air traffic rights on a bilateral basis been replaced by a multilateral approach, to which 17 states have so far subscribed, with more to follow as the European Union expands. A common set of economic and technical regulations enables carriers based in any of these countries to operate air services anywhere between and within the 17 nations. In essence, creating for European carriers a similar freedom to exploit a large *domestic* market as that enjoyed by US airlines in their, albeit larger, home territory.

To give an idea of the relative size of each country's international markets, Table 1.7 ranks the number of outbound seats supplied weekly by scheduled operators during the summer of 2000. As may be seen, when measured in this way the US has the largest international air transport markets. The gap between it and other countries is however not nearly so marked, as is the case with the supply of domestic services. The important role played by Singapore as an international hub is shown by its 9th ranking. China, which has the third largest domestic market seat supply, lies behind Singapore in terms of international seats supplied.

Table 1.7   Weekly outbound international seats supplied in 2000

USA	1,989,339	Turkey	175,869
UK	1,493,371	Malaysia	163,340
Germany	1,367,185	India	155,693
France	887,427	Portugal	143,063
Spain	656,596	Brazil	130,708
Japan	631,507	Norway	120,803
Italy	602,903	Argentina	105,696
Canada	481,182	Egypt	100,020
Singapore	385,138	South Africa	91,037
Thailand	305,957	New Zealand	82,347
China	279,404	Venezuela	53,936
Mexico	226,220	Chile	53,349
Australia	225,169	Morocco	46,816
Sweden	212,870	Kenya	41,977
Ireland	200,998	Peru	40,461
Taiwan	199,216		

Source: OAG.

It has however witnessed spectacular growth in both its domestic and international markets. Between June 1989 and June 2000, the number of outbound seats supplied in its international markets has been subject to a 585% increase. (Further details about the impact of deregulation in China are given in Chapter 3.) Table 1.8 shows that other countries have also experienced substantial growth in their international markets.

Table 1.8   Outbound seats supplied weekly 1989 and 2000

	1989	2000	% change
China	47,725	279,404	585
Spain	189,390	656,596	347
South Africa	28,883	91,037	315
Chile	18,357	53,349	291
Germany	479,208	1,367,185	285
Turkey	68,679	175,869	256
Malaysia	69,656	163,340	234
Portugal	61,123	143,063	234
Ireland	88,375	200,998	227
Italy	269,287	602,903	224
Sweden	95,975	212,870	222
Argentina	47,801	105,696	221
Peru	18,903	40,461	214
Singapore	190,753	385,138	202
UK	743,460	1,493,371	201
Australia	116,965	225,169	193
Thailand	161,327	305,957	190
Brazil	70,328	130,708	186
France	489,027	887,427	181
Taiwan	116,562	199,216	171
Japan	370,134	631,507	171
Mexico	133,502	226,220	169
Canada	289,111	481,182	166
USA	1,238,904	1,989,339	161
Kenya	28,235	41,977	149
New Zealand	56,224	82,347	146
Morocco	32,592	46,816	144
India	111,277	155,693	140
Venezuela	40,692	53,936	133
Egypt	89,549	100,020	112

Source: OAG.

Unlike in the case with domestic markets, all the countries analysed experienced more than a doubling of the number of international seats supplied.

Table 1.9 Change in the number of routes operated

	1989	2000	% change
China	47	188	400
Germany	366	998	273
Spain	164	447	273
Taiwan	19	45	237
South Africa	34	68	200
Japan	104	202	194
Turkey	94	180	191
Malaysia	50	90	180
Sweden	63	109	173
Mexico	84	145	173
Portugal	68	116	171
Chile	18	30	167
Italy	228	372	163
Ireland	55	88	160
Argentina	27	43	159
Thailand	66	101	153
USA	514	766	149
Singapore	59	86	146
India	89	129	145
Canada	180	237	132
Australia	77	101	131
Venezuela	39	50	128
Egypt	80	102	128
UK	357	439	123
New Zealand	32	39	122
France	382	420	110
Peru	23	24	104
Morocco	72	71	99
Kenya	41	39	95
Brazil	70	65	93

Source: OAG.

1.3 Contrasting the two

It is an interesting exercise to compare the ten largest domestic routes in the world with their international equivalents. Whilst the respective domestic markets have been deregulated, the international routes shown are still constrained by the terms contained in bilateral agreements. The ten busiest domestic routes in terms of seats supplied in summer 2000 are shown in Table 1.10, with an equivalent listing of international routes given in Table 1.11. As may be seen, four of the domestic city-pairs are in the Far East, three in the US, and one each in Australia, Europe and South America. The average weighted number of operating carriers on the ten routes is 3.17. The most concentrated is the one in Europe, Madrid - Barcelona, on which the privatised flag carrier Iberia provides nearly 75% of seat capacity. (For more details of the Spanish domestic market refer to Chapter 2.)

Table 1.10 World's ten busiest domestic routes in 2000

Seats	Route	HHI	Market share by Carrier (%)
210,820	Tokyo - Sapporo	0.31	All Nippon 34 Japan Airlines 35 Japan Air System 25 Hokkaido 6
202,345	Taipei - Kaohsuing	0.23	Far Eastern 34 Transasia 22 Mandarin 19 Uni 17 U-Land 8
185,148	Tokyo - Fukuoka	0.30	All Nippon 34 Japan Airlines 31 Japan Air System 28 Skymark 7
146,318	Rio de Janeiro - Sao Paulo	0.24	Varig 36 TAR 25 Vasp 20 Transbrasil 8 Rio-Sul 6 TAM 4*
143,426	Sydney - Melbourne	0.50	Qantas 58 Ansett 42
141,500	New York - Chicago	0.32	United 41 American 36 Continental 13 American Transair 8 Delta 1
133,120	Tokyo - Osaka	0.36	All Nippon 41 Japan Airlines 38 Japan Air System 21
132,715	New York - Washington	0.23	Delta 31 US Airways 27 United 20 Continental 15 American 4 TWA 3
126,764	Houston - Dallas	0.38	Southwest 54 American 23 Continental 20 Delta 3
125,781	Madrid - Barcelona	0.59	Iberia 74 Spanair 17 Air Europa 9

Source: OAG. (*2 other carriers serve the route each providing < 1% of the available seats.)

The two least concentrated of the ten routes are Taipei – Kaohsuing and New York - Washington. In summer 2000, five airlines were competing on the Taiwanese route and six on the US one. However, since then U-Land and Far Eastern have ceased operating, leaving the world's second busiest route in the hands of three airlines: Transasia, Mandarin (a subsidiary of China Airlines) and Uni Air. The number of carriers operating the US route has also fallen over the past year to five, as a result of American's takeover of TWA. Aside from size, there are a number of other differences between the ten routes. For example, four carriers, two of which use Boeing 747-400 aircraft equipped with 568 seats, serve the busiest route in the world, Tokyo - Sapporo. By contrast, the second busiest route, Taipei - Kaohsuing, is exclusively in the hands of narrow-bodied types.

Table 1.11 World's ten busiest international routes in 2000

Seats	Route	HHI*	Market share by Carrier (%)
129,000	Taipei - Hong Kong	0.34	Cathay 44 China Airlines 36 Thai 8 EVA Air 7 Japan Asia 3**
120,000	London - New York	0.24	BA 40 Virgin 21 American 15 United 11 Continental 7 Air India 5 Kuwait 1
115,000	London - Dublin	0.30	Aer Lingus 39 Ryanair 33 British Midland 19 BA 8 Jersey European 3
88,000	London - Amsterdam	0.21	BA 28 British Midland 22 KLM 21 KLM uk 18 easyJet 11
88,000	London - Paris	0.32	BA 43 Air France 34 British Midland 13 KLM uk 6 Suckling 1*
70,000	Bangkok - Hong Kong	0.31	Thai 45 Cathay 30 Emirates 7 China Airlines 7 Gulf Air 6*
68,000	London - Frankfurt	0.37	Lufthansa 50 BA 33 Ryanair 11 KLM uk 6*
66,000	Singapore - Bangkok	0.26	Thai 36 Singapore 34 Cathay 8 SAS 5 Swissair 3 Finnair 3 Turkish 3 Angel 3*
66,000	Singapore - Jakarta	0.23	Singapore 42 Garuda 18 Lufthansa 8 Cathay 7 Thai 7 KLM 6 Qantas 4 Emirates 4*
64,000	Singapore - Hong Kong	0.30	Singapore 44 Cathay 31 United 8 Garuda 6 China Airlines 6 Qantas 5

Source: OAG. (*Other carriers also operate the route but with very low frequencies.)

Of the top ten international city-pair markets, five involve London and three Singapore. The largest route in terms of seats supplied however, is Taipei - Hong Kong. By contrast, the busiest domestic sector has nearly double the number of seats on offer. Interestingly, the HHI ranges between

0.21 and 0.37 for the ten international routes and 0.23 and 0.59 for the ten domestic sectors, indicating greater concentration in the latter. The exercising of fifth freedom rights is apparent on certain international routes (for example, Air India and Kuwait Airways between London and New York). The growing presence of low cost, no-frills carriers is also apparent on both domestic and international short haul markets.

2 Impact in European domestic markets

This chapter seeks to examine the impact of airline deregulation in the domestic markets of three European countries: France, Norway and Spain. To have included all European countries in this analysis would not have possible. The countries selected however, have been specifically chosen as being representative of the range of different effects that air transport liberalisation has produced in the region.

It has only been since the mid 1990s that the domestic air transport markets of France and Spain have experienced any serious degree of competition, an outcome of the liberalising measures promulgated by the European Commission. Prior to this, virtually all of the domestic routes in these countries had been supplied on a monopolistic basis by the respective state-owned flag carrier or its subsidiary. The perceived need to provide essential air links between communities provided the justification for regulating the supply of air transport services in this way. Cross-subsidisation, entailing the profits generated by the relevant monopolist on its busier routes being used to cover the losses incurred on its more lightly trafficked city pairs, provided the means by which this policy could be carried out. To prevent the possible abuse of monopoly power, fare levels were subject to tight government regulation. The experience of other European countries, notably the UK, that competition on domestic routes was beneficial had not been considered pertinent.

It is apparent from Table 2.1 that entry to the domestic trunk routes of France and Spain has emanated from three sources, namely: existing scheduled carriers, charter airlines and new start-up companies.[1] Domestic market entry in the UK during the 1980s and early 1990s revealed that it was the former group that proved most successful. More recently, it has been new start-up carriers offering no frills services that have had the most impact. Interestingly, the greatest source of new entrant in France and Spain has been the charter sector. In the French market, Air Liberté and AOM played a major part in competing against Air Inter on the main trunk

15

routes, whilst Air Europa and Spanair have performed a similar role against Iberia and its subsidiary Aviaco in Spain.

Since 1994, entry has been permitted to the domestic routes of southern EU countries, transforming the busiest of them into highly competitive markets. The response of incumbents has been mainly centred on increasing service frequency, often involving the use of smaller aircraft. Extensive activity has been apparent in the range of discount fares on offer, but the price differential between incumbents and entrants with respect to fully flexible tickets has fallen over time.

Table 2.1 Entry to the main French and Spanish trunk routes

Routes	Entrant	Carrier Type	Period of Entry
Paris - Nice	AOM	Charter	1991 -
	Air Liberté	Charter	1996 -
Paris - Toulouse	Air Liberté	Charter	1995 -
	Euralair	Charter	1995 - 1996
	TAT	Scheduled	1996 - 1997
Paris - Marseilles	AOM	Charter	1995 -
	TAT	Scheduled	1995 - 1996
Madrid - Barcelona	Spanair	Charter	1994 -
	Air Europa	Charter	1994 -
Barcelona - Palma	Air Europa	Charter	1994 -
	Air Nostrum	New Entrant	1995 - 1996
	Spanair	Charter	1995 -
Madrid - Palma	Spanair	Charter	1994 -
	Air Europa	Charter	1994 -

Source: JP Airline-Fleets International.

2.1 Liberalisation of the French domestic market

In 1985, Air Inter was authorised by the French Government to continue operating its domestic route network on an exclusive basis for a further 15 years. Involvement of the European Commission over Air France's acquisition of UTA in 1990 however, forced an amendment to this arrangement.[2] Eight trunk routes were to be opened up to competition. In the event, only one of the routes identified became subject to any significant degree of entry. The charter operator Minerve, later renamed AOM after its merger with Air Outre Mer, began operating between Orly and Nice in 1991. Competition was concentrated in the areas of in-flight service and ground handling. Air Inter's sole response was to increase frequency on the route. Its policy of providing a basic, single class service utilising aircraft configured with high-density seating did not alter. Interestingly, the entry of AOM did not lead to any significant increase in capacity on the route due to the downsizing of aircraft employed by the flag carrier and its subsidiary. Air France and Air Inter increased the number of flights they provided between 1990 and 1994 by some 12%, but the total number of seats supplied by them fell by 6%, as may be seen in Figure 2.1.

Figure 2.1   Seats supplied on the Paris - Nice route

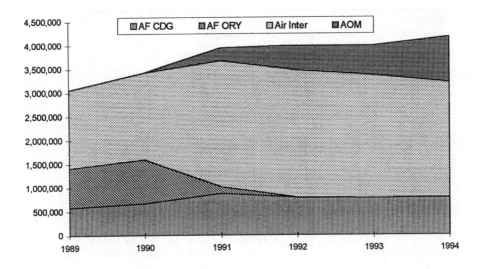

Source: OAG.   Note: AF CDG refers to Air France services from Charles de Gaulle and AF ORY to those from Orly.

It is clear that the French Government had not been keen to open up its domestic routes to competition. Only after a protracted battle with the European Commission and ultimately a decision by the European Court of Justice did other trunk routes become available for entry.[3] Table 2.2 lists the dates on which the seven busiest French routes serving Paris (Orly) were entered and gives details of the service frequency provided by each carrier before and after entry. Air Liberté, a charter airline established in 1987, began offering four services a day between Orly and Toulouse in

January 1995. During the following twelve months it commenced operations on four other trunk routes: Paris - Bordeaux, Paris - Montpellier, Paris - Nice and Paris - Strasbourg. AOM also expanded its domestic operations in 1995 by entering the Paris - Marseilles and Paris - Montpellier markets. TAT, a scheduled regional carrier in which British Airways had acquired a substantial shareholding in 1992, also entered the fray, commencing services between Orly and Marseilles in March 1995. Euralair, a small charter carrier, also began scheduled services between Paris and Toulouse in April 1995.

Table 2.2   Entry to Paris (Orly) trunk routes

Orly to	Frequency Pre Entry	New Entrant	Entry Date	Frequency Post Entry
Nice	Air Inter 9	AOM (IW)	4/1991	IT 15 IW 10
	Air France 5	Air Liberté (VD)	1/1996	IT 15 IW 11VD 5
			10/1996	IT 15 IW/VD 14
Toulouse	Air Inter 13	Air Liberté (VD)	1/1995	IT 13 VD 4
		Euralair (RN)	4/1995	IT 14 VD 6 RN 4
		TAT (IJ)	10/1995	IT 14 VD/RN 10 IJ 5
			10/1996	IT 14 VD 9 IJ 9
Marseilles	Air Inter 14	AOM (IW)	1/1995	IT 14 IW 7
		TAT (IJ)	3/1995	IT 14 IW 9 IJ 6
			10/1996	IT 14 IW 9 IJ 9
Bordeaux	Air Inter 9	Air Liberté (VD)	5/1995	IT 9 VD 6
			10/1996	IT 9 VD 6
Strasbourg	Air Inter 7	Air Liberté (VD)	9/1995	IT 8 VD 5
			10/1996	IT 9 VD 6
Montpellier	Air Inter 7	AOM (IW)	10/1995	IT 7 IW 4
		Air Liberté (VD)	1/1996	IT 7 IW 4 VD 3
			10/1996	IT 8 IW/VD 5
Toulon	Air Inter 5	AOM (IW)	4/1996	IT 6 IW 3
			10/1996	IT 6 IW 4

Source: OAG.

The most significant impact was achieved by Air Liberté, which adopted a much more aggressive stance than AOM. It actively engaged Air Inter in fare competition.[4] A good example of Air Liberté's approach is shown by its behaviour on the Paris-Toulouse route. After some initial aggressive discounting of the lowest fares available, prices stabilised with the new entrant undercutting Air Inter by some 21% for a fully flexible economy class return journey. Figure 2.2 contrasts the business class (C) return fares (in francs) charged by Air Liberté, Euralair and TAT with the economy (Y) return fare levied by Air Inter during 1995, the first year of competition.

Figure 2.3 compares the lowest fares available from each carrier on the route over the same period.

Figure 2.2   Highest return fares between Paris and Toulouse in 1995

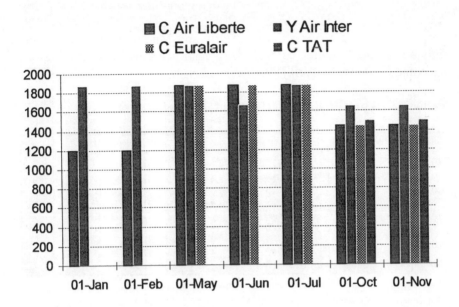

Note: C refers to business class fares and Y to economy class fares. Fares shown are in French francs.

Shortly before Air Liberté began operating the Orly - Toulouse route, Air Inter had been providing twelve services each weekday using mostly large capacity Airbus 300 and Airbus 330 aircraft. Table 2.3 shows the weekday departure times from Orly in November 1994 of Air Inter's services to Toulouse. A year later on the route the number of flights operated each weekday had increased to 31, with 65% more seats available overall. Table 2.4 shows the schedule of departures from Orly in November 1995. Growth in demand however, did not match this large increase in capacity. Between 1993 and 1995 passenger traffic increased by only 21%, as may be seen in Table 2.5. Not surprisingly, this substantial imbalance was not sustainable.

As well as competing on fares, Air Liberté provided its passengers with a superior in-flight service. Overall, consumers benefited from both lower and a wider choice of fares. In addition, they gained a substantial increase in frequency, in-flight meals and drinks, and a business class service with all the usual trimmings. Table 2.6 provides a list of the service features offered by new entrants, Air Liberté and TAT.

Figure 2.3 Lowest return fares between Paris and Toulouse in 1995

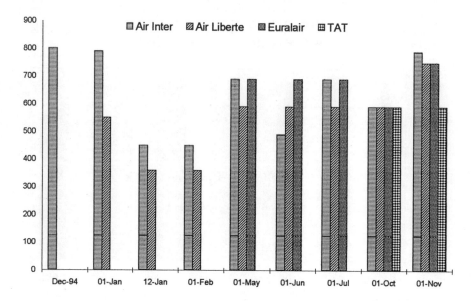

Note: Fares shown are in French francs.

Table 2.3   Air Inter services from Orly to Toulouse in November 1994

Departure Time	Aircraft Type	Seating Capacity
06.50	Airbus 330	412
08.15	Airbus 320	172
09.10	Airbus 330	412
11.30	Airbus 300	314
13.15	Airbus 320	172
14.25	Airbus 330	412
15.30	Airbus 300	314
16.20	Airbus 320	172
17.20	Airbus 330	412
19.15	Airbus 300	314
21.05	Airbus 330	412
21.55	Airbus 320	172

Sources: JP Airline-Fleets International & OAG.

Table 2.4   Services from Orly to Toulouse in November 1995

Departure Time	Airline	Aircraft Type	Seating Capacity
06.05	Air Liberté	MD-83	169
06.05	TAT	Fokker 100	99
06.10	Air Inter	Airbus 320	172
07.05	Air Inter	Airbus 330	412
07.30	Euralair	Boeing 737-200	130
07.55	Air Liberté	Airbus 310	275
08.15	Air Inter	Fokker 100	109
08.30	TAT	Fokker 100	99
09.05	Air Liberté	Airbus 300	345
09.05	Air Inter	Airbus 321	207
09.45	Euralair	Boeing 737-200	130
10.40	Air Inter	Airbus 320	172
11.15	TAT	Fokker 100	99
12.05	Air Inter	Airbus 320	172
12.25	Air Liberté	Airbus 310	275
13.25	Air Inter	Airbus 321	207
15.05	Air Liberté	MD-83	169
15.15	Air Inter	Airbus 321	207
16.10	TAT	Fokker 100	99
17.00	Air Inter	Airbus 320	172
17.00	Air Liberté	Airbus 310	275
17.20	Euralair	Boeing 737-200	130
17.50	Air Inter	Airbus 320	172
18.15	Air Inter	Airbus 300	314
18.45	TAT	Fokker 100	99
19.15	Air Inter	Airbus 321	207
19.45	Air Liberté	Airbus 300	345
20.00	TAT	Fokker 100	99
20.15	Air Inter	Airbus 320	172
20.35	Euralair	Boeing 737-200	130
21.10	Air Inter	Airbus 330	412

Sources: JP Airline-Fleets International & OAG.

The process of reducing the chronic over-supply situation on the route began in November 1995, when Air Liberté acquired Euralair's scheduled operations.[5] At the beginning of 1996, Air Liberté claimed that its 30% share of the Paris-Toulouse market was generating profits. Its intended launch of 23 new domestic routes during the first half of 1996 however, did not materialise. Its desire to take-over AOM, whose owners Credit Lyonnais were experiencing financial difficulties, was also not realised. An alliance established in June 1996 between Air Liberté and AOM, which involved the two carriers code-sharing on routes from Orly to Montpellier and Nice, was very short lived. The ambitious plans of Air Liberté came to an abrupt end in October 1996 with the carrier declaring itself bankrupt. Air Inter's (by then renamed Air France Europe) response to the forceful competitive approach of its rival had proved effective. Aside from matching the lowest fares offered by Air Liberté, the incumbent had substantially increased its service frequency and introduced in-flight catering. To further strengthen its grip on the domestic market, Air Inter introduced a shuttle service in October 1996, marketed under the name "Navette", on three of its major trunk routes.

Table 2.5 Traffic growth on French domestic trunk routes

Paris to:	1993	1995	1999
Nice	2,746,976	2,808,106	3,255,365
Marseilles	2,195,398	2,455,285	2,926,642
Toulouse	2,038,982	2,470,616	2,949,392
Bordeaux	1,306,576	1,411,899	1,600,476
Strasbourg	1,061,574	1,072,270	1,282,839
Montpellier	1,011,549	1,001,721	1,289,770
Toulon	683,710	621,368	664,987

Source: DGAC.

Table 2.6 Service features offered by the new entrants

Business class	Air Liberté	TAT
Separate check-in	✓	✓
Pre-flight seat allocation	✓	✓
Business lounge	✓	✓
Late check-in		✓
Separate boarding	✓	
Hot meals	✓	✓
Champagne	✓	✓
Hot towels		✓
Newspapers	✓	✓
Economy class		
Cold meals	✓	
Refreshments		✓
Towelettes		✓
Newspapers	✓	✓
Seat allocation	✓	✓

Source: Air Liberté and TAT timetables.

British Airways acquired Air Liberté in December 1996 and merged its two French subsidiaries in 1997, adopting the Air Liberté name. Combining the domestic operations of TAT with those of Air Liberté provided the prospect of a strong and durable competitor to Air France (Air Inter was merged into its parent company in 1997). This was not to prove the case, however. Further consolidation seemed a possibility in 1998 with the sale of AOM. Its sale triggered a bidding war involving Air France, British Airways, Swissair and others. In the event the SAir Group, Swissair's parent company, acquired a 49% shareholding in AOM in 1999, following its acquisition of a 44% stake in Air Littoral in September 1998. The SAir Group extended its involvement in the French market in May 2000, when as a result of continuing losses, British Airways sold its 86% shareholding in Air Liberté in May 2000 to Taitbout, the then joint owners with the SAir Group of AOM. (Taitbout also at this stage owned 17% of Air Littoral.)

The intention of the SAir Group and its French partners had then been to merge Air Liberté, Air Littoral and AOM during 2001 in order to compete more effectively with Air France and its regional associates. Air France had acquired a number of French regional carriers during 2000. In January of that year, the flag carrier began a process by which it would acquire a 42% shareholding in Protéus Airlines, based in Dijon, and followed this a month later by purchasing a 70% stake in Regional Airlines. Air France further increased its grip on the French market in June when it announced that it was to take a majority shareholding in Brit Air. As a result of these acquisitions, the French scheduled airline industry had consolidated by the end of 2000 into just two groupings - one controlled by the flag carrier and the other by Swissair in the guise of the SAir Group. Since then the SAir Group has been forced to relinquish its shareholdings in the French carriers, as a result of incurring heavy losses.

Examining the longer-term effects of deregulation on the French domestic market, it is clear that after an initial and dramatic upsurge in competition the market has evolved into one of duopolistic supply. Table 2.7 reveals that the total number of seats supplied in the domestic market reached a peak in 1996, representing a 27% increase over the equivalent 1992 figure when Air Inter supplied nearly all domestic services. By summer 2000 however, total seats supplied had been reduced by 11% compared to the 1996 level, reflecting the consolidation that had occurred.

The impact of competition can also be seen in terms of growth in the number of routes supplied by more than one carrier. As Table 2.8 shows, in 1992 only seven routes had more than one operating carrier. However, in six of these cases the operating airlines were Air France, Air Inter, Air Afrique and UTA, the latter two companies operating very infrequent services. The only route exhibiting any real competition was Paris – Nice. By 1996 however, 31 routes had more than one operating airline. This situation was relatively short-lived due to the market being substantially over-supplied. By summer 2000, although three routes are indicated as having three operating carriers, on two of them the third carrier was Air Afrique providing less than 1% of the seats offered. Table 2.9 lists the non-monopolistic routes being operated during summer 2000 and shows the percentage of seats supplied by each of the operating carriers. Table 2.10 lists the routes with over 10,000 seats supplied per week that are operated by only one carrier. The dominant position of Air France is clearly evident.

To complete the picture regarding the Orly – Toulouse route, Table 2.11 provides details of the current 41 weekday departures of which 25 are operated by Air France and 18 by Air Lib.[6] Table 2.12 provides a summary of the supply changes on the route between 1994 and 2000.

Table 2.7   Seats supplied on the top 30 routes

	1989		1992		1996		2000	
Routes	Seats	%	Seats	%	Seats	%	Seats	%
Top 3	167,674	29.1	203,625	31.7	268,850	33.0	241,288	32.9
Top 5	230,423	39.9	275,247	42.9	370,331	45.5	318,776	43.5
Top 10	314,536	54.5	367,631	57.2	493,081	60.6	418,442	57.0
Top 20	411,238	71.3	465,669	72.5	604,635	74.3	505,763	69.0
Top 30	461,667	80.0	519,065	80.8	664,789	81.7	561,666	76.6
Total	577,009		642,177		813,502		733,479	

Source: OAG.

Table 2.8   Evolving route competition

Routes with	1989	1992	1996	2000
1 carrier	161	157	160	136
2 carriers	7	4	22	21
3 carriers	2	3	4	3
4 carriers	0	1	4	0
5 carriers	0	0	1	0
	170	165	191	160

Source: OAG.

Table 2.9   Non-monopolistic routes operated in summer 2000

Route	Seats Supplied	% by Carrier 1	% by Carrier 2	% by Carrier 3
Paris - Nice	87,519	Air France 57%	AOM 24%	Air Liberté 19%
Paris - Toulouse	78,596	Air France 67%	Air Liberté 33%	-
Paris - Marseilles	75,173	Air France 77%	AOM 23%	Air Afrique <1%
Paris - Bordeaux	41,739	Air France 82%	Air Liberté 17%	Air Afrique 1%
Paris - Montpellier	35,749	Air France 71%	Air Liberté 29%	-
Paris - Toulon	20,310	AOM 52%	Air Liberté 48%	-
Paris - Perpignan	13,386	Air Liberté 54%	AOM 46%	-
Lyons - Nice	6,464	Air France 72%	Air Littoral 28%	-
Lyons - Toulouse	6,454	Air France 78%	Air Liberté 22%	-
Marseilles - Nantes	5,216	Air France 64%	Air Littoral 36%	-
Lyons - Strasbourg	4,672	Air France 79%	Regional 21%	-
Nice - Toulouse	4,504	Air Littoral 84%	Air France 16%	-
Nice - Cannes	4,270	Heli Inter R 79%	Nice Heli 21%	-
Nice - Strasbourg	4,214	Air Littoral 64%	Air France 36%	-
Marseilles - Figari	4,190	Air Littoral 51%	Air Liberté 49%	-
Nice - Bordeaux	3,906	Air Littoral 82%	Air France 18%	-
Nice - Lille	3,626	Air Littoral 58%	Air France 42%	-
Nice - Nantes	3,206	Air Littoral 78%	Air France 22%	-
Nice - Figari	2,750	Air Littoral 54%	Air Liberté 46%	-
Marseilles - Calvi	2,288	Air Littoral 56%	Air Liberté 44%	-
Nice - Rennes	2,100	Air Littoral 67%	Air France 33%	-
Nice - Calvi	1,804	Air Littoral 61%	Air Liberté 39%	-
Lyons - Mulhouse	1,128	Air France 67%	Air Liberté 33%	-
Lyons - Metz	1,009	Air Liberté 81%	Air France 19%	-

Source: OAG.

With the acquisition of Brit Air and Regional Airlines by Air France and the bankruptcy in June 2001 of AOM-Air Liberté, an opportunity may now exist for a no-frills carrier to establish itself in the domestic market. As a result of financial difficulties, the SAir Group was forced to sell AOM- Air Liberté in July 2001. Air Lib is currently in the process of downsizing its operations and appears likely to relinquish close to one half of its slots at Orly. Hence, the chance for another operator to set itself up in the market.

Table 2.10   Monopolistic routes operated in summer 2000

Routes	Seats Supplied	Carrier
Paris - Strasbourg	32,618	Air France
Paris - Lyons	18,544	Air France
Paris - Biarritz	14,808	Air France
Paris - Brest	13,348	Air France
Paris - Pau	13,226	Air France
Paris - Mulhouse	11,220	Air France

Source: OAG

Table 2.11   Services from Orly to Toulouse in January 2001

Departure Time	Airline	Aircraft Type	Seating Capacity
06.25	Air France	Airbus 319	142
06.55	Air France	Airbus 319	142
06.55	Air Liberté	Fokker 100	105
07.10	Air Liberté	MD-83	159
07.25	Air France	Airbus 320	159
07.55	Air France	Airbus 319	142
08.10	Air Liberté	MD-83	159
08.25	Air France	Airbus 320	159
08.55	Air France	Airbus 320	159
09.40	Air Liberté	MD-83	159
09.55	Air France	Airbus 320	159
10.40	Air Liberté	Fokker 100	105
10.55	Air France	Airbus 320	159
11.40	Air Liberté	MD-83	159
11.55	Air France	Airbus 320	159
12.40	Air Liberté	MD-83	159
12.55	Air France	Airbus 320	159
13.55	Air France	Airbus 319	142
14.10	Air Liberté	Fokker 100	105
14.25	Air France	Airbus 320	159
14.55	Air France	Airbus 319	142
15.10	Air Liberté	Fokker 100	105
15.25	Air France	Airbus 319	142
15.40	Air Liberté	MD-83	159
15.55	Air France	Airbus 319	142
16.25	Air France	Airbus 320	159
16.40	Air Liberté	MD-83	159
16.55	Air France	Airbus 319	142
17.10	Air Liberté	MD-83	159
17.25	Air France	Airbus 319	142
17.40	Air Liberté	Fokker 100	105
17.55	Air France	Airbus 319	142
18.25	Air France	Airbus 320	159
18.40	Air Liberté	Fokker 100	105
18.55	Air France	Airbus 319	142
19.10	Air Liberté	Fokker 100	105
19.25	Air France	Airbus 320	159
19.40	Air Liberté	MD-83	159
19.55	Air France	Airbus 320	159
20.25	Air France	Airbus 320	159
20.40	Air Liberté	MD-83	159
20.55	Air France	Airbus 319	142
21.10	Air Liberté	MD-83	159

Source: OAG.

Table 2.12   Supply changes on the Paris (Orly) - Toulouse route

	1994	1995	2000
Number of Carriers	1	4	2
Daily Frequency	12	31	43
Air France* share (%)	100	45	58
Daily Seats	3690	6074	6255
Air France* share (%)	100	51	60
Average aircraft seating capacity	308	196	145

*Air France subsidiary, Air Inter, operated the route in 1994 and 1995.
Data relates to a November weekday in each year.

2.2 Deregulation of the Spanish domestic market

Prior to 1994, Spanish domestic services were the preserve of the flag carrier Iberia and its subsidiary, Aviaco. A dramatic transformation however, occurred during 1994 when two charter operators, Air Europa and Spanair, began operating scheduled services on the country's trunk routes. Both carriers had been providing charter services within Spain before deregulation.[7] Air Europa, formerly a subsidiary of the failed International Leisure Group, was the first to take advantage of the new commercial freedom commencing eight rotations a day on the country's busiest domestic route, Madrid - Barcelona. Spanair, an SAS subsidiary, quickly followed suit with six daily services. By far the most important trunk route in Spain, and already the most frequently served domestic city-pair in Europe, it became subject to a large increase in capacity. Iberia responded to this encroachment in much the same manner as Air Inter did in its home market, namely by increasing frequency. Table 2.13 lists the dates on which the nine busiest trunk routes were entered and gives details of the service frequency provided by each carrier before and after entry.

Somewhat unusually, at least by the standards provided on domestic routes in other Southern European countries, Iberia operated a two-class service. Both new entrants offered a business class product, which came with all of the usual trimmings save for seat pitch. Both Spanair and Air Europa operated their aircraft in high density seating configurations. The improved in-flight service was not though the main means by which the new entrants challenged Iberia. The two companies substantially undercut the fares being charged by the flag carrier, typically by around 50%.

Table 2.13   Entry to Spanish domestic trunk routes

Route	Frequency Pre Entry	New Entrant	Entry Date	Frequency Post Entry
Madrid -	Iberia (IB)	Spanair (JK)	3/1994	IB 33 JK 7
Barcelona	31	Air Europa (UX)	4/1994	IB 35 JK 7 UX 9
			10/1996	IB 35 JK 10 UX 7
Barcelona	IB 11	Air Europa	4/1994	IB 11 UX 1
- Palma		Air Nostrum (YW)	6/1995	IB 12 UX 1 YW 2
		Spanair	7/1995	IB 12 UX 1 YW 2 JK 2
			10/1996	IB 10 UX 2 JK 3
Madrid -	IB 4	Spanair	3/1994	IB 4 AO 2 JK 2
Palma	Aviaco 2	Air Europa	4/1994	IB 4 AO 2 JK 2 UX 1
	(AO)		10/1996	IB 5 AO 2 JK 3 UX 3
Madrid -	IB 8	Air Europa	11/1994	IB 8 UX 1
Malaga			10/1996	IB 7 UX 2
Madrid -	IB 8	Air Europa	11/1994	IB 8 UX 1
Valencia		Air Nostrum	1/1995	IB 8 UX 1 YW 2
			10/1996	IB 7 YW 5
Madrid -	IB 7	Air Europa	11/1994	IB 7 UX 1
Bilbao		Air Nostrum	12/1995	IB 7 YW 1
			10/1996	IB 7 YW 1
Barcelona	AO 3	Air Nostrum	1/1995	AO 3 YW 1
- Menorca		Air Europa	10/1996	AO 5 YW 1 UX 1
Madrid -	IB 6	Air Europa	11/1994	IB 6 UX 1 JK 1
Santiago		Spanair		
			10/1996	IB 6 UX 2 JK 2
Barcelona	IB 4 AZ 1	Spanair	11/1994	IB 4 AZ 1 UX 1
- Malaga		Alitalia (AZ)		
			10/1996	IB 4 AZ 1 UX 1

Source: OAG.

For some while, Iberia did not attempt to match the lower fares of its new rivals, relying on the attraction of its large network. In October 1996 however, it responded aggressively by introducing APEX (Estrella) fares on six of the trunk routes it operated from Madrid. These new fares represented substantial reductions on the fares previously charged by the company, undercutting the lowest fares charged by Air Europa and Spanair on the country's busiest route, Madrid - Barcelona, by 25%. At the same time it introduced a flexible economy (S-class) fare on the Madrid-Barcelona route, providing passengers with a 37% reduction over its normal Y-class fare. The two newcomers to the scheduled scene had little option but to match the new fares charged by their larger rival. However, they did raise the matter with the European Commission arguing that a misuse of state aid by the flag carrier had occurred.[8] Figures 2.4 and 2.5 respectively trace the changes in business and economy class return fares (in pesetas) charged on this route by the three airlines between 1995 and 1998.

In January 1994, immediately before deregulation occurred, Iberia was providing all but one of the 29 daily services operated between Madrid and Barcelona, as Table 2.14 reveals. Iberia mostly employed Boeing 727-200 aircraft on the route equipped with 172 seats, providing a single class shuttle service that could not be booked in advance. The airline also operated flights on the route for which reservations could be made, but these consisted of services from Madrid to other European destinations that operated via Barcelona. The one non-Iberia service was provided by SAS and formed part of a through flight to Scandinavia.

By January 1995, Spanair and Air Europa had entered the route and SAS withdrawn its daily service. As Table 2.15 shows, the number of daily flights had increased to 45, 31 of which were operated by Iberia, two more than they had operated a year earlier. Spanair were providing eight flights using MD-83 aircraft configured in a high-density layout with 170 seats, but offering a separate business class. Air Europa, also retaining a charter configuration of its aircraft, operated six daily flights. They too provided a business class service on the route. Overall, in less than one year the number of daily flights between Madrid and Barcelona had increased by 55% and the number of seats offered by 51%. Unlike in the French market where the increased supply had vastly outstripped the growth in demand, a better balance was achieved in Spain. Between 1993 and 1995, the numbers of passengers flying between Madrid and Barcelona rose by 44%.

During the winter of 1996/97, Spanish consumers benefited from the lowest fares ever offered in their domestic air transport market. It was for them unfortunately, a situation that could not last. In April 1997, Air Europa and Spanair increased their fares substantially, citing higher costs as their justification. As Iberia choose not to alter its fares at this time, the price differential between the flag carrier and its rivals was reduced to around 15% for Y-class passengers. At the same time as the fare increases were being implemented, the three companies announced that an interline agreement had been established between themselves enabling passengers with full-fare tickets to transfer provided any difference in price was paid. Rather unsurprisingly, questions were raised about fare collusion.

Figure 2.4   Madrid - Barcelona business class fares 1995-1998

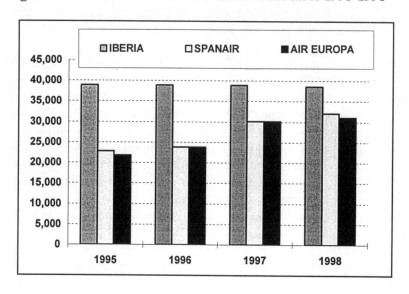

Figure 2.5   Madrid - Barcelona economy class fares 1995-1998

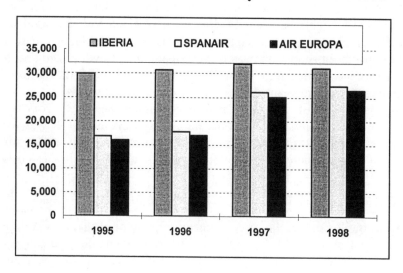

Table 2.14   Madrid to Barcelona services in January 1994

Departure Time	Airline	Aircraft Type	Seating Capacity
07.00	Iberia	Boeing 727	172
07.30	Iberia	Boeing 727	172
07.45	Iberia	MD-87	109
08.00	Iberia	Boeing 727	172
08.15	Iberia	Airbus 320	156
08.15	Iberia	Airbus 320	156
08.30	Iberia	Boeing 727	172
08.55	SAS	MD-87	110
09.00	Iberia	Boeing 727	172
09.45	Iberia	Boeing 727	172
10.00	Iberia	Boeing 727	172
11.00	Iberia	Boeing 727	172
11.50	Iberia	MD-87	109
11.55	Iberia	Airbus 320	156
12.00	Iberia	Boeing 727	172
14.00	Iberia	Boeing 727	172
15.00	Iberia	Boeing 727	172
16.00	Iberia	Boeing 727	172
16.30	Iberia	Boeing 727	172
17.00	Iberia	Boeing 727	172
17.30	Iberia	Boeing 727	172
18.00	Iberia	Boeing 727	172
18.30	Iberia	Boeing 727	172
19.30	Iberia	Boeing 727	172
20.00	Iberia	Boeing 727	172
20.30	Iberia	Boeing 727	172
21.00	Iberia	Boeing 727	172
22.00	Iberia	Boeing 727	172
22.45	Iberia	Boeing 727	172

Sources: JP Airline-Fleets International & OAG.

Six years after Iberia lost its monopoly position on the Madrid - Barcelona route, daily seat capacity had grown from 4,752 to 12,183 and frequency more than doubled, as Table 2.16 reveals. In terms of passenger demand, the route had become the busiest domestic city-pair market in Europe. By the beginning of 2001, Iberia were operating 49 daily flights in response to Spanair's 14 and Air Europa's 9, as shown in Table 2.17. Thirty four of Iberia's flights were operated as high frequency shuttle (Air Bridge) services, provided on a turn up and go basis at a standard fare and with no seat allocation. Passengers wishing to travel business class, reserve their seats in advance, or obtain discount fares had the use of the other 15 daily services provided by the company. The Air Bridge service has its own dedicated terminal facilities at Madrid and Barcelona, with flights operated every 15 minutes at peak times. To aid the marketing of the shuttle, flight numbers and departure times are one and the same. So, for example, IB0700 leaves Madrid for Barcelona at 07.00. By providing such a high service frequency, Iberia has ensured a relatively stable market share for itself of around 70%.

The above analysis has focussed on Spain's busiest domestic route, but what effects has deregulation had on the rest of its home market. As Table 2.18 reveals, the number of routes served in the Spanish domestic market contracted during the early 1990s. In 1992, all 91 routes were operated exclusively by Iberia or its wholly owned subsidiary, Aviaco.[9] As a result of liberalisation, by 1996 the situation had been considerably transformed. The number of routes served had increased to 123, 42 of which were operated by more than one carrier. In all, the number of seats provided in the domestic market had increased by 31% between 1992 and 1996, as Table 2.19 shows. Iberia and Aviaco were providing 74% of this capacity, Air Europa 11% and Spanair 9%. The country's ten busiest routes accounted for one half of all the seats provided.

Prior to 1994, Iberia and its subsidiary Aviaco were the sole suppliers of Spain's scheduled domestic air services. By 1996, when the market was at its most turbulent following deregulation, the combined share of seats supplied by Iberia and Aviaco on all domestic services amounted to 74%. Since 1996 though, there has been relatively little change in the overall supply situation, as Table 2.20 shows. The number of carriers providing domestic services however, has fallen since 1996. In April 1997, Air Nostrum entered into a franchise agreement with Iberia and has since operated all its flights on behalf of and in conjunction with the flag carrier. In addition, all of the other smaller Spanish carriers (Canarias, Paukn Air and Air Truck) have gone bankrupt and of the other non-Spanish airlines only Portugalia remains in the domestic market.

Table 2.15   Madrid to Barcelona services in January 1995

Departure Time	Airline	Aircraft Type	Seating Capacity
07.00	Iberia	Boeing 727	172
07.00	Spanair	MD-83	170
07.10	Air Europa	Boeing 737-300	148
07.15	Iberia	MD-87	109
07.30	Iberia	Boeing 727	172
07.45	Iberia	MD-87	109
08.00	Iberia	Boeing 727	172
08.20	Iberia	MD-87	109
08.25	Iberia	Boeing 727	155
08.30	Iberia	Airbus 320	156
08.30	Spanair	MD-83	170
08.50	Iberia	Boeing 727	155
08.50	Air Europa	Boeing 737-300	148
09.00	Iberia	Boeing 727	172
09.25	Air Europa	Boeing 737-300	148
09.35	Spanair	MD-83	170
09.45	Iberia	Boeing 727	172
10.00	Iberia	Boeing 727	172
11.00	Iberia	Boeing 727	172
11.50	Iberia	Airbus 320	156
12.00	Iberia	Boeing 727	172
13.00	Iberia	Boeing 727	172
14.00	Iberia	Boeing 727	172
14.45	Spanair	MD-83	170
15.00	Iberia	Boeing 727	172
16.00	Iberia	Boeing 727	172
16.15	Spanair	MD-83	170
16.30	Iberia	Boeing 727	172
17.00	Iberia	Boeing 727	172
17.20	Air Europa	Boeing 737-300	148
17.55	Air Europa	Boeing 737-300	148
18.00	Iberia	Boeing 727	172
18.20	Spanair	MD-83	170
18.30	Iberia	Boeing 727	172
19.00	Iberia	Boeing 727	172
19.30	Iberia	Boeing 727	172
19.45	Spanair	MD-83	170
20.00	Iberia	Boeing 727	172
20.25	Air Europa	Boeing 737-300	148
20.30	Iberia	MD-87	109
21.00	Iberia	Boeing 727	172
21.15	Spanair	MD-83	170
22.00	Iberia	Boeing 727	172
22.45	Iberia	Boeing 727	172
22.50	Iberia	MD-87	109

Sources: JP Airline-Fleets International & OAG.

Table 2.16 Supply changes on the Madrid - Barcelona route

	1994	1995	2000
Number of Carriers	2	3	3
Daily Frequency	29	45	71
Iberia share (%)	97	69	68
Daily Seats	4,752	7,199	12,183
Iberia share (%)	98	69	69
Average aircraft seating capacity	164	160	172

Data relates to a January weekday of each year.
Sources: JP Airline-Fleets International and OAG.

Table 2.17 Madrid to Barcelona services in January 2001

Departure Time	Airline	Aircraft Type	Seating Capacity
07.00	Iberia	Airbus 320	156
07.00	Spanair	MD-83	170
07.15	Iberia	Boeing 757	202
07.30	Iberia	Boeing 757	202
07.30	Spanair	MD-83	170
07.45	Iberia	Boeing 757	202
07.55	Iberia	Airbus 320	156
08.00	Iberia	Boeing 757	202
08.00	Spanair	MD-83	170
08.05	Air Europa	Boeing 737-400	168
08.10	Iberia	Airbus 320	156
08.15	Iberia	Airbus 320	156
08.20	Iberia	Boeing 727	155
08.30	Iberia	Boeing 727	155
08.30	Iberia	Airbus 321	186
08.35	Iberia	Boeing 727	155
08.45	Iberia	Boeing 767	211
08.50	Iberia	MD-87	109
09.00	Iberia	Boeing 757	202
09.10	Iberia	Airbus 320	156
09.10	Spanair	MD-83	170
09.20	Air Europa	Boeing 737-300	148
09.30	Iberia	Airbus 320	156
09.30	Spanair	MD-83	170
09.50	Air Europa	Boeing 737-300	148
10.00	Iberia	Boeing 757	202
11.00	Iberia	Boeing 757	202
11.20	Spanair	MD-83	170
11.40	Iberia	Boeing 757	202
12.00	Iberia	Boeing 757	202
12.30	Iberia	Airbus 320	156
13.00	Air Europa	Boeing 737-300	148
13.00	Iberia	Boeing 757	202
13.30	Spanair	MD-83	170

Table 2.17 Continued

Departure Time	Airline	Aircraft Type	Seating Capacity
14.00	Iberia	Boeing 757	202
14.30	Iberia	Airbus 320	156
15.00	Iberia	Boeing 757	202
15.15	Iberia	Airbus 320	156
15.15	Spanair	MD-83	170
15.30	Iberia	Airbus 320	156
16.00	Iberia	Boeing 757	202
16.10	Iberia	Airbus 320	156
16.40	Spanair	MD-83	170
17.00	Iberia	Boeing 757	202
17.00	Air Europa	Boeing 737-300	148
17.30	Iberia	Boeing 757	202
17.40	Spanair	MD-83	170
17.55	Air Europa	Boeing 737-400	168
18.00	Iberia	Boeing 757	202
18.15	Iberia	Airbus 320	156
18.15	Iberia	Airbus 320	156
18.30	Iberia	Airbus 320	156
19.00	Iberia	Boeing 757	202
19.00	Air Europa	Boeing 737-800	184
19.15	Iberia	Airbus 320	156
19.15	Spanair	MD-83	170
19.30	Iberia	Airbus 320	156
19.50	Iberia	MD-87	109
20.00	Iberia	Boeing 757	202
20.30	Iberia	Boeing 757	202
20.45	Spanair	MD-83	170
21.00	Iberia	Boeing 757	202
21.00	Air Europa	Boeing 737-300	148
21.05	Spanair	MD-83	170
21.30	Iberia	Boeing 757	202
21.40	Spanair	MD-83	170
21.50	Air Europa	Boeing 737-300	148
22.00	Iberia	DC9-30	110
22.15	Iberia	Airbus 320	156
22.45	Iberia	Boeing 757	202
23.30	Iberia	MD-87	109

Sources: JP Airline-Fleets International and OAG.

Table 2.18   Competition on Spanish domestic routes

Routes with	1989	1992	1996	2000
1 carrier	87	85	81	76
2 carriers	11	6	31	21
3 carriers	2	0	8	17
4 carriers	0	0	3	4
	100	91	123	118

Source: OAG.

Table 2.19   Seats supplied on Spanish domestic routes

	1989		1992		1996		2000	
Routes	Seats	%	Seats	%	Seats	%	Seats	%
Top 3	108,256	24.5	129,277	29.1	147,095	26.6	199,430	25.7
Top 5	145,393	33.0	162,568	36.5	193,363	35.0	266,929	34.4
Top 10	210,851	47.8	227,741	51.2	276,240	50.0	394,795	50.8
Top 20	294,243	66.7	307,857	69.2	372,179	67.3	536,021	69.0
Top 30	345,299	78.3	356,080	80.1	435,547	78.8	619,652	79.8
	441,119		444,794		552,862		776,435	

Source: OAG.

Table 2.20   Spanish domestic market concentration 1992-1998

Airline	1992		1996		1998	
	Capacity	%	Capacity	%	Capacity	%
Iberia	279,156	63	234,523	43	442,649	72
Aviaco	165,086	37	168,818	31		
Spanair			48473	9	84,560	14
Air Europa			62,728	11	56,000	9
Canarias					10,944	2
Paukn Air			8,400	1.5	8,625	1
Air Truck			3,680	0.5	4,800	1
Alitalia			4,788	1	4,718	1
Portugalia					2,470	<1
Luxair			363	<1	363	<1
Air Nostrum			14,850	3		
Total	444,242	100	546,623	100	615,429	100
HHI	1.0		0.57		0.55	

Source: OAG. Note: The services operated by Iberia subsidiaries, Binter Canarias and Binter Mediterraneo, are excluded from this listing due to a lack of relevant data. In 2001, Binter Mediterraneo was acquired by Air Nostrum.

Table 2.19 revealed that nearly 80% of domestic seat capacity is provided on the top 30 routes. In summer 2000, 42 of the 118 routes operated had more than one operating carrier (see Table 2.18). Details of the market shares of the carriers providing services on 40 of these routes are contained in Table 2.21.

Of the 40 routes shown in Table 2.21, Iberia is the largest provider of capacity on all but nine. In addition, the company's subsidiary, Binter Canarias, provides the largest number of seats on a further six. Despite this dominance, competition is strongly evident with Air Europa and/or Spanair providing services on all but the most lightly trafficked routes. For a while it had looked as if Air Europa would be acquired by Iberia, following an arrangement between the two involving the flag carrier wet leasing one third of Air Europa's fleet for a period of five years. Towards the end of 2000, discussions took place between the two companies regarding a possible purchase but in the event no sale was agreed. The other major provider in the domestic market, Spanair, is a subsidiary of SAS and as such is likely to play an increasing part in Star Alliance activities. It is likely to remain however, as the stronger of Iberia's competitors. Since deregulation, it is clear the air transport market in Spain has experienced strong and durable competition. (Table 2.22 provides a listing of the carriers that have operated scheduled services in Spain between 1990 and 2000.)

Table 2.21   Non-monopolistic routes operated in summer 2000

Route	Seats Supplied	% by Carrier 1	% by Carrier 2	% by Carrier 3
Madrid - Barcelona	125,781	Iberia 74%	Spanair 17%	Air Europa 9%
Barcelona - Palma*	37,938	Iberia 46%	Spanair 36%	Air Europa 15%
Madrid - Palma	35,711	Iberia 40%	Spanair 35%	Air Europa 25%
Madrid - Tenerife	34,879	Iberia 64%	Spanair 18%	Air Europa 18%
Madrid - Malaga	32,620	Iberia 65%	Spanair 25%	Air Europa 10%
Madrid - Las Palmas	31,608	Iberia 69%	Spanair 25%	Air Europa 6%
Madrid - Bilbao	27,612	Iberia 65%	Spanair 23%	Air Europa 12%
Madrid - Valencia	24,220	Iberia 70%	Spanair 30%	-
Madrid - Santiago de C	23,890	Iberia 61%	Spanair 28%	Air Europa 11%
Madrid - Alicante	20,536	Iberia 60%	Spanair 29%	Air Europa 11%
Madrid - Oviedo	17,882	Iberia 59%	Spanair 32%	Air Europa 9%
Madrid - Sevilla	16,360	Iberia 70%	Spanair 30%	-
Madrid - Vigo	16,358	Iberia 71%	Spanair 29%	-
Barcelona - Sevilla	16,200	Iberia 76%	Spanair 13%	Air Europa 11%
Madrid - La Coruna	13,838	Iberia 82%	Air Europa 18%	-
Barcelona - Malaga	13,014	Iberia 83%	Spanair 17%	-

Table 2.21 Continued

Barcelona - Ibiza	12,314	Iberia 78%	Air Europa 22%	-
Barcelona - Bilbao**	12,120	Iberia 66%	Spanair 17%	Air Europa 13%
Barcelona - Mahon	11,240	Iberia 78%	Air Europa 22%	-
Las Palmas - Tenerife	10,888	Binter 99%	Air Atlantic 1%	-
Palma - Mahon	9,266	Iberia 58%	Spanair 26%	Air Europa 16%
Madrid - Arrecife	9,328	Iberia 45%	Spanair 37%	Air Europa 18%
Valencia - Palma	8,542	Air Europa 51%	Iberia 43%	Portugalia 6%
Madrid - Jerez	7,997	Iberia 81%	Air Europa 19%	-
Barcelona - Tenerife	7,908	Iberia 39%	Spanair 36%	Air Europa 25%
Las Palmas - Fuerteventura	7,868	Binter 97%	Air Atlantic 3%	-
Madrid - Ibiza	7,024	Iberia 75%	Air Europa 25%	-
Las Palmas - Arrecife#	6,957	Binter 82%	Air Europa 8%	Spanair 7%
Palma - Ibiza	6,936	Iberia 87%	Air Europa 13%	-
Tenerife - Arrecife	5,390	Binter^	Spanair^	Air Europa^
Barcelona - Las Palmas	4,836	Iberia 55%	Spanair 45%	-
Palma - Alicante	4,312	Air Europa 67%	Iberia 33%	-
Barcelona - La Coruna	4,036	Iberia 71%	ERA 29%	-
Sevilla - Tenerife	2,836	Iberia 74%	Air Europa 26%	-
Tenerife - Valverde	2,592	Binter 94%	Air Atlantic 6%	-
Barcelona - Valladolid	2,096	Iberia 57%	Air Europa 43%	-
Las Palmas - La Palma	2,048	Binter 93%	Air Atlantic 7%	-
Barcelona - Vitoria	1,580	ERA 62%	Iberia 38%	-
Malaga - Tenerife	1,268	Iberia 71%	Air Europa 29%	-
Bilbao - Alicante	1,112	Iberia 67%	Air Europa 33%	-

Source: OAG.   Notes: *European Regions Airlines provided 3% of the seat capacity. The company has since gone out of business. **Portugalia provided 4% of the seat capacity. #Air Atlantic provided 3% of the seat capacity. ^As a result of Spanair and Air Europa providing very different seating capacities in each direction on this route, it is not possible to provide an accurate % split.

Table 2.22 Spanish scheduled domestic service operators

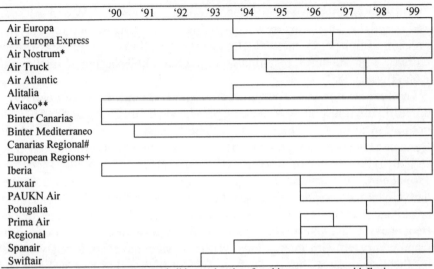

	'90	'91	'92	'93	'94	'95	'96	'97	'98	'99
Air Europa										
Air Europa Express										
Air Nostrum*										
Air Truck										
Air Atlantic										
Alitalia										
Aviaco**										
Binter Canarias										
Binter Mediterraneo										
Canarias Regional#										
European Regions+										
Iberia										
Luxair										
PAUKN Air										
Potugalia										
Prima Air										
Regional										
Spanair										
Swiftair										

(*Since 1997, Air Nostrum has operated all its services in a franchise arrangement with Iberia.
**Aviaco's operations were merged with those of Iberia in 1999.
#Canarias Regional ceased trading in January 1999.
+European Regions Airline ceased trading in 2000.)
Source: JP Airline-Fleets International.

2.3 Competition in the Norwegian domestic market

Historically, three airlines have provided the vast majority of Norway's domestic air services. Until 1987, all routes had a single operator. In 1956, SAS, the multinational "flag" carrier, had been granted rights to operate routes in the north of the country and between the north and the south, whilst Braathens, the Norwegian then privately owned carrier, had rights to serve the south.[10] In addition to its allocation of routes, SAS were awarded the licence to operate the busiest route in the country, Oslo-Bergen. The third operator, Widerøe connected remoter communities located along Norway's extensive coastline.

As in many other countries, the Government ensured that smaller regional towns were provided with air services by allowing the two carriers to each operate on a sufficient number of profitable routes in order to cover the losses incurred on their less dense links. This policy of encouraging cross-subsidisation resulted in high load factors (particularly on routes to the north) and relatively little fare discounting.

In 1966, Braathens was allowed to operate between Oslo and Ålesund and to add the latter to its route connecting towns along the west coast. In a revision of this policy in 1973, Braathens were allowed to connect western Norway with the north, resulting in an overall 40:60 sharing of traffic with SAS (Burns, 1997).

The first attempt at introducing some limited competition into Norway's domestic air transport was made in 1987, when Braathens and SAS were both allowed to serve the country's three busiest city-pair routes (Oslo to Bergen, Stavanger and Trondheim). However, the newcomer in each case, Braathens in respect of Bergen and SAS with regards to Stavanger and Trondheim, were restricted to providing no more than four frequencies per day. Given the considerable amount of business traffic on these routes, the advantage clearly lay with the carrier that provided the higher service frequency. A fare war did not ensue, partly because fares were already low when compared with international services. Maximum fare levels were set by the Government, but aside from this restriction the two airlines had pricing freedom. As a consequence, the effect of allowing two operators on the three routes was muted.

The aim of the Norwegian Administration in controlling the number of frequencies that the second operator on each of the three routes could provide was clearly aimed at preventing a serious excess supply situation occurring, the effects of which would have been a fare war and losses for both airlines. Ensuring the survival of both carriers in the domestic market was an important Government objective. As will be made clear below, the contrast between the effects of this enlightened interventionist policy, in which the State placed a limit on the commercial freedom of the two carriers, and that of an unconstrained market a decade or so later, would perhaps find many Norwegians now thinking that the former was preferable.

Although Norway is not a member of the European Union, it has adopted all of the measures contained in the Third Package. As such, from 1997 Norway's domestic market became subject to entry by any commercial carrier registered and controlled within any of the EU Member States. To enable Norwegian airlines to be in a position to face competitors, the Norwegian Government opted to fully deregulate its domestic air transport market in April 1994. Widerøe's STOL services, which were subsidised by the state, were exempted from this policy until 1997 when the Passenger Service Obligation (PSO) system was adopted.

With commercial freedom, the aim of both SAS and Braathens was to build up their previously constrained frequencies and to develop their networks to incorporate those areas of the country that had previously been denied to each of them. As may be seen in Table 2.23, which details the daily service frequencies provided by each operating carrier on 14 of the country's top routes between 1994 and 2000, the former policy was quickly realised. On the country's busiest trunk route, Oslo - Bergen, Braathens increased its service frequency from four to seven, to compete with SAS' 14. The company continued with this policy of building frequency on the route for the next few years, so that by 1998 it was providing 12 daily flights in contrast to the 16 offered by SAS. In the same way in the Oslo - Stavanger route, SAS, which had been restricted to operating three flights per day, had built up its daily service frequency to 14 by 1998, matching the number provided by Braathens.

The clear beneficiary of liberalisation though has been SAS. Right from the outset its ability to outperform its rival, particularly in terms of attracting high yield traffic, was evident. Table 2.24 shows the changes in the full fare market shares of the two carriers on the country's three busiest routes (Oslo-Bergen, Oslo-Stavanger, Oslo-Trondheim) between 1992 and 1996. The experience of SAS on the two routes it was seeking to strengthen its position is in marked contrast to that of Braathens on the Bergen route. While SAS was quickly able to attract over one third of the full fare paying passengers on the Stavanger and Trondheim routes, Braathens struggled to achieve a little over 20% in respect of Bergen. In terms of discount fare travellers, the opposite was the case with SAS gaining 33% of the Oslo-Stavanger traffic by 1996, whilst Braathens equivalent figure for Oslo-Bergen was 43%, as Table 2.25 reveals.

The net effect of these market share changes is revealed by the yields achieved by the two companies on the three routes in question. As may be seen in Figure 2.6, while in 1992 on the Bergen route SAS and Braathens had identical yields, deregulation saw the former company quickly establish a significant lead over its rival. By 1996, SAS' yield on the route was 37% higher than that of Braathens. An even more dramatic change however, occurred on the other two routes. Pre-deregulation, Braathens obtained higher yields on the two routes on which it had long been established, namely: Oslo-Stavanger and Oslo-Trondheim. Despite SAS being the relative newcomer, the situation was quickly reversed as Figures

2.7 and 2.8 reveal. By 1996, SAS was achieving significantly higher yields than Braathens on both routes.

Table 2.23 Weekday non-stop service frequencies by carrier

Oslo to:	1994	1995	1996	1997	1998	1999	2000
Aalesund	BU 5	BU 6	BU 6	BU 7	BU 7	SK 5 BU 7 G2 4	SK 4 BU 6
Bardufoss	SK 1	-	SK 1	SK 1	SK 1	BU 1	SK 1 BU 1
Bergen	SK 15 BU 7	SK 15 BU 9	SK 16 BU 11	SK 15 BU 12	SK 16 BU 12	SK 18 BU 16 G2 5	SK 16 BU 13
Bodo	SK 5 BU 2	SK 5 BU 2	SK 6 BU 3	SK 6 BU 3	SK 6 BU 3	SK 7 BU 4	SK 6 BU 5
Harstad	SK 3 BU 2	SK 3 BU 2	SK 3 BU 2	SK 3 BU 2	SK 3 BU 2	SK 4 BU 3	SK 4 BU 3
Haugesund	SK 9	SK 10	SK 5	SK 5	SK 5	SK 5 BU 4	SK 6
Kristiansand	BU 7	BU 8	BU 8	BU 9	BU 11	SK 5 BU 9	SK 4 BU 8
Stavanger	SK 10 BU 16	SK 10 BU 15	SK 10 BU 15	SK 12 BU 15	SK 13 BU 15	SK 14 BU 14	SK 12 BU 13
Tromso	SK 7 BU 2	SK 7 BU 4	SK 7 BU 3	SK 7 BU 3	SK 7 BU 4	SK 8 BU 4	SK 8 BU 4
Trondheim	SK 8 BU 14	SK 8 BU 14	SK 11 BU 18	SK 11 BU 15	SK 11 BU 16	SK 16 BU 18 G2 5	SK 13 BU 15
Bergen to:							
Stavanger	SK 5 BU 14	SK 5 BU 12	SK 5 BU 12	SK 2 BU 10	SK 6 BU 10	SK 6 BU 13	SK 7 BU 13
Trondheim	BU 6	BU 5	BU 6	BU 7	BU 7	BU 7	BU 7
Bodo to:							
Tromso	SK 2 BU 2	SK 2 BU 2	SK 3 BU 3	SK 2 BU 3	SK 2 BU 3	SK 3 BU 3	SK 4 BU 3
Trondheim	SK 4 BU 3	SK 5 BU 3	SK 5 BU 2	SK 4 BU 4	SK 5 BU 3	SK 5 BU 4	SK 5 BU 3

Data refers to a Thursday in mid - September for each year shown. (SK=SAS, BU=Braathens, G2=Color Air)
Source: OAG.

   Braathens weaker performance in the deregulated market is also reflected in the load factors achieved by the two carriers on the three routes. Table 2.26 shows the changes in the two rivals' load factors between 1992 and 1996. While SAS was able to fill 59% of its seats on the Bergen route in 1996 despite the large increase in capacity provided by its competitor, Braathens was struggling on the Stavanger route to achieve much more than 50%. Of critical significance however, is the relationship between the large increases in capacity provided by the two carriers in their respective new markets and the proportion of full fare passengers they were each able to attract. An enormous difference is apparent between the two, as Figure 2.9, which shows the correlation on the Bergen route for Braathens, and Figure 2.10, which shows the same for SAS in respect of Stavanger, reveal.

Table 2.24   Full fare market shares

	Bergen		Stavanger		Trondheim	
	SAS	Braathens	SAS	Braathens	SAS	Braathens
1992	84.2	15.8	14.6	85.4	19.4	80.6
1993	89.1	10.9	16.9	83.1	23.4	76.6
1994	83.5	16.5	33.4	66.6	31.7	68.3
1995	75.4	24.6	33.0	67.0	30.1	69.9
1996	78.0	22.0	37.7	62.3	38.7	61.3

Source: Burns, 1997.

Table 2.25   Discount fare market shares

	Bergen		Stavanger		Trondheim	
	SAS	Braathens	SAS	Braathens	SAS	Braathens
1992	72.6	27.4	14.8	85.2	26.4	73.6
1993	72.6	27.4	14.0	86.0	25.5	74.5
1994	65.2	34.8	24.7	75.3	29.5	70.5
1995	59.4	40.6	30.0	70.0	33.4	66.6
1996	57.0	43.0	33.0	67.0	36.6	63.4

Source: Burns, 1997.

Table 2.26   Load factors (%)

	Bergen		Stavanger		Trondheim	
	SAS	Braathens	SAS	Braathens	SAS	Braathens
1992	64.0	56.5	60.8	61.1	56.7	56.2
1993	66.8	57.2	60.2	57.0	61.4	58.5
1994	66.2	49.4	49.6	49.7	63.4	58.1
1995	59.0	48.0	43.7	51.3	61.0	60.8
1996	59.0	47.1	48.0	53.2	61.0	58.8

Source: Burns, 1997.

Whilst SAS was able to increase its capacity on the Stavanger route and gain a commensurate proportion of the full fare traffic, Braathens on the Bergen route with nearly 40% of the overall capacity was achieving only around one half of this proportion of the high yield traffic. This placed Braathens at a serious disadvantage to its rival; a situation that was exacerbated when low cost carrier Color Air entered the fray in 1998, ultimately leading to the parlous state in which the airline currently finds itself.

Figure 2.6   Oslo - Bergen yields by carrier (NKR per RPK)

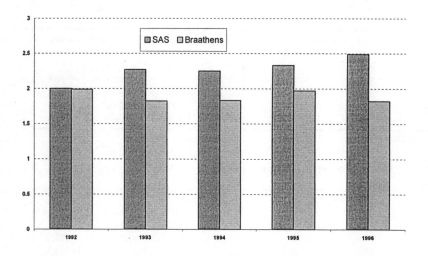

Figure 2.7   Oslo - Stavanger yields by carrier (NKR per RPK)

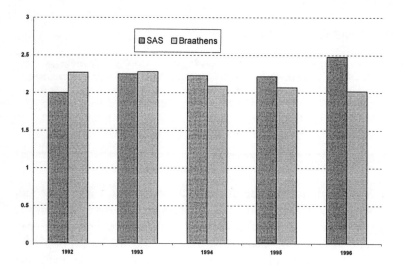

Figure 2.8   Oslo - Trondheim yields by carrier (NKR per RPK)

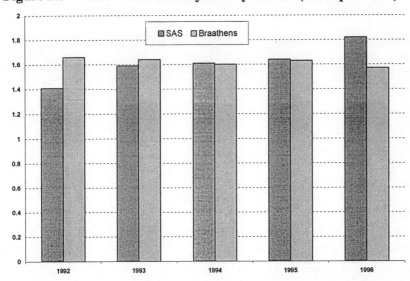

**Figure 2.9   Braathens' full fare market versus capacity share:
Oslo - Bergen**

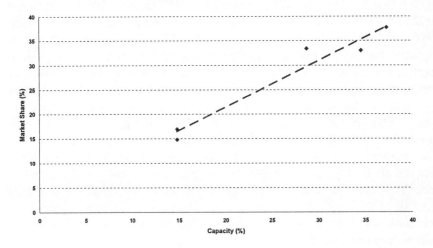

**Figure 2.10   SAS' full fare market versus capacity share:
Oslo - Stavanger**

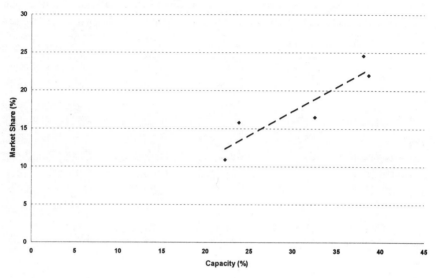

As may be seen in Table 2.27, the total number of seats supplied in the Norwegian domestic market increased by 34% to over 380,000 between 1992 and 1996, and was subject to a further dramatic rise of 31% between 1996 and 1999, taking the total to over 500,000. Close on one half of this capacity was supplied on the top five routes, up from the pre-deregulation level of just under 40%. Part of this increase in capacity was the result of low cost no-frills Color Air entering the market in September 1998. A subsidiary of the car ferry operator Color Line, it served three domestic routes: Oslo-Bergen, Oslo-Trondheim and Oslo-Ålesund. (Table 2.28 shows that no fewer than seven routes had three operating carriers in 1999.) The increase in passenger demand however, did not match the large increase in supply. For example, while capacity on the top three routes grew by over 40% between 1996 and 1999, traffic increased by less than one half of this amount. As a result of this large over-capacity, Color Air's existence was very short, the company folding only a year after it had commenced operations.

The imbalance between supply and demand further weakened Braathens, which as has already been mentioned not been faring as well as SAS in the aftermath of deregulation. In 1997, KLM acquired a 30% shareholding in

Braathens and became associated with the Wings alliance. Braathens' moves to establish itself in the Swedish market through its takeover of Malmo Aviation had also not proved a success. Irrespective of its link with KLM, losses continued to mount. By the beginning of 2001, it was clear that KLM no longer was interested in maintaining its shareholding in the loss-making company. In a dramatic development in summer 2001, Braathens announced that in view of its dire financial state and KLM's desire to sell its stake in the airline, it had reached an arrangement with SAS whereby the latter would acquire a 69% shareholding (including the KLM stake), in effect taking over the Norwegian company. The approach for this very unusual development had come from Braathens itself. At first, the Competition Authority in Norway (Konkurransetilsynet) indicated that it would not approve the takeover due to concerns over the likely monopolistic supply of domestic air services and its view that Braathens' financial condition was not as parlous as was being claimed. In October 2001 however, approval was granted for SAS to acquire a majority shareholding in its long-term rival. The prospects for competition in the Norwegian domestic market it would seem do not look too promising.

Table 2.27   Capacity of top 30 routes 1992-2000

	1992		1996		1999		2000	
Routes	Seats	%	Seats	%	Seats	%	Seats	%
Top 3	81,029	28.2	126,086	32.8	185,876	37.0	131,890	32.0
Top 5	112,161	39.0	173,037	45.0	237,125	47.2	179,646	43.6
Top 10	151,131	52.6	228,179	59.3	329,509	65.6	252,040	61.2
Top 20	200,741	69.8	283,931	73.8	398,425	79.3	314,737	76.4
Top 30	224,627	78.1	310,249	80.7	424,898	84.5	344,423	83.6
	287,441		384,487		502,670		412,040	

Source: OAG.

Table 2.28   Route competition 1992-2000

Routes with	1992	1996	1999	2000
1 carrier	117	109	104	87
2 carriers	9	17	17	19
3 carriers	0	1	7	0
	126	127	128	106

Source: OAG.

2.4 Concluding comments

What can be concluded from the domestic markets of Europe with regards to the effects of deregulation? While it is clear that not all countries have had the same experiences, there are a number of similarities. New entrants have been successful in establishing themselves in Greece, Ireland, Italy, Spain and the UK. Low cost, no-frills carriers in particular have had a major impact in the UK and Ireland, and have now set their sights on establishing a significant presence in continental Europe. By contrast, the domestic markets of Norway and Sweden are characterised by the near complete monopoly status of the flag carrier, SAS. In Germany, Lufthansa has a very dominant share of the market. Only Deutsche BA, which has at best been marginally profitable, provides any serious competition to the flag carrier. In France, the new entrants have also not been able to operate profitably, even when owned by European majors. Given that the French domestic market is one of Europe's largest, it would seem very odd if one successful competitor to Air France could not eventually emerge.

Why has this seemingly contradictory mix come about? How is it that the experience with deregulation in certain countries has been beneficial, whilst in others the effects have been disappointing to say the least? Market size would not appear to be the differentiating factor, witness the contrasting evidence from two of Europe's largest domestic markets, France and Spain. (Table 2.29 shows the number of seats supplied weekly between 1989 and 2000 in a selection of European countries.) In both countries, established charter carriers were the main source of the new entrants to the scheduled sector. However, whilst in Spain seven years on Air Europa and Spanair both remain in competition with Iberia on nearly all of the country's trunk routes, in France, Air Liberté, AOM and TAT have all failed in their endeavours against Air France, despite being owned by two of Europe's major players. It remains to be seen how effective the carrier that eventually emerges from the bankrupt Air Liberté-AOM (now renamed Air Lib) will be.

Much would appear to depend on how large and rapid an increase in capacity has occurred as a result of deregulation. As has been shown above, the experience in France was of a dramatic increase in capacity on the country's trunk routes (for example, 65% between Paris and Toulouse between 1994 and 1995), which was not matched by anything approaching a corresponding growth in passenger demand, despite the availability of very low fares. In Spain, whilst the number of seats supplied in the domestic market was also subject to increase, it was nowhere near as large. For example, capacity on the country's top three trunk routes grew by only 14% between 1992 and 1996. A key reason for this more restrained approach by Air Europa and Spanair may have been the fact that both had been providing charter flights in the domestic market prior to deregulation and therefore had some knowledge of how extensive the market was likely to be.[11] They would also have had some prior experience of how Iberia and its then subsidiary Aviaco could be expected to react when faced with increased competition. Air Liberté, the most aggressive of the new entrant's to France's domestic market, had neither experience of how responsive consumers would be to the large availability of low fares nor of the likely response of the incumbent, Air Inter. It would have been easy to have been lulled into thinking that the flag carrier's subsidiary would not react in a very aggressive way, given its former monopoly position and therefore rather non-commercial attitude.

Table 2.29   Weekly seat supply by country 1989-2000

	1989	1992	1996	2000
France	577,009	642,177	813,502	733,479
Germany	476,694	521,038	568,169	652,241
Italy	446,307	484,395	557,692	742,074
Norway	na	287,441	384,487	412,040
Spain	441,119	444,794	552,862	776,435
UK	370,244	439,880	476,426	564,961

Source: OAG.

The problems faced by Air France in the mid 1990s may also have added weight to the view that the flag carrier and its subsidiary would not fare well when faced with competition from a carrier with substantially lower costs. In the event, Air Inter's and its parent's ability to withstand a fares war was to prove greater than their new entrant rivals.

In Norway, commercial freedom allowed a larger carrier with an extensive regional and international route network to capture high yield traffic from Braathens. The Frequent Flyer Program of SAS, later reinforced through its membership of the Star Alliance, made the airline much more of an attractive proposition to business users. Braathens' later involvement with KLM did little fundamentally to redress this imbalance.

Greece, the most recent of the EU-Member States to fully deregulate its domestic market, has experienced the consolidation of its new entrant carriers with Aegean acquiring Air Greece in 1999 and Cronus in 2001. As in Spain, a number of the new entrants had been operating domestic charter services prior to the scheduled market being deregulated.

Overall it is clear that carriers offering a conventional product that have challenged a strong incumbent in an aggressive and substantial way have mostly come unstuck. Given the deep purses of flag carriers and their subsidiaries, replenished in certain instances with state aid, a full-scale assault on an incumbent's heartland has been successfully rebuffed. The offering of an altogether more secure existence to new entrants, coupled with the prospect of greater opportunities to come, seems a wise move on the part of flag carriers. The franchising strategy of British Airways provides the best example of this approach in Europe. Others have been following suit, more recently Alitalia with Alpi Eagles and Iberia with Air Nostrum. Operating marginal routes with a lower cost airline makes both economic sense and has the effect of deterring entry. With very few exceptions, only the no-frills providers have any real hope of competing directly against the combined force of flag carriers and franchised regional airlines.

As may be seen in Table 2.30, France, the UK, Italy and Spain have the busiest domestic city-pair markets in Europe. Prospects for competition on domestic routes are undoubtedly better if a capital city is equipped with more than one airport. Even countries whose sole capital city airport is not currently slot constrained are likely at some stage to face a capacity shortage.

Prospects for future competition in the domestic markets of Europe are inexorably linked to the low cost airlines. Whilst it seems clear that flag carriers and their subsidiaries have found ways of keeping in check the conventional breed of entrant, the elimination of all of the new generation of no-frills operator is unlikely. Certainly Lufthansa could operate Paris-Madrid if choose to, but would it be worth the hassle given the likelihood of easier, more secure options elsewhere?

Table 2.30 Distribution of the busiest domestic routes by country

| | > 50,000 seats per week | | | |
	1989	1992	1996	2000
France	2	3	4	3
Germany	1	1	0	0
Italy	1	1	1	1
Norway	0	0	0	0
Spain	1	1	1	1
UK	0	2	2	2

| | 40,000 - 49,999 seats per week | | | |
	1989	1992	1996	2000
France	1	0	2	1
Germany	1	0	2	3
Italy	0	0	0	0
Norway	0	0	2	3
Spain	0	0	0	0
UK	1	0	1	2

| | 30,000 - 39,999 seats per week | | | |
	1989	1992	1996	2000
France	1	2	0	2
Germany	1	2	2	3
Italy	0	0	0	3
Norway	0	0	1	0
Spain	0	1	1	5
UK	2	2	1	0

| | 10,000 - 29,999 seats per week | | | |
	1989	1992	1996	2000
France	10	9	10	7
Germany	15	13	11	16
Italy	11	13	14	15
Norway	4	4	4	7
Spain	11	9	12	14
UK	4	3	4	6

Source: OAG.

Notes

1. Another source of route entry in certain other EU states has been the air taxi sector.
2. UTA, a privately owned airline, operated long haul scheduled services.

3. Air France's state aid had been conditional on allowing competitors access to domestic routes.
4. This included season tickets, which provided substantial discounts for frequent travellers.
5. In return, Euralair gained a 10% shareholding in Air Liberté (Flight International, 13-19 December 1995, p.6).
6. AOM–Air Liberté was renamed Air Lib in August 2001 following its sale by the SAir Group to the HOLCO Group.
7. Some three million passengers were carried annually on charter services within Spain during the early 1990s.
8. The Commission decided not to investigate the matter.
9. Six routes were served by both carriers, but not in a competitive way.
10. In the domestic market Braathens is viewed as the Norwegian flag carrier.
11. Around three million passengers were carried annually on domestic charter services in the early 1990s.

Reference

'The Prospects for Airline Competition in Norway and Southern Scandinavia', S.J. Burns, MSc Thesis, Cranfield University, 1997.

3 Impact in other regions' domestic markets

Having examined the differing effects of deregulation in a number of European domestic markets, this chapter seeks to establish whether the experience has been much the same in other countries around the world. As with Europe, it is beyond the scope of a text of this nature to do other than explore in some detail a sample of domestic air transport markets. Five countries (Brazil, Canada, China, India and South Africa) have been selected to represent both the different regions of the world and the different types of liberalisation policy that have been implemented.

3.1 Effects of liberalisation in the Brazilian domestic market

The process of deregulating Brazil's domestic air transport sector has been a gradual one. Prior to 1992, aside from Varig, VASP and Transbrasil, which were licensed to operate the main national air routes, there were only five regional carriers in existence and these were tightly restricted as to where they could fly. The five regional airlines were Rio Sul, a subsidiary of Varig serving the south; TAM operating in the affluent south east; Nordeste supplying services in the north east; Brasil Central[1] covering the central west; and TABA serving the Amazon region. In 1992 however, the DAC amended its policy to allow regional carriers to operate any route they wished except for those connecting the state capitals. Rapid growth of regional carriers ensued thereafter, such that by 1996 the number of such airlines had increased to 14 and their share of the domestic traffic had grown from 5% to 20%. The largest of the regional operators, TAM, rapidly expanded its route network. By including short stops at small regional airports, it was able to serve several major national routes. Its success led to the TAM Group receiving Government approval in 1996 to form the country's fourth national carrier, also known as TAM. Table 3.1 provides a listing of Brazil's passenger carriers since 1991.

Table 3.1 Brazil's passenger airlines since 1991

Airline	'91	'92	'93	'94	'95	'96	'97	'98	'99	'00	'01
Airvias			├──	──	──	──	──┤				
Brasil Central	├──	──	──	──	──	──┤					
Fly					├──	──	──	──	──	──┤
GOL										├──┤
Interbrasil Star					├──	──	──	──	──┤		
Nacional											
Nordeste	├──	──	──	──	──	──	──	──	──	──┤
Pantanal		├──	──	──	──	──	──	──	──	──┤
Passaredo						├──	──	──	──	──┤
Penta						├──	──	──	──	──┤
Rico	├──	──	──	──	──	──┤				
Rio Sul	├──	──	──	──	──	──	──	──	──	──┤
Skyjet Brasil	├──	──	──┤						
TABA	├──	──	──	──	──	──	──	──	──	──┤
TAM	├──	──	──	──	──	──	──	──	──	──┤
Tavaj	├──	──	──	──┤					
Total			├──	──	──	──	──	──	──	──┤
Transair Int'al							├──	──	──	──┤
Transbrasil	├──	──	──	──	──	──	──	──	──	──┤
Trip							├──	──	──	──┤
VARIG	├──	──	──	──	──	──	──	──	──	──┤
VASP	├──	──	──	──	──	──	──	──	──	──┤
Via Brasil							├──	──	──┤	
Unex Airlines						├──	──	──	──┤	

Source: JP Airline-Fleets International.

Until 1998, airline fares compared to other countries in South America had been high. Price competition was almost nonexistent, with carriers charging the same full fares and offering very few discounts. For example, on the Ponte Aerea shuttle service between Rio de Janeiro and Sao Paulo Varig, VASP and Transbrasil operated a joint service, with the three companies providing respectively 50%, 30% and 20% of capacity and pooling their costs and revenues. It was clear that the high fares were having a constraining effect on the development of tourism and so in August 1997 the Brazilian Government set up a Commission to investigate the matter. The realisation that the DAC was likely to introduce measures promoting lower prices led the three companies to begin offering highly discounted fares.

In January 1998, the DAC announced that in future domestic charter flights operated by Brazilian owned airlines would have no fare restrictions placed upon them, provided tickets were purchased at least 48 hours in advance. Prior to this all seats on charter flights had to be sold as part of a package that included accommodation. The regulator also gave its approval for the maximum discount that could be offered on full fares to increase from 50% to 65%. Restrictions were also removed on carriers operating into the downtown airports of the major cities. The effects of these policy changes on capacity can be observed in Table 3.2, which shows the number of seats offered per week in the country's top 30 routes between 1989 and 2000.

Table 3.2 Seats supplied in the top 60 Brazilian domestic sectors

	1989		1992		1996		2000	
Sectors	Seats	%	Seats	%	Seats	%	Seats	%
Top 6	141,721	22.1	143,339	23.0	156,066	19.4	251,699	21.6
Top 10	182,172	28.5	179,716	28.9	206,050	25.7	327,228	28.0
Top 20	255,713	40.0	247,825	39.8	292,992	36.5	442,151	37.9
Top 40	352,273	55.2	347,427	55.8	391,021	48.7	576,141	49.4
Top 60	421,809	65.9	416,622	66.9	465,547	58.0	682,199	58.5
Total	639,961		622,824		802,852		1,166,708	

Source: OAG. Note: the top six sectors equate to the busiest three routes.

The liberalisation measures announced by the DAC in January 1998 had a dramatic effect in terms of fare competition. In anticipation of the policy change, the main players began offering discount fares during the latter part of 1997. The new pricing freedom also triggered the break up of the collusive operation of the Rio–Sao Paulo air-bridge service by Varig, VASP and Transbrasil. In March 1998, TAM reduced fares between Rio and Sao Paulo, leading other carriers to follow suit. By spring 1998, Varig was offering fares on its night operations at 55% below the full price level with 30% discounts on its daytime services, whilst Transbrasil was offering fares with at 45% discount and VASP 60%. The overall effect of the discounting was to reduce average fares by between 25% and 30% (Airline Business, October 1998). With the large fall in yield coinciding with the poor economic conditions prevailing in Brazil, the impact on the financial performance of the country's four largest carriers has been dramatic, as Table 3.3 reveals.

The arrival of the country's first no-frills operator, GOL, in January 2001 has exacerbated the already dire situation faced by the main players. The new airline operating a fleet of Boeing 737-700 has based its philosophy on the tried and well-tested Southwest model. It competes by offering substantially lower fares than those charged by the full service providers. For example, between Sao Paulo and Brasilia the carrier charges a maximum fare of Real$199, compared to the Real$308 charged by TAM and Varig, and the Real$270 by VASP. The incumbents have also faced an increasing supply of seats in the domestic market from charter airlines. Table 3.4 shows the market shares of carriers in the country's ten busiest routes, whilst Table 3.5 reveals the impact of the above developments in terms of the overall number of sectors with competing carriers.

Table 3.3   Net results of Brazil's major airlines ($millions)

	1996	1997	1998	1999	2000
Varig	-60.4	25.8	-21.9	- 52.5	- 97.6
VASP	154.6	44.8	-157.0	-51.1	62.5
Transbrasil	-38.1	68.0	165.9	-48.6	-116.3
TAM	55.6	12.6	13.2	-71.5	22.7

Source: Airline Business. (TAM's 1997-2000 results refer to TAM Holdings.)

Table 3.4   Brazil's ten busiest domestic routes in 2000

Seats	Route	HHI	Market share by Carrier (%)
146,318	Rio de Janeiro - Sao Paulo	0.24	Varig 36 TAR 25 Vasp 20 Transbrasil 8 Rio-Sul 6 TAM 4*
57,251	Sao Paulo - Brasilia	0.19	TAR 27 Nordeste 19 Varig 18 Transbrasil 16 Vasp 15 TAM 5
48,130	Sao Paulo - Curitiba	0.25	TAR 42 Rio-Sul 18 Varig 14 TAM 11 Vasp 10 Transbrasil 4
44,138	Sao Paulo - Belo Horizonte	0.27	TAR 32 Rio-Sul 30 VASP 25 Varig 8 TAM 5
30,537	Rio de Janeiro - Brasilia	0.25	Varig 38 Vasp 22 Transbrasil 16 Rio-Sul 14 TAM 10
30,537	Sao Paulo - Salvador	0.28	Varig 40 Transbrasil 23 TAM 21 Vasp 16
25,862	Rio de Janeiro - Belo Horizonte	0.36	Rio-Sul 50 TAR 34 Transbrasil 10 Varig 6
23,634	Sao Paulo - Porto Alegre	0.35	Varig 52 Vasp 22 Transbrasil 16 TAM 10
19,986	Rio de Janeiro - Salvador	0.27	Varig 36 Vasp 26 Transbrasil 23 TAM 15
17,397	Brasilia - Goiania	0.31	TAM 47 Vasp 31 Rio-Sul 12 Varig 10

Source: OAG. (*2 other carriers serve the route each providing < 1% of the available seats.)

Table 3.5 Evolving competition in Brazil

Sectors with	1989	1992	1996	2000
1 carrier	315	283	464	280
2 carriers	73	60	89	96
3 carriers	35	37	38	60
4 carriers	20	25	12	35
5 carriers	6	2	6	22
6 carriers	0	6	4	2
7 carriers	0	2	2	3
8 carriers	0	0	0	1
Total	449	415	615	499

Source: OAG.

Transbrasil, VASP and Varig have all been badly affected by the price wars, currency devaluations and economic slowdown. During 2001, Transbrasil has had some of its aircraft repossessed by lessors and is currently in the process of reducing its workforce of 2,900 by one third. Of its fleet of three Boeing 767-200 and seven Boeing 737-300, three aircraft are currently out of service. (Table 3.6 provides details of the fleets currently operated by Brazil's larger airlines.) While there was some speculation a year earlier that the company might merge with TAM, this outcome did not materialise. The carrier has since entered into a code-sharing agreement with Varig between Rio and Sao Paulo, effectively abandoning its own operations between the two cities. It also has allowed Varig to operate additional services to Portugal using traffic rights it had abandoned.

VASP also has faced major problems, which have forced it to completely withdraw from international operations. After incurring heavy losses in 1998 and 1999, the company has returned to profitability by concentrating its activities in the domestic market. Between 1998 and 2000, VASP halved its workforce and withdrew its fleet of ten MD-11 aircraft. Its fleet currently consists of three Airbus 300B2, 21 Boeing 737-200, three Boeing 737-300 and two Boeing 727-200 freighters. With exception of the three Boeing 737-300 aircraft, its fleet has an average age of over 20 years.

As may be seen from Table 3.3, Varig has not made a profit since 1997. Its most recent announcement concerning its finances have indicated an even worse result however, with a loss of US$199 million being posted for the first six months of 2001. The company blames currency devaluation against the US dollar and high taxes for its deteriorating financial condition. Large debt interest payments are another cause of its poor state.

Set against the troubles of these three long established carriers, the new low cost entrant GOL has quickly established itself in the domestic market. Only six months after commencing service, the company was accounting for a little over 5% of the overall market. By the end of 2001, with a fleet of ten Boeing 737-700 aircraft it expects this to have grown to 9%.

Table 3.6   Brazil's airlines' fleets in summer 2001

Airline	Fleet
Fly	3 Boeing 727-200
GOL	9 Boeing 737-700
Interbrasil Star	6 Brasilia
Nacional	2 Boeing 737-200
Nordeste	4 Boeing 737-500, 5 Fokker 50, 3 Brasilia
Pantanal	7 ATR 42
Passaredo	3 Brasilia
Penta	3 Brasilia, 2 Bandeirante
Rico	3 Brasilia, 4 Bandeirante
Rio Sul	3 Boeing 737-300, 14 Boeing 737-500, 14 Embraer RJ145, 1 Fokker 50, 8 Brasilia
TABA	2 FH-227, 1 Bandeirante
TAM	7 Airbus 330, 18 Airbus 320, 6 Airbus 319, 50 Fokker 100, 1 Fokker 50
Tavaj	2 F27-600, 1 Brasilia, 7 Bandeirante
Total	4 ATR 42, 2 Boeing 727-200F, 1 Bandeirante
Transbrasil	3 Boeing 767-200, 7 Boeing 737-300
Trip	1 ATR 42, 2 Brasilia
VARIG	16 MD-11, 6 Boeing 767-300, 6 Boeing 767-200, 1 Boeing 737-800, 5 Boeing 737-700, 4 Boeing 737-400, 36 Boeing 737-300, 10 Boeing 737-200, 3 DC-10F, 7 Boeing 727-100F
VASP	3 Airbus 300B2, 21 Boeing 737-200, 3 Boeing 737-300, 2 Boeing 727F
Via Brasil	1 Boeing 727-200

Sources: JP Airline-Fleets International, ATI database.

Faced with the problems of currency devaluation, high taxes, economic slowdown and increased competition from low cost scheduled and charter airlines, it is highly unlikely that all three of the incumbent carriers will survive. Consolidation of the old guard is inevitable. The level of competition that deregulation has unleashed into the Brazilian domestic market is substantial. By way of example, Table 3.7 lists the services that are currently available every weekday morning from Rio to Sao Paulo. Between 06.15 and noon each day there is a flight every 6.5 minutes in each direction, providing nearly 14,000 seats between the two cities.

Table 3.7   Rio to Sao Paulo morning services summer 2001

Departure	Airline	Aircraft type	Seats
06.16	Vasp	Boeing 737-300	132
06.23	TAM	Airbus 319	122
06.30	Rio-Sul	Boeing 737-300	132
06.30	Varig	Boeing 737-300	132
06.44	Rio-Sul	Boeing 737-500	117
06.46	TAM	Airbus 319	122
07.00	Vasp	Boeing 737-300	132
07.00	Rio-Sul	Boeing 737-300	132
07.00	Varig	Boeing 737-300	132
07.00	*Varig*	*Boeing 737-300*	*132*
07.14	Varig	Boeing 737-300	132
07.15	*TAM*	*Fokker 100*	*100*
07.16	TAM	Airbus 319	122
07.20	Varig	Boeing 737-300	132
07.30	Rio-Sul	Boeing 737-300	132
07.40	***GOL***	***Boeing 737-700***	***144***
07.44	TAM	Airbus 319	122
07.45	*Varig*	*Boeing 737-200*	*109*
07.56	Varig	Boeing 737-300	132
08.16	TAM	Airbus 319	122
08.32	Varig	Boeing 737-300	132
08.40	*TAM*	*Fokker 100*	*100*
08.44	TAM	Airbus 319	122
08.46	Vasp	Boeing 737-300	132
09.00	Varig	Boeing 737-300	132
09.14	TAM	Airbus 319	122
09.16	Varig	Boeing 737-300	132
09.30	Vasp	Boeing 737-300	132
09.34	Varig	Boeing 737-300	132
09.44	TAM	Airbus 319	122
09.46	Varig	Boeing 737-300	132
09.50	Rio-Sul	Boeing 737-500	117
09.50	Varig	Boeing 737-300	132
10.10	Varig	Boeing 737-300	132
10.16	TAM	Airbus 319	122
10.28	Rio-Sul	Boeing 737-300	132
10.34	Vasp	Boeing 737-300	132
10.35	*Transbrasil*	*Boeing 737-300*	*133*
10.44	TAM	Airbus 319	122
11.00	*TAM*	*Fokker 100*	*100*
11.02	Varig	Boeing 737-300	132
11.10	*Varig*	*Boeing 737-400*	*158*
11.10	*TAM*	*Fokker 100*	*100*
11.10	*Vasp*	*Airbus 300*	*240*
11.14	TAM	Airbus 319	122
11.20	Vasp	Boeing 737-300	132
11.30	***GOL***	***Boeing 737-700***	***144***
11.32	Varig	Boeing 737-300	132
11.35	*Fly*	*Boeing 727-200*	*163*
11.40	*TAM*	*Fokker 100*	*100*

Table 3.7 Continued

Departure	Airline	Aircraft type	Seats
11.44	TAM	Airbus 319	122
11.46	*Vasp*	*Boeing 737-200*	*109*
11.58	Vasp	Boeing 737-300	132

Source: OAG. (Flights shown in italics operate to and from the two cities international airports, except for those operated by GOL, which are between Rio International and Sao Paulo's downtown airport.)

3.2 Effects of liberalisation in the Canadian domestic market

For the eleven years following the acquisition of Wardair by Canadian Airlines in 1989, Air Canada and Canadian Airlines dominated Canada's internal market. While in 1984 deregulation had enabled the charter carrier Wardair to provide scheduled services, rapid consolidation of the other scheduled carriers into the Air Canada and CP Air (renamed Canadian in 1986) camps had also occurred. The large increases in capacity and Wardair's low fares policy had resulted in all three carriers incurring losses, and as was inevitable the company with the least financial ability to shoulder these failed. Compared with the sizes of their US counterparts, the two surviving Canadian carriers were quite small and it seemed unlikely that in the long term both could survive as independent companies. (Williams, 1994) Even though both carriers were facing severe financial problems in the early 1990s, there was strong resistance to allowing the two to merge. In the event, they went their separate ways and linked up with US airlines, Air Canada with Continental and Canadian with American.

Until the latter part of the 1990s, the only operators of large aircraft in the country, aside from Air Canada, Canadian and their affiliates, were a number of charter carriers, whose activities were mostly focussed on international operations. Table 3.8 provides details of the carriers operating scheduled and charter services in Canada since 1990. This situation began to alter in 1996, when WestJet, a no-frills airline modelled on Southwest, commenced operations from Calgary. By the beginning of 2001, the company was operating to 16 destinations (of which 12 were in western Canada) and had a fleet of 22 Boeing 737-200, giving it an estimated 14% share of the domestic market.[2] As with other no-frills scheduled carriers around the world, WestJet generated new traffic for the sector and therefore avoided challenging the two incumbents for their core business traffic.

Table 3.8   Canada's scheduled and charter airlines since 1991

Airline	'91	'92	'93	'94	'95	'96	'97	'98	'99	'00	'01
Air Canada											
Air Club											
Air Transat											
Canada 3000											
Canadian											
CanJet											
Royal											
Skyservice											
WestJet											

Source: JP Airline-Fleets International.

By the end of the 1990s, Canadian's financial position had deteriorated to such an extent that the Government had little option than to let Air Canada take it over, which it did in January 2000. A hostile bid had been made by Onex in autumn 1999 to take over both Air Canada and Canadian prior to merging them, but it failed. With the combined Air Canada and Canadian accounting for some 80% of domestic traffic, concern was high that a monopoly situation had been created and therefore that other companies should be encouraged to enter the market and compete. In the event, this hoped for rivalry has mostly emanated from the existing charter carriers. Royal Aviation, which was merged with Canada 3000 in spring 2001, had been operating domestic and international charter services since 1992, but took the opportunity to enter the scheduled market in October 1999. Immediately prior to its take-over, Royal was the largest low fares carrier serving cities in eastern Canada. The enlarged Canada 3000, itself a former charter airline established in 1988, now operates a fleet of 40 short and long haul aircraft, and has a similar share of the domestic market as that of WestJet.

Aside from Canada 3000, Royal and Westjet, two other low cost airlines entered the market, both though for only very short periods of time. CanJet, a Halifax based no-frills operator, began operations in September 2000, but faced a very aggressive response from Air Canada. The flag carrier reduced its fares by up to 80% on the routes on which it and CanJet competed. Despite winning a court case against Air Canada over its predatory pricing, the company was taken over by Canada 3000 after only eight months. Roots Air, a no-frills operator set up by charter airline Skyservice, lasted for only six weeks. Air Canada had been considering setting up its own no-frills operation, but another possibility was for it to use Roots Air for this purpose. In the event, Air Canada was able to reach agreement with its own employees and is likely to follow the former route.

To provide an impression of the competitive conditions currently existing on Canada's trunk routes, details of the daily operations on three such routes (Montreal - Toronto, Toronto - Vancouver, Vancouver - Calgary) are given in Tables 3.9, 3.10 and 3.11. As may be seen, on the country's busiest city-pair Air Canada provides 24 daily services using a wide mix of aircraft types. Air Nova, a subsidiary company, also operates six flights each weekday between Dorval and Toronto's downtown airport. In all, this results in the flag carrier providing 75% of the seat capacity and 73% of the service frequency. Competition comes predominantly from Canada 3000, which provides ten daily flights, all but one with Boeing 737-200 aircraft operated by Royal. This equates to 22% of the seats provided on the route and 25% of the service frequency. The one other operator, Air Transat, provided only one flight and this formed part of a through service from Montreal to Vancouver.

Between Toronto and Vancouver Air Canada currently provides 16 daily services again using a mix of aircraft types, which equates to 78% of the overall seat capacity and 80% of the service frequency on the route. As with Montreal - Toronto, competition comes predominantly from Canada 3000, which provides three daily non-stop flights with Boeing 757 aircraft. (The carrier also operates two indirect flights, but these have been excluded from this analysis.) This gives the company 14% of the seats provided on the route and 15% of the service frequency. The one other operator, Air Transat, provides only one flight using a 362 seat Lockheed Tristar, representing 8% of overall capacity.

Between Vancouver and Calgary, WestJet provides 28% of the seat capacity on a typical weekday involving nine direct flights with Boeing 737-200 aircraft. Air Canada, as on the previous two routes, offers the greatest number of seats and service frequency. Its share of traffic however, is not as high as in eastern Canada and on transcontinental routes. On this western route it provides 21 daily services using mainly Boeing 737-200 aircraft, which gives it 60% of the overall seat capacity and 64% of the service frequency. Canada 3000 also provides three daily non-stop flights, equating to 14% of the seats provided on the route and 15% of the service frequency.

Table 3.9   Montreal to Toronto services summer 2001

Departure	Airline	Aircraft type	Seats
06.00	Air Canada	Airbus 319	112
06.15	Air Canada	Canadair RJ	50
06.30	Air Canada	Boeing 767-200	191
06.30	Air Nova*	Dash 8-100	37
06.45	Air Canada	Airbus 320	132
07.00	Canada 3000	Boeing 757	226
07.00	Air Transat	L-1011	362
07.00	Air Canada	Boeing 767-300	203
07.00	Air Nova*	Dash 8-100	37
07.30	Air Canada	Airbus 320	132
07.45	Canada 3000	Boeing 737-200	122
08.00	Air Canada	Boeing 767-300	203
09.00	Canada 3000	Boeing 737-200	122
09.00	Air Canada	Boeing 767-300	203
09.00	Air Nova*	Dash 8-100	37
10.00	Air Canada	Airbus 340	284
10.30	Canada 3000	Boeing 737-200	122
11.00	Air Canada	Boeing 767-300	203
11.40	Canada 3000	Boeing 737-200	122
12.00	Air Canada	Airbus 320	132
13.00	Air Canada	Boeing 767-200	191
13.30	Canada 3000	Boeing 737-200	122
14.00	Air Canada	Airbus 330-300	292
14.15	Air Nova*	Dash 8-100	37
15.00	Air Canada	Boeing 767-300	203
16.00	Canada 3000	Boeing 737-200	122
16.00	Air Canada	Airbus 330-300	292
16.15	Air Nova*	Dash 8-100	37
16.30	Air Canada	Airbus 320	132
17.00	Air Canada	Boeing 767-300	203
17.30	Air Canada	Airbus 320	132
18.00	Canada 3000	Boeing 737-200	122
18.00	Air Canada	Boeing 767-200	191
18.15	Air Nova*	Dash 8-100	37
18.30	Air Canada	Boeing 767-200	191
19.00	Air Canada	Boeing 767-300	203
20.00	Canada 3000	Boeing 737-200	122
20.00	Air Canada	Boeing 767-300	203
21.00	Air Canada	Boeing 737-200	111
22.00	Canada 3000	Boeing 737-200	122
22.00	Air Canada	Airbus 319	112

Source: OAG. (*Air Nova is a subsidiary of Air Canada. Its flights operate to
Toronto's downtown airport. Flights are shown for a Thursday in September.)

Table 3.10   Toronto to Vancouver services summer 2001

Departure	Airline	Aircraft type	Seats
07.15	Air Canada	Boeing 767-300	203
08.15	Air Canada	Airbus 340	284
08.45	Air Canada	Airbus 340	284
09.15	Air Canada	Boeing 747-400	421
09.20	Canada 3000	Boeing 757	226
09.30	Air Transat	L-1011	362
10.15	Air Canada	Boeing 767-200	191
11.15	Air Canada	Boeing 767-200	191
12.15	Air Canada	Boeing 767-300	203
13.15	Air Canada	Boeing 767-300	203
14.10	Canada 3000	Boeing 757	226
14.15	Air Canada	Boeing 767-200	191
15.15	Air Canada	Boeing 767-200	191
16.15	Air Canada	Boeing 767-300	203
17.15	Air Canada	Airbus 330-300	292
18.30	Air Canada	Boeing 767-200	191
18.30	Canada 3000	Boeing 757	226
19.30	Air Canada	Boeing 767-300	203
20.30	Air Canada	Boeing 767-200	191
21.45	Air Canada	Boeing 767-300	203

Source: OAG. (Only non-stop services are listed.)

Table 3.11   Vancouver to Calgary services summer 2001

Departure	Airline	Aircraft type	Seats
06.50	Air Canada	Boeing 737-200	110
07.00	WestJet	Boeing 737-200	120
07.55	Air Canada	Airbus 320	132
08.30	Air Canada	Airbus 319	112
08.45	WestJet	Boeing 737-200	120
09.00	Air Canada	Boeing 737-200	110
09.05	Canada 3000	Boeing 737-200	122
10.00	Air Canada	Boeing 737-200	110
10.10	WestJet	Boeing 737-200	120
10.30	Air Canada	Boeing 737-200	110
11.00	Air Canada	Boeing 737-200	110
11.30	Air Canada	Boeing 737-200	110
11.30	WestJet	Boeing 737-200	120
12.00	Air Canada	Boeing 767-300	203
12.30	Air Canada	Airbus 319	112
13.00	Air Canada	Boeing 737-200	110
13.05	Canada 3000	Boeing 757	226
13.15	Air Canada	Fokker 28	55
13.30	Air Canada	Airbus 319	112
14.00	WestJet	Boeing 737-200	120
14.00	Air Canada	Boeing 737-200	110
15.15	Air Canada	Boeing 737-200	110
15.35	WestJet	Boeing 737-200	120

Table 3.11 Continued

Departure	Airline	Aircraft type	Seats
16.15	Air Canada	Airbus 320	132
17.15	Air Canada	Boeing 737-200	110
18.15	Air Canada	Boeing 737-200	110
18.20	Canada 3000	Boeing 737-200	122
18.55	WestJet	Boeing 737-200	120
19.15	Air Canada	Airbus 319	112
20.15	WestJet	Boeing 737-700	140
20.15	Air Canada	Boeing 737-200	110
21.20	WestJet	Boeing 737-200	120
21.30	Air Canada	Boeing 737-200	110

Source: OAG. (Only non-stop services are listed.)

To provide an indication of the impact of deregulation on the overall Canadian domestic market, Table 3.12 shows the number of seats supplied weekly during the summers of 1989, 1992, 1996 and 2000 in the country's busiest routes. As may be seen, whilst total seat capacity fell between 1989 and 2000 the proportion of seats accounted for by the busiest routes increased.

Table 3.12   Seats supplied in the top 60 Canadian domestic sectors

Sectors	1989		1992		1996		2000	
	Seats	%	Seats	%	Seats	%	Seats	%
Top 6	167,684	16.0	163,378	17.1	183,148	18.0	181,923	20.4
Top 10	247,977	23.7	233,886	24.4	266,740	26.2	254,832	28.6
Top 20	390,210	37.3	353,676	36.9	393,695	38.6	381,321	42.8
Top 40	528,787	50.6	486,469	50.8	516,999	50.7	482,374	54.2
Top 60	604,728	57.9	557,353	58.2	599,993	58.8	554,365	62.3
Total	1,045,256		958,179		1,019,659		890,340	

Source: OAG. Note: the top six sectors equate to the busiest three routes.

Increased competition in the country's busiest sectors is indicated by Table 3.13, which shows the changes in the level of route competition between 1989 and 2000. Only 41 routes of the 908 indicated by OAG as being served in 2000 had services provided by more than two carriers. In 1989, the equivalent figure had been 47. Several of these routes were served by individual carriers at very low frequencies, so tending to overstate the level of competition being experienced. Table 3.14, which lists the seat supply shares of carriers serving the country's top ten routes in

2000, clearly reveals the dominant position of Air Canada in the domestic market.

Table 3.13   Evolving competition in Canada

Sectors with	1989	1992	1996	2000
1 carrier	775	749	655	689
2 carriers	250	259	276	178
3 carriers	35	20	34	27
4 carriers	6	3	9	12
5 carriers	0	2	2	0
6 carriers	6	1	0	2
7 carriers	0	1	0	0
8 carriers	0	0	2	0
Total	1072	1035	978	908

Source: OAG.

Table 3.14   Canada's ten busiest domestic routes in 2000

Seats	Route	HHI	Market share by Carrier (%)
81,601	Montreal - Toronto	0.44	Air Canada 62 Canadian 17 Royal 15 Air Transat 6
53,020	Toronto - Vancouver	0.43	Air Canada 57 Canadian 31 Royal 4 Air Transat 8
47,302	Toronto - Ottawa	0.48	Air Canada 60 Canadian 35 Royal 5
41,879	Vancouver - Calgary	0.32	Canadian 42 Air Canada 30 Westjet 24 Air Transat 4
30,566	Toronto - Calgary	0.60	Air Canada 74 Canadian 22 Air Transat 4
28,850	Calgary - Edmonton	0.54	Canadian 63 Westjet 29 Air Canada 8
28,196	Vancouver - Victoria	0.25	Air Canada 37 Canadian 27 West Coast Air 11 Helijet 11 Pacific Coastal 7 Harbour Air 7
27,898	Toronto - Halifax	0.40	Air Canada 54 Canadian 30 Royal 12 Air Transat 4
21,994	Toronto - Winnipeg	0.40	Air Canada 53 Canadian 32 Royal 11 Air Transat 4
19,551	Vancouver - Edmonton	0.30	Canadian 33 Westjet 32 Air Canada 30 Air Transat 5

Source: OAG.

3.3 Effects of liberalisation in the Chinese domestic market

Until the mid 1980s, the Civil Aviation Administration of China (CAAC) operated all of China's air services. The process of transforming what had been a division of the military into an air transport industry based on commercial principles had begun in the late 1970s. In 1979, the six regional aviation bureaus that formed one of the four administrative tiers of CAAC became what in effect were cost and profit centres. In 1987, a second stage in the reform process began, the aim of which was to separate the CAAC's regulatory function from its role as operator of air services and airports. This consisted of four elements: reducing the number of administrative layers in CAAC to two, setting up a trunk carrier where each of the six regional bureaus was located, separating airport and airline operations, and easing market entry conditions (Wang, 1989). China Southwestern and China Eastern were the first trunk airlines to be established, the policy being implemented initially in the Chengdu and Shanghai regional bureaus in response to the market entry of Sichuan Airlines and Shanghai Airlines. Following the successful inauguration of these two carriers, operators were formed in the remaining four bureaus (Zhang, 1998). In the absence of local competition however, the Guangzhou and Shenyang bureaus were not spun off until 1991. Table 3.15 lists the six carriers and their main operating bases.

Table 3.15   Establishment of China's trunk airlines

Carrier	Base	Initial operation
China Southwestern	Chengdu	1987
China Eastern	Shanghai	1987
Air China	Beijing	1988
China Northwestern	Xian	1989
China Northern	Shenyang	1991
China Southern	Guangzhou	1991

Under the new aviation policy, the setting up of locally owned carriers by provincial and municipal authorities and large enterprises was encouraged. These non-CAAC owned companies began to be established from 1984. The impact of these reforms on the demand for air travel was dramatic. In 1985, when CAAC was virtually the sole provider of air services the number of passengers carried was just under 7.5 million. Just two years later the figure had risen to over 13 million, by 1994 it had reached a staggering 40 million and today at over 60 million it is the third largest domestic market in the world. In terms of capacity provided, between 1989 and 2000 the number of seats offered rose from 275,000 per week to 1.75 million, as Table 3.16 reveals.

Table 3.16   Seats supplied in the top 60 Chinese domestic sectors

	1989		1992		1996		2000	
Sectors	Seats	%	Seats	%	Seats	%	Seats	%
Top 6	42,166	15.3	47,180	12.8	105,322	9.2	137,319	7.8
Top 10	60,621	22.0	68,564	18.6	141,842	12.4	198,999	11.3
Top 20	88,358	32.1	106,058	28.7	215,194	18.8	309,305	17.6
Top 40	125,222	45.4	155,016	42.0	330,213	28.9	471,961	26.8
Top 60	150,387	54.6	187,803	50.8	419,526	36.7	601,641	34.2
Total	275,582		369,408		1,143,314		1,759,184	

Source: OAG.

By the early 1990s, a large number of airlines were operating in the domestic market. Table 3.17 provides a listing of the carriers that have operated domestic services during the 1990s. The impact of the influx of carriers on competition can be seen from the data contained in Table 3.18. By summer 2000, 95 domestic routes had four or more competing carriers compared to only eight in 1992. The number of routes operated increased from under 250 in 1989 to just over 600 in 2000. The number of seats offered per week by each carrier on the country's ten busiest routes in summer 2000 is shown in Table 3.19.

The rapid growth in the number of carriers and the services they operated placed a great strain on the available infrastructure and raised major concerns over safety. In response to these worries, in July 1994 the CAAC stopped issuing licences to newly formed airlines and cancelled the licences of several smaller carriers (Zhang 1998). This had the effect of reducing the number of operating airlines from over 40 to around 30.

Aside from restricting the number of carriers licensed to operate in the domestic market, the CAAC controls entry at the route level as well as pricing. The CAAC's policy has been to grant rights first to carriers with a home base at either end of a route. Additional airlines are then only allowed to enter when the average load factor has reached 75%. As for fares, the

CAAC establishes the standard price to be charged on each route, although airlines can apply for these to be altered. Until July 1996, carriers were allowed to offer discounts of up to 20% on the fares charged to residents. The prices charged to foreigners have traditionally been considerably higher than those paid by locals, although this is altering with China joining the World Trade Organisation. The fares paid by locals are now rising to match those charged to foreigners.

Table 3.17 China's airlines

CAAC Airlines	'91	'92	'93	'94	'95	'96	'97	'98	'99	'00
Air China										
China Eastern										
China Northern										
China Northwest										
China Southern										
China Southwest										
Air Great Wall										
China General Avn										
China Xinjiang										
China Yunnan										
Other Airlines	**'91**	**'92**	**'93**	**'94**	**'95**	**'96**	**'97**	**'98**	**'99**	**'00**
Air Guizhou										
Changan Airlines										
China United										
China Xinhua										
CNAC-Zhejiang										
Fujian Airlines										
Hainan Airlines										
Nanjing Airlines										
Shandong Airlines										
Shanghai Airlines										
Shanxi Aviation										
Shenzhen Airlines										
Sichuan Airlines										
Wuhan Air Lines										
Xiamen Airlines										
Zhongyuan A/lines										

Source: JP Airline-Fleets International.

Despite the controls on route entry and fares, considerable over supply has been apparent. The smaller regional carriers competing solely in terms of price have been major contributors to falling yields and the industry's accompanying large financial losses. In the first six months of 1999, China's airlines produced an aggregate loss of over $200 million. These unwelcome developments have led the Chinese Government to encourage airlines to merge in order to reduce the imbalance between supply and demand. In April 2001, the CAAC confirmed the arrangements for the consolidation of the ten carriers under its direct control into three groups and that it would relinquish its shareholdings in the companies.

Table 3.18 Evolving competition in China

Sectors with	1989	1992	1996	2000
1 carrier	483	395	649	704
2 carriers	0	123	289	267
3 carriers	0	28	101	137
4 carriers	0	8	54	63
5 carriers	0	0	12	20
6 carriers	0	0	6	12
7 carriers	0	0	0	0
8 carriers	0	0	2	0
9 carriers	0	0	2	0
Total	483	554	1,115	1,203

Source: OAG.

Given the Government's strong desire that the industry consolidates there is some doubt over the future of the non-CAAC carriers. Responding to the growing power in the marketplace of the big three, the first non-CAAC airline to be established, Hainan Airlines, has taken over three of its fellow carriers (Changan, China Zinhua and Shanxi). Shandong Airlines has also been keen to acquire shareholdings in other carriers, but has failed so far to do so, settling instead for a loose alliance with four passenger airlines (Shanghai, Shenzhen, Sichuan and Wuhan) and China Postal Airlines. The one remaining airline, China United, is the commercial division of the Chinese Air Force. The constituents of the five groupings are shown in Table 3.20 and their fleets in Table 3.21.

One additional control over the sector exercised by the central Government has been aircraft acquisition. The China Aviation Supply Corporation (CASC), a subsidiary of CAAC, used to be responsible for the purchasing of all commercial aircraft. It now no longer exercises this function in respect of the three largest carriers (Air China, China Eastern and China Southern), however. Even these airlines though require the consent of the SPC and CAAC, the former with responsibility for trade and foreign currency and the latter over concerns in respect of the airworthiness of aircraft. Interestingly, the CAAC only approves the acquisition of aircraft that are in production. Political factors have also been seen to play a part in terms of which manufacturers have been favoured at particular points in time.

Table 3.19   China's ten busiest domestic routes in 2000

Seats	Route	HHI	Market share by Carrier (%)
63,433	Beijing - Shanghai	0.29	China Eastern 38 China Airlines 32 Shanghai 18 China Northern 6 China Northwest 5 China Xinjiang 1
40,956	Beijing - Guangzhou	0.41	China Southern 52 China Airlines 37 China Xinjiang 2 China Northwest 9
32,930	Guangzhou - Shanghai	0.36	China Southern 45 China Eastern 34 Shanghai 21
32,506	Guangzhou - Haikou	0.56	China Southern 72 Hainan 21 Shandong 4 China Southwest 3
29,174	Shanghai - Shenzhen	0.22	Shanghai 29 China Southern 25 China Eastern 20 China Northern 13 Shenzhen 9 China Southwest 4
25,840	Beijing - Shenzhen	0.43	China Airlines 55 China Northern 2 China Southern 35 Shenzhen 8
23,682	Beijing - Shenyang	0.46	China Northern 57 China Xinhua 3 China Airlines 36 China National 4
23,324	Beijing - Xian	0.45	China Northwest 57 China Xinhua 7 China Airlines 35 China Northern 1
20,286	Beijing - Chengdu	0.65	China Southwest 78 China Airlines 22
17,736	Kunming - Jinghong	0.78	China Yunnan 88 Shanghai 10 China Xinhua 2

Source: OAG.

Table 3.20   Airline consolidation

Air China	China Eastern	China Southern	Hainan
China Southwest	Air Great Wall	China Northern	Changan
CNAC-Zhejiang	Air Guizhou	China Xinjiang	China Zinhua
	China Northwest	Fujian Airlines	Shanxi
	China Yunnan	Xiamen Airlines	
	Nanjing Airlines	Zhongyuan A/l	
Shandong			
Shanghai			
Shenzen			
Sichuan			
Wuhan			

Source: Air Transport Intelligence.

Table 3.21   China's airlines' fleets in summer 2001

CAAC Airlines	Fleet
Air China	6 B747-400, 8 B747-400 Combi, 10 B777-200, 3 A340-300, 4 B767-300, 6 B767-200, 7 B737-800, 19 B737-300, 4 BAe 146-100, 4 Y7.
China Eastern	4 MD-11, 2 MD-11F, 5 A340-300, 10 A300-600, 18 A320, 9 MD-90, 4 MD-82, 4 A319, 7 B737-300, 4 Y7.
China Northern	6 A300-600, 13 MD-90, 24 MD-82, 10 Y7.
China Northwest	3 A300-600, 3 A310-200, 13 A320, 7 BAe 146-300, 3 BAe 146-100.
China Southern	9 B777-200, 18 B757, 20 A320, 22 B737-300, 12 B737-500.
China Southwest	3 A340-300, 13 B757, 3 B737-800, 17 B737-300.
Air Great Wall	3 B737-200.
China Xinjiang	3 IL-86, 7 B757, 5 Tu-154, 2 B737-300, 5 ATR-72.
China Yunnan	3 B767-300, 4 B737-700, 13 B737-300.
Other Airlines	
Air Guizhou	1 B737-300, 7 Y7.
Changan Airlines	2 DHC-8-400, 7 Y7.
China United	15 Tu-154, 2 B737-300, 20 IL-76F.
China Xinhua	3 B737-400, 6 B737-300.
CNAC-Zhejiang	5 A320, 3 DHC8-300.
Fujian Airlines	1 B737-700, 2 B737-500.
Hainan Airlines	7 B737-800, 7 B737-400, 5 B737-300, 20 FD328 JET.
Nanjing Airlines	2 Y7.
Shandong Airlines	6 B737-300, 6 Canadair RJ, 8 Saab 340.
Shanghai Airlines	3 B767-300, 7 B757, 6 B737-700, 2 Canadair RJ.
Shanxi Aviation	3 Y7.
Shenzhen Airlines	5 B737-700, 6 B737-300.
Sichuan Airlines	4 Tu-154, 2 A321, 5 A320, 1 B737-300, 5 Y7, 2 MA-60, 4 Embraer RJ145.
Wuhan Air Lines	2 B737-800, 6 B737-300, 6 Y7.
Xiamen Airlines	5 B757, 5 B737-700, 3 B737-300, 4 B737-500, 2 B737-200.
Zhongyuan A/lines	5 B737-300, 2 Y7.

Source: JP Airline-Fleets International.

3.4   Effects of liberalisation in the Indian domestic market

The Air Corporations Act of 1953 gave Air India and Indian Airlines the sole rights to provide respectively the country's international and domestic air transport services. The Act was to remain in force until 1994, despite considerable long-term dissatisfaction with the level and quality of services provided by the state-owned Indian Airlines. As late as 1990, the carrier was accounting for over 99% of demand in the market. Its monopoly position was only very slowly eroded, the result of the government's desire to protect the company from private competitors. Government interference in the airline was substantial. As a result, decisions on such issues as fleet replacement were monumentally time-consuming and often decided upon by Ministers on the basis of non-technical and non-commercial factors. (Mhatre, 2000) The many-layered bureaucracy slowed everything to a snail's place, changes in government making the situation even more difficult for the airline's management. As has been the case with Olympic Airways in Europe, numerous changes of Chief Executive Officer occurred. Everyone wanting and seeming to have his or her say made any hope of change being realised a very long and tortuous affair.

The long process of change began in 1988, when the Government authorised the operation of domestic charter flights by private companies using aircraft equipped with no more than 20 seats. The companies that took advantage of this change in policy did not prove commercially successful, however. Pressure for a fuller liberalisation policy was growing all the time. The inability of Indian Airlines to cater adequately for the overseas tourist market and growing backlogs of air cargo led first to the implementation of the cargo "Open Skies" policy for international flights in 1990. This was followed a year later by the Air Taxi Scheme, which permitted such companies to operate jet aircraft, albeit with highly restrictive conditions attached. The fatal crash of an Indian Airlines A320 in 1990 had added to the pressure for private operators to enter the market with larger capacity aircraft.

One of the more bizarre conditions applied to the air taxi scheme was that whilst the companies could operate scheduled services they could not publish timetables. To protect Indian Airlines in a more substantial way, the country's routes were divided into three categories. The first category consisted of the twelve main city pairs; the second, routes to the Kashmir area, those to and within the northeast States, and those to islands in the Bay of Bengal and off the southwest coast; and the third all other sectors. Whatever capacity an air taxi company operated on the trunk routes they had to provide 10% of this amount (measured in ASK's) on category 2 routes and 50% on category 3 routes. These conditions made life very tough for the new entrants and not surprisingly few survived the experience. The companies that failed during this phase of liberalisation included Air Link, Air Asiatic, Continental and UB Air. Table 3.22 lists the carriers operating domestic services and when they provided them.

The grounding of the Indian Airlines Airbus 320 fleet for nearly a year in 1992, together with their ongoing industrial relation difficulties, provided the so-called air taxi companies with an opportunity to establish themselves in the market. The strike by pilots of Indian Airlines in 1993 was strongly beneficial to the private companies. By the end of 1993, air taxi companies were operating flights on 54 routes, reducing Indian Airlines' overall market share to around 70%. (Malik and Malik, 1996) The pressure for change was now overwhelming, so much so that the Government announced in 1993 that it intended to repeal the 1953 Air Corporations Act, which it did the following year. In 1994, Air India and Indian Airlines were made public limited companies and six air taxi operators (Archana, Damania, East-West, Jet, ModiLuft and NEPC Airlines) had scheduled airline status conferred upon them. Four other air taxi operators (India International, Jagson, Rajair and Sahara Indian Airlines) were also approved in principle for scheduled airline status, subject to meeting certain minimum criteria set by the DGCA.

Table 3.22 Indian carriers providing domestic services

Airline	'91	'92	'93	'94	'95	'96	'97	'98	'99	'00	'01
Air Asiatic	■	■									
Air India	■	■	■	■	■	■	■	■	■	■	■
Alliance Air							■	■	■	■	■
Archana A/l			■	■	■						
City Link				■	■						
Continental		■	■								
Damania*			■	■	■	■	■				
East West A/l			■	■	■	■					
Gujurat A/l					■	■	■	■	■	■	■
Indian A/l	■	■	■	■	■	■	■	■	■	■	■
Jagson A/l			■	■	■	■	■	■	■	■	■
Jet Airways			■	■	■	■	■	■	■	■	■
Modiluft				■	■	■					
NEPC A/l				■	■	■					
Rajair			■	■	■						
Sahara A/l**			■	■	■	■	■	■	■	■	■
Spanair				■	■						
Trans Bharat	■	■	■								
UB Air				■	■						
UP Air***					■	■	■	■	■	■	■
VIF Airways		■	■	■							

Source: JP Airline-Fleets International. (*Damania was renamed Skyline NEPC in 1996. **Now trading as Air Sahara. UP Air was renamed SGS Air in 1998.)

By the beginning of 1995, the private airlines had a 35% share of the overall market. This has since grown to around 45%, with Indian Airlines accounting for 50% and Air India the remaining 5%. Despite the obvious success of the privately owned carriers in terms of market share, only two of the ten former air taxi operators remain as providers of mainstream services. The largest of the air taxi companies in 1994, East-West Airlines, then with ten Boeing 737-200 aircraft in operation, eventually had its right to serve category 1 routes rescinded due to non-payment of fees. Poor financial management and the general lack of experience of its management with air transport were the reasons cited for its failure. Several of the other failures were also the result of inexperience of the sector. Many based their operational and marketing standards on those of Indian Airlines, which were by the mid-1990s very out-dated and inappropriate in a competitive marketplace.

The two privately owned carriers that have survived the liberalisation process and remain in competition with the two state-owned airlines are Jet Airways and Air Sahara (formerly known as Sahara Airlines). Jet Airways is by far the larger of the two companies, with a current market share of 40%. Naresh Goyal founded the company in 1993 and unlike many of his counterparts had wide experience of the airline industry. In 1974, he had set up a marketing company, Jetair, which acted as a general sales agent to foreign carriers in India. The management of the new carrier comprised of experienced air transport practitioners, a feature which differentiated the carrier from other new entrants. Right from the outset, Jet decided to distinguish itself from other operators, and in particular, Indian Airlines, by conveying a business class image. Rather than commencing operations with elderly Boeing 737-200 aircraft, as most other new entrants had done, the company leased in four Boeing 737-300. The quality image quickly paid off, with the airline capturing 7% of total domestic traffic by the end of its first year.

Jet Airways now has a fleet of 33 aircraft, comprising ten Boeing 737-400, eight 737-700, ten 737-800 and five ATR-72. The average age of its fleet is only three years, in marked contrast to that of Indian Airlines. The company operates to 30 destinations and provides a hot meal service on virtually every route it operates. Indian Airlines, which now also serves international destinations, serves 59 domestic points and is acknowledged as providing an inferior service to that of its new entrant rivals. It is estimated that close to 85% of passengers in the Indian domestic market are travelling on company business. (Malik and Malik, 1996) Given the type of demand in the domestic market, it is not surprising that Jet has been so successful.

Three other operators currently provide services with jet aircraft in the domestic market: Air India, Air Sahara and Royal Airways. Air India and Air Sahara each have a market share of round 5%, the former serving 11 domestic cities and the latter operating to 14 destinations. Royal Airways is a resurrected ModiLuft, a carrier that had been established with support from Lufthansa in 1993 but which collapsed in 1996 after the German flag carrier withdrew. To provide an idea of the level of competition experienced in the domestic market, Table 3.23 provides details of the carriers operating the country's top ten routes in summer 2000 and their respective market shares. A more recent picture still of the competitive conditions prevailing on the country's trunk routes is given in Tables 3.24 and 3.25, which respectively list the services operated from Delhi to Mumbai, the country's busiest, and from Goa to Mumbai, on a typical weekday in September 2001.

As may be seen, competition on the country's busiest ten routes is thriving. At the time of writing seven of the ten routes have two of the new entrants competing against one or both of the state owned carriers. Of the privately owned carriers, Jet Airways provides by far and away the largest number of flights. In 2000, the airline's passenger traffic grew by 23% compared to 1999, achieving an average load factor of 72%. The company had 5,965 employees and generated 6,700 million ASKs. The productivity of its labour force was more than double that of Indian Airlines, which had over 20,000 employees. If Jet Airways continues to expand at its current rate, within the next two to three years it overtake Indian Airlines and become the largest carrier in the domestic market. Much will depend on when and the manner in which the state owned carrier is privatised. Like with deregulation, the privatisation of Air India and Indian Airlines is proving to be a long drawn out affair.

The impact of deregulation on the domestic market can be analysed both in terms of changes in the total number of seats supplied (see Table 3.26) and in the number of carriers operating each route (see Table 3.27). As may be seen, overall capacity increased by 31% between 1992 and 1996, and by 18% over the next four year period. In terms of competition, the number of routes operated by more than one carrier increased dramatically following liberalisation. While in 1992, only 15 routes had more than one operator, by 1996, two routes had five carriers providing flights, eight had four operating airlines, eleven had three companies competing, and a further 39 had two operators, making an equivalent figure of 60. It should be borne in mind that the two operating carriers in 1992 were Air India and Indian Airlines. So the change in the marketplace has been even more substantial than it would at first appear.

Table 3.23   India's ten busiest domestic routes in 2000

Seats	Route	HHI	Market share by Carrier (%)
57,725	Delhi - Mumbai	0.29	Indian 36 Jet 29 Air India 27 Sahara 6
24,183	Mumbai - Madras	0.27	Jet 31 Indian 30 Air India 23 Sahara 16
23,780	Mumbai - Bangalore	0.33	Indian 39 Jet 37 Sahara 14 Air India 10
19,738	Bangalore - Madras	0.35	Jet 44 Sahara 28 Indian 28
15,625	Mumbai - Hydrabad	0.41	Jet 46 Indian 43 Air India 11
13,514	Mumbai - Ahmedabad	0.40	Indian 45 Jet 42 Air India 13
13,510	Delhi - Bangalore	0.35	Indian 44 Sahara 28 Jet 28
12,398	Mumbai - Goa	0.34	Jet 44 Indian 36 Sahara 14 Air India 6
12,251	Delhi - Madras	0.34	Indian 45 Jet 34 Sahara 17 Air India 4
11,084	Mumbai - Calcutta	0.47	Indian 49 Jet 47 Air India 4

Source: OAG.

Table 3.24   Delhi to Mumbai services September 2001

Departure	Airline	Aircraft type	Seats
04.45	Air India	Boeing 747-300 Combi	281*
06.00	Indian	Airbus 320	145
06.45	Royal	Boeing 737-400	155
06.50	Jet	Boeing 737-800	160
07.00	Air Sahara	Boeing 737-400	150
07.00	Indian	Airbus 320	145
08.00	Jet	Boeing 737-400	136
08.00	Indian	Airbus 320	145
09.00	Indian	Airbus 320	145
09.30	Royal	Boeing 737-400	155
13.00	Indian	Airbus 320	145
14.00	Jet	Boeing 737-800	160
16.50	Jet	Boeing 737-400	136
17.00	Indian	Airbus 320	145
17.00	Air India	Airbus 310	210*
17.15	Royal	Boeing 737-400	155
17.25	Jet	Boeing 737-800	160
17.55	Air Sahara	Boeing 737-400	150
18.00	Indian	Airbus 320	145
19.00	Indian	Airbus 320	145
19.35	Jet	Boeing 737-800	160
19.50	Royal	Boeing 737-400	155
20.00	Indian	Airbus 320	145

Table 3.24 Continued

20.30	Jet	Boeing 737-800	160
22.30	Jet	Boeing 737-800	160
23.00	Alliance	Boeing 737-200	119
23.35	Air India	Boeing 747-400	448*

(* It should be noted that Air India's flights between Delhi and Mumbai are the domestic legs of through international services and therefore only a portion of the available seats indicated will have been allocated for domestic traffic.)
Sources: OAG and JP Airline-Fleets International.

Table 3.25   Goa to Mumbai services September 2001

Departure	Airline	Aircraft type	Seats
14.05	Jet	Boeing 737-800	160
14.05	Indian	Airbus 320	145
14.40	Jet	Boeing 737-400	136
15.10	Air Sahara	Boeing 737-400	150

Sources: OAG and JP Airline-Fleets International.

Table 3.26   Seats supplied in the top 60 Indian domestic sectors

	1989		1992		1996		2000	
Sectors	Seats	%	Seats	%	Seats	%	Seats	%
Top 6	62,230	18.7	57,852	18.5	94,865	23.2	105,688	21.8
Top 10	81,150	24.4	74,734	24.0	120,931	29.6	141,051	29.1
Top 20	122,750	36.9	110,745	35.5	174,620	42.7	203,808	42.1
Top 40	174,076	52.3	159,477	51.1	247,830	60.6	276,516	57.1
Top 60	202,348	60.8	188,938	60.6	287,246	70.2	324,889	67.1
Total	332,840		311,961		409,112		484,393	

Source: OAG. Note: the top six sectors equate to the busiest three routes.

Table 3.27   Evolving competition in India

Sectors with	1989	1992	1996	2000
1 carrier	334	273	145	147
2 carriers	50	30	78	77
3 carriers	0	0	22	26
4 carriers	0	0	16	10
5 carriers	0	0	5	0
Total	384	303	266	260

Source: OAG.

3.5 Effects of liberalisation in South Africa

The domestic air transport market in South Africa is considerably smaller than those of the above four countries. Even so, deregulation has produced a number of significant changes in terms of the supply of air services. A key characteristic of the country's domestic market is the large concentration of resources on a very small number of trunk routes. As may be seen from Tables 3.28 and 3.29, in summer 2000 a little over 60% of all the seats supplied in the market involved the country's top two routes (Johannesburg-Cape Town and Johannesburg-Durban). This contrasts with the under 20% of overall seat capacity provided in the top three routes of the other four countries discussed in this chapter.

Table 3.28   Seats supplied in the top 60 domestic sectors

	1989		1992		1996		2000	
Sectors	Seats	%	Seats	%	Seats	%	Seats	%
Top 6	78,595	51.6	95,102	59.5	116,419	64.2	145,169	67.2
Top 10	93,309	61.2	109,373	68.4	133,188	73.4	164,545	76.2
Top 20	121,615	79.8	133,639	83.6	154,386	85.1	187,249	86.7
Top 40	141,955	93.1	150,814	94.3	171,326	94.4	204,723	94.5
Top 60	147,683	96.9	156,215	97.7	179,267	98.8	211,975	98.1
Total	152,449		159,855		181,433		215,971	

Source: OAG. Note: the top six sectors equate to the busiest three routes.

The domestic market in South Africa was deregulated in 1991. Since then a number of new entrants have sought to establish themselves on the country's two trunk routes, but with varying degrees of success. Flight Star was the first such carrier to take advantage of liberalisation. Established in 1991 and making use of commuter carrier Trek Air's operating licence, Flight Star quickly gained a reputation for service quality. Using a fleet of modern aircraft comprised of Airbus 320 and ATR 42, the carrier was able to take a significant share of the market away from South African Airways (SAA). SAA responded to this threat through aggressive price competition and by helping Comair to establish itself as a jet operator. Comair had been formed in 1949 and until 1992 operated propeller aircraft in the domestic market. In 1992 it began to operate between Johannesburg and Cape Town using Boeing 737-200 aircraft. As a result of these actions, Flight Star became loss making and was sold by its shareholders to SAA in 1994. As a condition of the sale, SAA required the airline's owners to sign a restraint of trade thereby precluding them from further competition with the flag carrier. Once the sale was completed SAA closed the carrier down, a policy it was to repeat in 1999 with Sun Air.

Over time Comair established itself as the second largest carrier in the domestic market and in 1996 entered into a franchise agreement with British Airways, subsequently operating all its flights in BA colours and using the BA code. In January 2000, BA acquired an 18.3% shareholding in the airline. Comair has a fleet of Boeing 727-200 and Boeing 737-200 aircraft, some of which it acquired from BA. Most recently, it has established a low fare subsidiary, Kulula.com, to operate no-frills services between Johannesburg and Cape Town using a Boeing 727-200. In instigating the new Internet orientated company, Comair is competing directly with Intensive Air, a provider of discounted air services. SAA has also lowered its fares on the route, undercutting Kulula.com's single fare by one Rand. Unlike the new discount carrier, SAA offers an in-flight meal and frequent flyer points at these fares.

As mentioned above, Sun Air has been the most recent airline to fail in the South African market. Originally formed in 1979 as Mmabatho Air service, the carrier operated as the national airline of Bophuthatswana under the name BOP Air until 1997. Following Bophuthatswana's re-incorporation into South Africa in 1994, the carrier became wholly owned by the South African government and adopted the name Sun Air. Until 1994, the airline had operated a small fleet of turbo-prop aircraft, but following Flight Star's demise Sun Air acquired jets and began filling the gap left in the domestic market by the new entrant. Like Flight Star before it, the carrier quickly attained a reputation for service excellence (Bell, 2000). In 1997, the South African government privatised the company. Comair was one of the parties to take a stake, acquiring a 25% shareholding in its rival.

Sun Air grew rapidly and by the beginning of 1999 was operating a fleet of 11 aircraft, comprising five MD-80, five DC-9, and one Boeing 727-200. Aggressive price competition from SAA however, coupled with conflicts between the airline's shareholders and general poor management, resulted in heavy financial losses. As a consequence, Sun Air's shareholders decided to sell the company to SAA in August 1999, which immediately closed the airline down.

Aside from Comair (and its Kalula.com subsidiary), SAA currently faces competition on its main domestic routes from Nationwide Airlines and Intensive Air. The former company, a subsidiary of Nationwide Air Charter, was established in 1995 and began operations in 1996 using a fleet of BAe 1-11 aircraft. As may be seen from Table 3.29, it currently provides 7% of capacity on the country's busiest route using Boeing 737-200 aircraft. The carrier's use of older aircraft was reflected in the lower fares it charged. This also has been a feature of Intensive Air, which began services in 1997 and now operates a small fleet of Fokker F28 aircraft each equipped with 75 seats. SAA and Comair however, provide the lion's share of capacity between Johannesburg and Cape Town, both in terms of seats (SAA 62%, Comair 30%) and service frequency (SAA 58%, Comair 30%). Table 3.30 lists all the services operated from Johannesburg to Cape Town on a typical weekday in October 2001. A full listing of South Africa's passenger airlines since 1991 is contained in Table 3.31.

Table 3.29   South Africa's ten busiest domestic routes in 2000

Seats	Route	HHI	Market share by Carrier (%)
78,596	Johannesburg - Cape Town	0.41	South African 58 Comair 24 Nationwide 10 African Star 7 Air Zimbabwe 1
51,557	Johannesburg - Durban	0.45	South African 62 Comair 25 Nationwide 13
15,016	Johannesburg - Port Elizabeth	0.54	South African 64 Comair 36
12,896	Cape Town - Durban	0.52	South African 59 Comair 41
6,280	Johannesburg - East London	1.0	South African 100
5,272	Johannesburg - George	0.71	South African 83 Nationwide 17
5,166	Durban - Port Elizabeth	1.0	South African 100
4,900	Johannesburg - Bloemfontein	1.0	South African 100
2,400	Johannesburg - Richards Bay	1.0	South African 100
2,300	Johannesburg - Kimberley	1.0	South African 100

Source: OAG.

Table 3.30   Johannesburg to Cape Town services October 2001

Departure	Airline	Aircraft type	Seats
06.00	South African	Boeing 737-200	107
06.30	South African	Boeing 737-800	157
06.30	Comair	Boeing 737-200	108
07.00	Comair	Boeing 727-200	148
07.00	Nationwide	Boeing 737-200	110
07.00	South African	Boeing 737-800	157
07.30	South African	Boeing 737-800	157
07.40	Comair	Boeing 727-200	148
08.00	South African	Boeing 737-800	157
08.30	South African	Boeing 737-800	157
08.50	South African	Boeing 737-800	157
09.30	South African	Boeing 737-200	107
10.00	Comair	Boeing 727-200	148
10.00	South African	Boeing 747-200	291
11.00	South African	Boeing 737-800	157
11.30	Comair	Boeing 727-200	148
11.30	South African	Boeing 737-200	107
11.45	Nationwide	Boeing 737-200	110
12.00	South African	Boeing 737-200	107
12.45	Comair	Boeing 727-200	148
13.00	South African	Boeing 737-800	157
14.00	South African	Boeing 737-800	157
14.15	Comair	Boeing 727-200	148
14.45	Nationwide	Boeing 737-200	110
15.00	South African	Boeing 737-800	157
15.30	Comair	Boeing 727-200	148
15.30	South African	Boeing 737-200	107
16.00	South African	Boeing 737-800	157
16.10	Comair	Boeing 737-200	108
16.15	Intensive Air	Fokker F28	75
17.00	South African	Boeing 737-800	157
17.15	Comair	Boeing 727-200	148
17.30	South African	Boeing 737-800	157
17.45	Comair	Boeing 737-200	108
18.00	Nationwide	Boeing 737-200	110
18.00	South African	Boeing 737-800	157
18.25	Comair	Boeing 727-200	148
18.30	South African	Boeing 737-200	107
19.00	South African	Boeing 737-800	157
19.00	Comair	Boeing 737-200	108
19.30	South African	Boeing 737-200	107
20.00	South African	Boeing 737-800	157
21.05	South African	Boeing 737-800	157

Source: OAG.

Table 3.31   South Africa's passenger airlines since 1991

Airline	'91	'92	'93	'94	'95	'96	'97	'98	'99	'00	'01
Comair	▓	▓	▓	▓	▓	▓	▓	▓	▓	▓	▓
Flight Star	▓	▓	▓	▓							
Intensive Air						▓	▓	▓	▓	▓	▓
Inter Air							▓	▓	▓	▓	▓
Million Air					▓	▓	▓				
Nationwide					▓	▓	▓	▓	▓	▓	▓
Phoenix				▓	▓	▓	▓	▓	▓	▓	▓
SA Airlink				▓	▓	▓	▓	▓	▓	▓	▓
SA Express				▓	▓	▓	▓	▓	▓	▓	▓
South African	▓	▓	▓	▓	▓	▓	▓	▓	▓	▓	▓
Sun Air				▓	▓	▓	▓	▓	▓		

Source: JP Airline-Fleets International.

3.6   Concluding comments

What conclusions can be drawn from the experiences that the above five countries have had as a result of liberalising their domestic air transport markets?   Unlike the three European countries analysed in the previous chapter, there are wide differences in terms of the degree to which Brazil, Canada, China, India and South Africa have deregulated their air transport markets.   China and India have yet to remove all restrictions, whilst near complete freedom is the order of the day in the other three countries. Another differentiating factor in terms of regulatory change between these five countries and their European counterparts is that liberalisation did not occur at the same point in time, nor progress at the same pace.   Whilst there are significant differences in terms of the effects each country has experienced, there are a number of common features.

The three countries discussed in this chapter that have fully deregulated their markets (Brazil, Canada and South Africa) have low cost, no-frills carriers providing services on their main trunk routes. In Europe, Norway has had Color Air (albeit for only a year), Spain has Air Europa and Spanair (not no-frills operators admittedly but certainly low cost), and France would seem very likely to have its first experience of a no-frills airline operating domestic services within the very near future following the tribulations of AOM-Air Liberté. Another common feature has been the severe difficulties faced by incumbent carriers when faced with competition from lower cost, new entrants. As a result of its financial difficulties, Brazil's flag carrier Varig is currently exploring the possibility of merging with its rival TAM. The country's other two incumbent airlines Transbrasil and VASP have also faced severe problems, their futures as independent entities in no way assured. India's two long established airlines Air India and Indian Airlines have also faced extreme difficulties when faced with competition from well organised and efficiently run new entrant carriers. Despite the best efforts of the government to protect its two nationally owned airlines, JET Airlines now accounts for around 40% of domestic traffic.

China has followed a different path to the other countries in terms of responding to excessive competition in its domestic markets. The proliferation of scheduled airlines in the country led to substantial over supply with the resulting financial problems facing many companies and an overall unstable situation. While purists would no doubt disapprove, in response to this imbalance between demand and supply the government instigated a policy of airline consolidation. It would seem probable that four airline groups will remain, with the prospect that in the longer term a more stable and efficient market in air transport services will result. No doubt market forces would eventually have produced a similar outcome, but it would have taken much longer to achieve with enormous upheaval occurring in the process. The guiding hand of the regulator in this instance rather than allowing the full rigours of the marketplace to unfold would in this instance seem to have been justified.

Overall though it is apparent from these widely differing countries that the liberalising of their domestic air services has proved to be beneficial. Even where governments have been sceptical about letting go completely of the reins, as in India, consumers have benefited greatly. When faced with a major adverse outcome of unfettered market forces however, government intervention that is both wisely applied and designed to ensure that competition remains neither excessive nor deficient would seem common sense.

Notes

1. Brasil Central was merged into TAM in 1996.
2. Airline Business, September 2000.

References

A decade of turmoil, Air Transport World, Mahtre, K., May 2000.

'Indian liberalisation – how to avoid repeating the mistakes of the past', Malik, H. and Malik, P., *Avmark Aviation Economist*, July/August 1996.

Civil Aviation in Modern China, Wang, Y., China Social Science Press, Beijing, 1989.

The Airline Industry and the Impact of Deregulation, Williams, G., Avebury Aviation, 1994.

'Industrial reform and air transport development in China', Zhang, A., *Journal of Air Transport Management*, Vol. 4, 1998.

4 Impact of low cost carriers in Europe

Low cost scheduled airlines have revolutionised short haul air travel in many parts of the world. Such carriers now account for around 25% of demand in the US, but as yet only 5% in Europe. The spectacular growth and strong financial performance of Southwest has set an important standard for the rest of the industry. Its simple philosophy, from which it has not faltered, has been copied by new entrant carriers in other parts of the world. Several countries have now experienced the low cost phenomenon, one very recent example being Brazil.[1] It would be surprising if the phenomenon were not to continue to spread.

To convey the impression however that low cost carriers account for only round 5% of passenger traffic in Europe would be wholly untrue. If travellers using charter flights were included, then a figure of around 35% of RPKs would be indicated. Given the significance of the charter sector and the fact that charter airlines achieve the lowest operating costs of all, it would seem appropriate to begin this analysis of the impact of low cost carriers in Europe with this component of the market.

4.1 Europe's charter sector

By comparison with other regions of the world, Europe is unusual in that such a large proportion of its passenger traffic is carried on charter flights. Table 4.1 reveals that the vast majority of passengers travelling on charter services originate in Germany and the UK. An estimated 80% of Europe's charter traffic comprises travellers on inclusive tour package holidays.[2] The remainder is made up of independent seat only users, who fly on the same flights as package tour customers, and those passengers on ad hoc charter services, such as those that are operated in connection with sporting events. Interestingly, Belgium comes a close second to the UK in terms of number of charter passengers per head of population.

Table 4.1 Numbers of passengers travelling on charter flights in 1996

Country	Population (millions)	Passengers (m)#	Ratio*
Austria	8.0	1.3	0.16
Belgium	10.1	4.3	0.43
Denmark	5.2		
Norway	4.3	5.0	0.27
Sweden	8.7		
Finland	5.1	0.7	0.14
France	57.7	4.3	0.07
Germany	81.2	23.7	0.29
Italy	57.1	1.6	0.03
Netherlands	15.3	4.6	0.30
Portugal	9.9	0.3	0.03
Spain	39.1	5.0	0.13
UK	57.8	25.9	0.45

Source: The Single European Aviation Market: The First Five Years, CAP 685,
UK Civil Aviation Authority, June 1998.

Very few charter carriers now exist that are not owned by tour operating companies. Most form part of vertically integrated organisations incorporating tour operator, travel agency chain, airline and, more often than not, hotels and providers of ground transportation. Typically, in-house charter airlines provide between 70% and 90% of their parent's flight requirements.[3] However, while providing for the needs of their tour operator owners forms the main activity of this type of carrier, flying is often undertaken for other tour companies[4] and, when circumstances permit, ad hoc charters are undertaken.

As in many other sectors, market forces have led to the disappearance of many medium-sized companies.[5] The extent of this trend towards integration and consolidation in the UK is revealed in Table 4.2, which shows the current position of the largest four tour operating groups. Together these organisations account for around 80% of the UK inclusive tour market. Two of these companies are now German owned. During the 1990s, the number of inclusive tour passengers carried on charter flights from the UK has more than doubled as Figure 4.1 reveals.

Table 4.2   Vertical integration in the UK inclusive tour market

Tour Operator	Share	Owner	Airline	Travel Agent	Outlets
Airtours	25%	Airtours	Airtours	Going Places	730
Thomson	23%	Preussag	Britannia	Lunn Poly	795
Thomas Cook	18%	C&N	jmc	Thomas Cook	800
First Choice	15%	First Choice	Air 2000	Travel Choice	650

Sources: Aviation Strategy, February 2001; Annual reports of the tour operators.

Figure 4.1   UK demand for inclusive tours

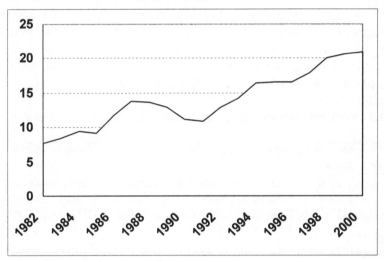

Source: ATOL Statistics, UK Civil Aviation Authority.

In Germany, Europe's other large charter market, vertical integration has been a much more recent phenomenon. The move towards merging German tour operating companies with local airlines and travel agency chains followed moves by Airtours and Thomson to acquire tour operators in other European countries.[6] The tables have been turned recently though, with Preussag, owners of the largest German tour operator, TUI, acquiring Thomson in summer 2000; and C&N taking control of Thomas Cook at the beginning of 2001. As Table 4.3 shows, the degree of vertical integration and consolidation that has occurred recently in the German inclusive tour market mirrors what took place in the UK during the late 1980s and early 1990s.

Table 4.4 provides details of French, German, Spanish and UK charter carriers and indicates whether they form part of vertically integrated tour operating organisations. As may be seen, very few charter airlines now exist as independent companies. Those that do, with the notable exceptions of Aero Lloyd and Air Berlin, operate small fleets. Unlike the past, the vast majority of charter carriers today employ the most modern jet aircraft available, often being the launch customers for particular types (e.g. Boeing 757-300). The average seating capacity of the UK charter fleet is currently around 225. For short haul operations, the Airbus 320 equipped with 180 seats, the Airbus 321 with 220 seats and the Boeing 757-200 with 235 seats predominate. This contrasts with the 148 seats available on the aircraft most commonly in use with the low cost scheduled airlines, the Boeing 737-300. Average load factors typically are in the low 90's, some 10% above those of the no-frills carriers and 15% to 20% above the full service operators (Mason, Whelan and Williams, 2000).

Table 4.3   Vertical integration in the German inclusive tour market

Tour Operator	Market Share	Owner	Airline
TUI	28%	Preussag, WestLB & Scickedanz	Hapag Lloyd
C&N	20%	Lufthansa & Karstadt	Condor
LTU	13%	Rewe (40%), SAir Group (49.9%)	LTU
Frosch Touristik	5%	Airtours & D Guntz	Fly FTI

As to the future, it would seem most probable that further consolidation involving cross-border mergers and acquisitions will occur. The very recent purchase of Poland's largest charter company, White Eagle, by Preussag is further evidence of this trend. The dire financial difficulties of Swissair undoubtedly will lead to the sale of the SAir Group's charter airlines, LTU and Volare (comprising Air Europe and Volare). Within two years, it is likely that over 80% of Europe's charter fleets will controlled by three, or possibly four, pan-European tour operating organisations. (Table 4.5 provides a summary of the current three pan-European tour operators.) A few independent airlines will remain, both home and destination based, to fulfil the needs of niche market tour operators and to provide ad hoc charter services. For example, a major element of the work undertaken by four of the five independent UK charter airlines (British World, European Air Charter, Flightline, Titan) consists of ad-hoc operations and wet leasing.

Table 4.4   French, German, Italian, Spanish and UK charter airlines

	Number of Aircraft	Vertically Integrated	Independent	Scheduled Subsidiary
France				
Aeris	4		✈	
Aerolyon	2	✈		
Aigle Azur	3		✈	
Air Jet	2		✈	
Air Lib*	(53)		✈	
Air Mediterranee	3		✈	
Corsair	12	✈		
Euralair	6		✈	
Star Europe	5	✈		
Total	*90*			
Germany				
Aero Lloyd	20		✈	
Air Berlin	24		✈	
Condor	37	✈		✈
Condor Berlin	12	✈		✈
Germania	10	✈		
Hamburg Int'al	3		✈	
Hapag Lloyd	35	✈		
LTU	28	✈		✈
Total	*172*			
Spain				
Air Europa*	26	✈		
Air Plus Comet	5	✈		
Futura	12			✈
Iberworld	6	✈		
LTE	3	✈		
Spanair*	44			✈
Total	*96*			
UK				
Air Scandic	2		✈	
Airtours	26	✈		
Air 2000	29	✈		

Table 4.4 Continued

Britannia	33	✈	
British World	12		✈
Excel	9	✈	
European AC	16		✈
Flightline	8		✈
jmc	29	✈	
Monarch	22	✈	
Titan	6		✈
Total	*192*		

Source: JP Airline-Fleets International 2000-01. (* Indicates the carrier also operates scheduled services.)

Table 4.5 Pan-European tour operators and their charter airlines

Tour Group	Revenues	RPKs (000)	Airline(s)	Country	Fleet
World of Tui (Preussag)	$10,052m	44,544	Hapag Lloyd	Germany	B737-800 A310-200
			Britannia	UK	B737-800 B757 B767-300
			Corsair	France	B747 A330-200 B737-400
Thomas Cook	$7,066	31,886	Condor	Germany	A320 B757 B767-300
			jmc	UK	A320 B757 A330-200
Airtours	$6,631	26,226	Airtours	UK	A320 A321 B757 B767-300 A330-200 DC-10
			Premiair	Denmark	A320 A300B4 A330-300

Source: Airline Business, October 2001.

4.2 Emergence of Europe's no-frills sector

While there are over fifty charter airlines currently registered in Europe, the number of no-frills carriers that have existed can be counted on the fingers of one's hands. In all, there have only been nine low cost scheduled European airlines, three of which have failed (see Table 4.6).

Table 4.6 Europe's low cost scheduled airlines

Airline	'92	'93	'94	'95	'96	'97	'98	'99	'00	'01
AB Airlines*			▬	▬	▬	▬	▬	▬		
Basiq Air									▬	▬
Buzz							▬	▬	▬	▬
Color Air*					▬	▬	▬	▬		
Debonair*					▬	▬	▬	▬		
easyJet				▬	▬	▬	▬	▬	▬	▬
GO						▬	▬	▬	▬	▬
Ryanair	▬	▬	▬	▬	▬	▬	▬	▬	▬	▬
Virgin Express			▬	▬	▬	▬	▬	▬	▬	▬

(*AB Airlines operated a small network of routes from Gatwick using B737-300 and BAe 1-11 aircraft. Color Air, a subsidiary of the ferry company Color Line, operated three domestic trunk routes in Norway and to two international destinations, using Boeing 737-300 aircraft. Debonair, a Luton based operator, relied mainly on a fleet of BAe 146-200 aircraft. It differentiated itself from other low cost carriers by offering generous seat pitch (32") and in-flight catering.)

Ryanair, the first of Europe's new low cost players, was originally established as a regional carrier offering conventional services using a mixed fleet. Experiencing financial difficulties during the recession at the beginning of the 1990s, the airline reinvented itself as a no-frills, low cost airline closely emulating the Southwest philosophy. It quickly established itself as a major player on the Irish Sea routes, providing cheap travel for the large VFR market between the UK and Ireland (see Section 4.3). Widely acknowledged as the most successful of Europe's no-frills operators, it has spent the past few years building up an extensive network of services from London's third airport at Stansted. As may be seen from Table 4.7, the carrier now serves 34 destinations from London. The majority of points served attract a mix of customers travelling for business and leisure. Most involve the use of secondary airports, which enables the company to keep its operating costs low. For example, the airport it uses to serve Frankfurt is Hahn, located some 100kms to the west of the city. Most recently, Ryanair has started to develop a network of services from Chaleroi, a location advertised by the company as Brussels South.

Table 4.7 Destinations served from London in summer 2001

	easyJet	Ryanair	BUZZ	GO	Virgin Express
Domestic	Aberdeen Belfast Edinburgh Glasgow Inverness	Derry Prestwick	-	Belfast Edinburgh Glasgow	-
Business / City break / VFR	Amsterdam Athens Barcelona Geneva Madrid Zurich	Aarhus Brescia Chaleroi Cork Dublin Esbjerg Genoa Gothenburg Hahn Lubeck Malmo Oslo Pisa St. Etienne Salzburg Shannon Stockholm Treviso Trieste Turin Vasteras	Berlin Bordeaux Cologne Dusseldorf Frankfurt Helsinki Lyons Marseilles Milan Paris Toulouse Vienna	Barcelona Bilbao Bologna Copenhagen Milan Munich Naples Prague Reykjavik Rome Venice	Brussels
Holiday / VFR	Nice	Ancona Biarritz Carcassonne Dinard Kerry Knock Nimes Perpignan Pescara	Jerez La Rochelle Montpellier Poitiers	Nice	-
Holiday	Malaga Palma	Alghero Rimini	Gerona Murcia	Alicante Faro Ibiza Malaga Palma	-
Total	14	34	17	20	1

Source: Sunday Times, Travel Section, 2 September 2001.

EasyJet, which commenced services in November 1995 from Luton, one of London's then under-utilised airports, has concentrated on providing a high frequency of services to a smaller number of destinations, linking up many of the points it serves from its main operating bases in the UK,

Switzerland and, most recently, the Netherlands (see Table 4.7 for details). Like Ryanair, the company has kept closely to the Southwest model. From the outset it avoided conventional distribution methods, providing its own call centre for reservations. During the last few years it has increasingly been relying on the Internet to sell its flights. Recently, it has been achieving over 90% of its sales via this medium.

The third largest of the no-frills carriers, GO, which until recently was a British Airways subsidiary, began operations from Stansted in May 1998. Initially, the company focussed its attentions on providing international services from its London base, the only exception being its route to Edinburgh. In the past two years however, it has added Belfast and Glasgow to its domestic portfolio, but of more significance has been its decision to establish a second UK base at Bristol (see Table 4.7 for details). The move followed easyJet's decision in 1998 to operate from Liverpool, an airport with plenty of capacity and a potentially large catchment area. GO was the first of the low cost scheduled operators to offer seasonal services to traditional package holiday destinations, such as Ibiza and Faro. Unlike easyJet and Ryanair, the company undertakes seat assignment, but in most other respects their philosophies are very similar. British Airways divested itself of GO in spring 2001, seeking to concentrate its resources on its mainstream product. The recent decision of GO to enter the lion's den by taking on Ryanair at its Dublin hub promises to provide those wishing to travel between Edinburgh or Glasgow and the Irish capital with some incredibly low fares. In the main, the low cost players have sought to avoid competing head to head with each other, but Ryanair's decision to match GO by introducing services from Dublin to Edinburgh promises to provide spectators with a rare opportunity to witness what promises to be a very aggressive contest.

The second longest established low no-frills carrier, Virgin Express, is the first, and until very recently the only, such operator to be based in continental Europe. The company was originally established in 1992 as a charter carrier under the name Euro Belgian Airlines. In 1994, however, the company began operating low fare scheduled services from its Brussels base to a small number of European cities. In May 1996, the name Virgin Express was adopted when Richard Branson's Virgin Group acquired a 90% shareholding in the company. During 1998, in an attempt to reduce the high costs of operating from Brussels, a subsidiary, Virgin Express Ireland, was established at Shannon. The venture was relatively short-lived however, due to industrial relations difficulties and financial problems.

Charter flights had formed a significant element of the company's operations, but most recently the airline has withdrawn from this activity. Virgin Express currently operates from its Brussels hub to eight destinations (Barcelona, Copenhagen, London Heathrow, Madrid, Malaga, Milan, Nice and Rome), three of which are flown under a code-share arrangement with Sabena. This rather unusual tie-up has seen the low cost airline operating all of the Belgian flag carrier's services on the prestigious Heathrow - Brussels route.

The third and most recent no-frills carrier to establish itself at Stansted is Buzz, a wholly owned subsidiary of KLM. Buzz is not entirely a new airline, however, having in an earlier incarnation formed part of KLM uk. At the beginning of 2000, the former operations of KLM uk were divided into those routes feeding KLM at Amsterdam, which continued to be provided under the KLM uk name, whilst most other routes operated from Stansted were transferred to Buzz. While other low cost carriers have started from scratch, Buzz has had the difficult task of transform a full cost carrier into a low cost one.

The most recent of the no-frills airlines is Basiq Air, a subsidiary of Transavia, the charter airline owned by KLM. Basiq Air began operations from Amsterdam in December 2000, using Transavia's aircraft. The company is currently operating daily services to Barcelona and Nice from both Amsterdam and Rotterdam. The decision of Tranasvia to establish Basiq Air may just have had something to do with easyJet announcing that Amsterdam was to form its next traffic hub! Quite what parent KLM's longer-term strategy vis à vis its two no-frills carriers will be remains to be seen. It would unlikely though, that there is scope for three low cost scheduled airlines at Stansted.

In terms of aircraft, most of the no-frills carriers have relied on the Boeing 737, as Table 4.8 reveals. The most commonly used version of the 737 has been the 300 series, equipped with 148 or 149 seats. Ryanair however, based its earlier operations on the older 200 series, which were acquired second-hand. Its most recent acquisitions though have been the 800 series, which provide the largest passenger carrying capability of any of the types used by the low cost companies. EasyJet is also a committed Boeing operator, but with the 300 series no longer in production the airline has opted for the long range 700 series, which offers the same seating capacity as its earlier aircraft. GO's and Virgin Express' fleets consist entirely of 300 series aircraft. The one exception is BUZZ, whose fleet is comprised of eight 110 seat BAe 146-300 and two 737-300 aircraft. Aside from the disadvantage of operating two different types of aircraft, the unit costs of its BAe 146 are significantly higher than that of the aircraft used by its competitors. For passengers however, the seat pitch is some two inches better on the 146 than the 737-300.

Table 4.8   Fleets operated by no-frills airlines - summer 2001

Airline	Fleet	Seating capacity	Operating base(s)
Buzz	8 x BAe 146-300 2 x B737-300	1176	Stansted
EasyJet	18 x B737-300 3x B737-700	3129	Luton Liverpool Geneva Amsterdam
GO	17 x B737-300	2516	Stansted Bristol
Ryanair	20 x B737-200 16 x B737-800	5624	Dublin Stansted Prestwick Charleroi
Virgin Express	9 x B737-300	1332	Brussels

Source: JP Airline-Fleets International, 2001.

As may be seen from the information contained in Table 4.9, not all of the current low cost carriers are as yet financially strong. Based on US experience, it would be surprising if all six were to survive. A more realistic forecast would suggest two or at the most three.

Table 4.9   Financial wellbeing of the no-frills airlines

Airline	Net Result ($million)		
	1998	1999	2000
EasyJet	8.3	2.1	34.4
GO	-	-24.5	4.1
Ryanair	61.2	70.8	94.9
Virgin Express	0.7	-6.0	-60.1

4.3   Impact of the no-frills carriers on scheduled markets

From the outset easyJet has been involved in providing domestic services, concentrating mainly on the London - Scotland market. The two busiest destinations, Edinburgh and Glasgow, are now also served by GO from Stansted. Ryanair also serves the Glasgow market, operating between

Stansted and Prestwick, which is located 30 miles to the south of the city. The net impact of these three low cost airlines on the London-Glasgow route has been substantial. Between 1995 and 2000, passenger demand increased by 53%, compared to 10% between 1990 and 1995. Figure 4.2 shows the growth in demand between each pair of airports between 1990 and 2000. The low cost companies collectively accounted for 33% of the traffic in 2000 and by the end of the current year this proportion is likely to reach 40%.

Figure 4.2   London - Glasgow passenger demand 1990-2000

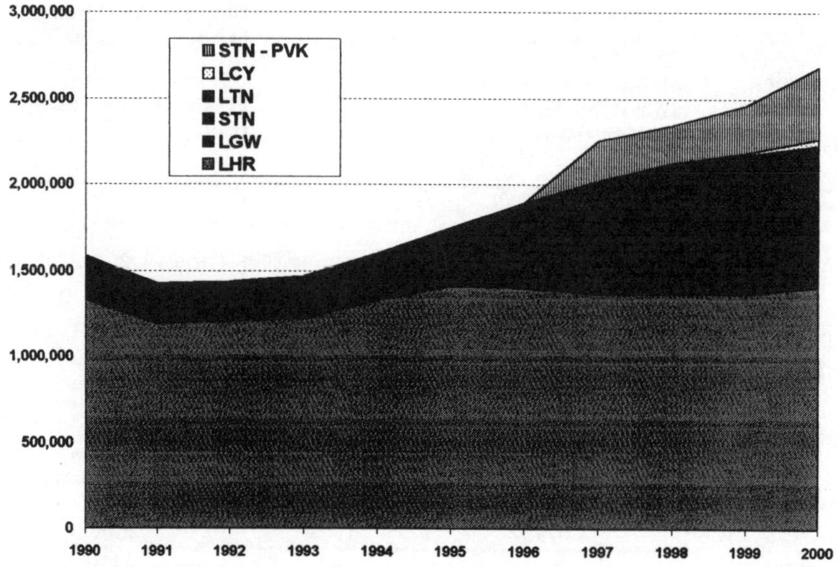

Source: UK Airlines, CAA.

To give an idea of the enormous range of options currently available to those wishing to travel between the two cities, Table 4.10 lists the flights available on a typical weekday in September 2001. As may be seen, the total number of services provided was 48, of which 39.6% were operated by the no-frills airlines. In terms of the total number of seats available, the low cost players accounted for 40.1%. With competition so extensive, some passengers have been paying more in airport charges and taxes than for the fare. The full one-way fare from Heathrow to Glasgow is currently £169,

Table 4.10   Services on the London - Glasgow route in summer 2001

Departure	Airline	Airport(s)	Aircraft type	Seats
06.40	Ryanair	Stansted – Prestwick	Boeing 737-200	130
06.40	British Midland	Heathrow	Airbus 320	160
06.45	GO	Stansted	Boeing 737-300	148
07.15	British Airways	Heathrow	Airbus 319	126
07.15	British Airways	Gatwick	Boeing 737-300	130
07.50	easyJet	Luton	Boeing 737-300	149
08.15	British Airways	Heathrow	Boeing 757	195
08.25	Ryanair	Stansted – Prestwick	Boeing 737-200	130
08.50	British Midland	Heathrow	Airbus 320	160
09.15	British Airways	Heathrow	Boeing 757	195
09.25	easyJet	Luton	Boeing 737-700	149
09.25	Scot Airways	City	Dornier 328	31
09.40	British Airways	Gatwick	Boeing 737-300	130
09.50	GO	Stansted	Boeing 737-300	148
10.50	British Midland	Heathrow	Airbus 320	160
11.05	easyJet	Luton	Boeing 737-300	149
11.15	British Airways	Heathrow	Boeing 757	195
11.35	Ryanair	Stansted – Prestwick	Boeing 737-200	130
12.15	British Airways	Gatwick	Boeing 737-300	130
12.45	Ryanair	Stansted – Prestwick	Boeing 737-800	189
13.05	British Midland	Heathrow	Airbus 320	160
13.15	British Airways	Heathrow	Boeing 757	195
14.15	British Airways	Heathrow	Boeing 757	195
14.35	easyJet	Luton	Boeing 737-300	149
14.50	GO	Stansted	Boeing 737-300	148
15.00	British Midland	Heathrow	Airbus 320	160
15.15	British Airways	Heathrow	Boeing 757	195
15.15	British Airways	Gatwick	Boeing 737-300	130
15.50	Ryanair	Stansted – Prestwick	Boeing 737-800	189
16.15	British Airways	Heathrow	Airbus 319	126
16.50	Scot Airways	City	Dornier 328	31
17.00	British Airways	Gatwick	Boeing 737-300	130
17.15	British Airways	Heathrow	Boeing 757	195
17.25	British Midland	Heathrow	Airbus 320	160
17.50	easyJet	Luton	Boeing 737-300	149
18.15	British Airways	Heathrow	Airbus 319	126
18.40	GO	Stansted	Boeing 737-300	148
19.10	British Midland	Heathrow	Airbus 320	160
19.15	Ryanair	Stansted – Prestwick	Boeing 737-800	189
19.15	British Airways	Heathrow	Boeing 757	195
19.45	British Airways	Gatwick	Boeing 737-400	130
20.10	Ryanair	Stansted – Prestwick	Boeing 737-200	130
20.10	Scot Airways	City	Dornier 328	31
20.15	British Airways	Heathrow	Boeing 757	195
20.55	GO	Stansted	Boeing 737-300	148
21.05	easyJet	Luton	Boeing 737-300	149
21.40	British Midland	Heathrow	Airbus 320	160
22.35	easyJet	Luton	Boeing 737-300	149

Source: OAG.

but a flight from Luton or Stansted can be obtained for as little as £37.50 (including taxes). For those willing to vary their travel plans in order to obtain the lowest fares available, the option of travelling instead by rail or coach would often prove more expensive.

To provide an overall idea of the impact of low cost carriers on this domestic route, the services supplied on a typical weekday in summer 1995 are shown in Table 4.11. In order to make comparison with Table 4.10 easier to undertake, a summary of the changes that have occurred between 1995 and 2001 is provided in Table 4.12. The proportion of passengers that have been carried by the no-frills sector over this period is depicted in Figure 4.3.

Table 4.11   Services on the London - Glasgow route in summer 1995

Departure	Airline	Airport(s)	Aircraft type	Seats
07.00	Air UK	Gatwick	BAe 146-300	108
07.05	British Midland	Heathrow	Boeing 737-500	117
07.15	British Airways	Heathrow	Boeing 737-400	141
08.15	British Airways	Heathrow	Boeing 757	195
08.30	Air UK	Stansted	BAe 146-300	108
09.00	British Midland	Heathrow	Boeing 737-500	117
09.05	Air UK	Gatwick	BAe 146-300	108
09.15	British Airways	Heathrow	Boeing 737-400	141
10.15	British Airways	Heathrow	Boeing 757	195
11.00	British Midland	Heathrow	Boeing 737-500	117
12.15	British Airways	Heathrow	Boeing 757	195
12.40	Air UK	Gatwick	BAe 146-300	108
13.00	British Midland	Heathrow	Boeing 737-500	117
14.15	British Airways	Heathrow	Boeing 757	195
15.00	British Midland	Heathrow	Boeing 737-500	117
15.15	British Airways	Heathrow	Boeing 737-400	141
15.20	Air UK	Stansted	BAe 146-300	108
16.15	British Airways	Heathrow	Boeing 757	195
16.40	Air UK	Gatwick	BAe 146-300	108
17.00	British Midland	Heathrow	Boeing 737-300	131
17.15	British Airways	Heathrow	Boeing 737-400	141
18.15	British Airways	Heathrow	Boeing 767-300	247
19.00	British Midland	Heathrow	Boeing 737-500	117
19.10	Air UK	Stansted	BAe 146-300	108
19.15	British Airways	Heathrow	Boeing 757	195
20.15	British Airways	Heathrow	Boeing 757	195
20.35	Air UK	Gatwick	BAe 146-300	108
21.00	British Midland	Heathrow	Boeing 737-500	117

Source: OAG.

Table 4.12   Supply changes on the London - Glasgow route

	1995	2001
Number of Carriers	3	6
Daily Frequency	28	48
No frills frequency share	0%	39.6%
British Airways frequency share	42.9%	37.5%
Daily Seats	3990	7156
No frills capacity share	0%	40.1%
British Airways capacity share	54.5%	40.7%
No frills average seating capacity	-	151
Full frills average seating capacity	143	148

Data relates to a summer weekday in each year.

Figure 4.3   Low cost airlines' share of London - Glasgow traffic

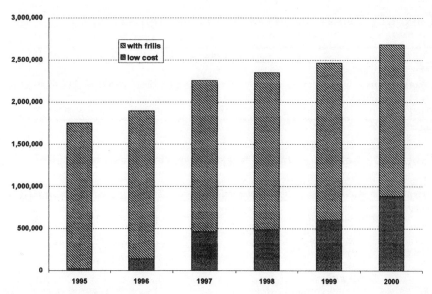

Source: UK Airlines, CAA.

Since the entry of the low cost carriers, total capacity between London and Glasgow has increased by around 80%. Six airlines now compete on the route, with all five London airports connected to the Scottish city. No-frills operators are currently providing 40% of the seats offered and in 2000 accounted for 33% of the traffic. Travellers have clearly benefited from this situation and future prospects for competition on the route appear to be healthy.

This has not been the experience though on all short haul routes with no-frills services. On short haul international sectors, the capacity share of the low cost carriers varies widely, ranging for example from the 32% that Ryanair currently provides between London and Dublin to the 18% offered by the same carrier between London and Oslo. Table 4.13 reveals the phenomenal growth in the number of seats and service frequency supplied between the UK and Irish capital cities during the 1990s. Between 1992 and 2000, seat capacity increased by 85%. More recently still, on a typical weekday in September 2001, there were 58 flights offered between the two cities, of which Ryanair operated 20. Aer Lingus provided the most number of flights at 24, involving three of London's airports. The HHI of 0.30 confirms the high degree of choice available to consumers. Table 4.14 provides a summary of the flights offered by the five operating airlines.

Table 4.13 Supply changes on the London - Dublin route

	1989	1992	1996	2000
Number of Carriers	6	3	5	5
Weekly Seats	67,630	62,137	96,878	114,697
No frills capacity share	11%	26%	32%	33%
HHI	0.33	0.39	0.33	0.30

Source: OAG.

Table 4.14 London - Dublin weekday services - summer 2001

Airport	Airline	Frequency	% of total	Seats	% of total
Heathrow	Aer Lingus	15	25.9	2671	30.3
	British Midland	8	13.8	1568	17.8
		23	*39.7*	*4239*	*48.1*
Gatwick	Cityflyer Express	6	10.3	660	7.5
	Ryanair	4	6.9	520	5.9
	Aer Lingus	3	5.2	468	5.3
		13	*22.4*	*1648*	*18.7*
Stansted	Ryanair	11	19.0	1607	18.3
Luton	Ryanair	5	8.6	650	7.4
City	Aer Lingus	6	10.3	660	7.5

Source: OAG.

The impact of the no-frills operators has not been nearly so marked on the more business-orientated routes of northern Europe. For example between London and Oslo, Ryanair currently operates two flights per day, between the two cities. Ryanair began operating to Sandefjord[7] in 1997 and to combat the threat of no frills carriers operating from Stansted, SAS introduced services from London's third airport to Copenhagen, Oslo and Stockholm. Previously, the company had concentrated its activities at Heathrow.[8] As a result of low traffic and perhaps because the threat from Ryanair was not as large as it had originally anticipated, SAS withdrew its Stansted service to Oslo within a year. It has subsequently withdrawn totally from Stansted and once again is concentrating all its operations at Heathrow. Figure 4.4 shows each carrier's share of passenger traffic on the route between 1990 and 2000. As Table 4.15 reveals, there is a total of 13 daily services currently provided on the route involving four carriers.

Figure 4.4   London - Oslo passenger demand 1990-2000

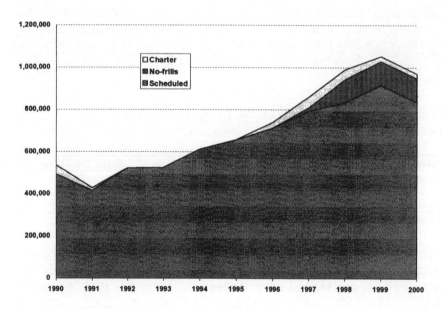

Source: UK Airlines, CAA.

Table 4.15   Services on the London - Oslo route in summer 2001

Departure	Airline	Airport(s)	Aircraft type	Seats
07.40	SAS	Heathrow	MD-82	130
07.45	Ryanair	Stansted-Sandrefjord	Boeing 737-200	130
07.50	British Airways	Heathrow	Airbus 319	126
10.20	SAS	Heathrow	MD-90	147
11.30	Braathens	Gatwick	Boeing 737-700	134
13.05	British Airways	Heathrow	Airbus 319	126
13.05	SAS	Heathrow	MD-82	130
16.20	British Airways	Heathrow	Airbus 319	126
17.35	SAS	Heathrow	MD-90	147
17.40	Braathens	Gatwick	Boeing 737-500	119
18.25	Ryanair	Stansted-Sandrefjord	Boeing 737-800	189
18.45	British Airways	Heathrow	Airbus 319	126
19.35	SAS	Heathrow	MD-82	130

Source: OAG.

The overall supply situation on the London - Oslo route between 1989 and 2000 is summarised in Table 4.16. As may be seen, overall seat capacity increased by 130%, substantially more than between London and Dublin over the same period. The number of operating carriers has fluctuated between three and four and market concentration as measured by the HHI has rarely fallen below 0.30. The proportion of capacity provided by low cost carriers has remained at less than half that achieved on the Irish Sea route.

Table 4.16   Supply changes on the London - Oslo route

	1989	1992	1996	2000
Number of Carriers	3	4	3	4
Weekly Seats	12,280	18,330	21,066	28,282
Low cost capacity share	13%	0%	0%	12%
HHI	0.40	0.28	0.41	0.32

Source: OAG.

This section concludes by examining the penetration of no-frills carriers on one of Europe's busiest business routes, London - Frankfurt. Table 4.17 lists the flights provided on a typical weekday in summer 2001. As may be seen, out of the 32 services operated six are by no-frills operators. Ryanair and Buzz each fly three times daily from Stansted, the former using Hahn airport located 100 kms to the west of Frankfurt. The daily seat capacity on the route is 5,385, of which Lufthansa accounts for 52.3% and British Airways 30.8%. The German flag carrier operates to Frankfurt from all but one of London's airports. Its three daily Stansted services being in direct response to competition from the two no-frills carriers on the route. Lufthansa has a reputation for tackling new competition in an aggressive manner, making no attempt to disguise its undercutting of the low fares charged by the likes of Buzz and Ryanair. Wide differences have been apparent between the fares charged by Lufthansa for similarly timed journeys from Frankfurt to Stansted and those to Heathrow. By contrast, British Airways has continued to focus its Frankfurt services at Heathrow and Gatwick.

Table 4.17   London - Frankfurt services in summer 2001

Departure	Airline	Airport(s)	Aircraft type	Seats
06.50	Buzz	Stansted	BAe 146-300	110
07.00	Ryanair	Stansted – Hahn	Boeing 737-800	189
07.00	Lufthansa	Heathrow	Airbus 310	222
07.15	British Airways	Heathrow	Boeing 767-300	252
07.45	British Airways	Gatwick	Boeing 737-400	147
08.55	Lufthansa	City	Avro RJ 85	80
09.15	Lufthansa	Heathrow	Airbus 300-600	270
10.05	Lufthansa	Heathrow	Airbus 321	182
10.30	British Airways	Heathrow	Airbus 319	126
10.55	Lufthansa	Stansted	Boeing 737-300	123
11.50	Lufthansa	Heathrow	Boeing 737-500	103
11.55	British Airways	Heathrow	Boeing 757	180
12.05	Buzz	Stansted	BAe 146-300	110
12.10	Ryanair	Stansted – Hahn	Boeing 737-800	189
13.05	Lufthansa	Heathrow	Airbus 300-600	270
13.40	British Airways	Gatwick	Boeing 737-400	147
13.45	Lufthansa	City	Dash 8-100	37
14.00	Lufthansa	Stansted	Airbus 320	144
14.05	Lufthansa	Heathrow	Airbus 310	222
15.00	British Airways	Heathrow	Boeing 757	180
15.50	British Airways	Heathrow	Airbus 320	149
16.35	Buzz	Stansted	BAe 146-300	110
17.00	Lufthansa	Heathrow	Airbus 300-600	270
17.55	Lufthansa	Stansted	Airbus 320	144
18.05	Lufthansa	Heathrow	Airbus 300-600	270
18.45	British Airways	Heathrow	Boeing 757	180
18.55	Lufthansa	City	Avro RJ 85	80
19.00	Lufthansa	Heathrow	Airbus 300-600	270
19.15	British Airways	Gatwick	Boeing 737-400	147
20.25	Ryanair	Stansted – Hahn	Boeing 737-800	189
20.25	British Airways	Heathrow	Airbus 320	149
21.05	Lufthansa	Heathrow	Airbus 320	144

Source: OAG.

The overall supply changes on the route between 1989 and 2000 are summarised in Table 4.18. As may be seen, while the number of operating carriers has fallen from nine to five over this period, the total number of seats on offer has increased by 59%. It should be pointed out however, that this earlier figure includes the low frequency fifth freedom operations of several non-European carriers. Direct comparison is therefore not entirely appropriate. The share of capacity of the no-frills operators was 17% in 2000, a situation that has remained the same in 2001.

Table 4.18   Supply changes on the London - Frankfurt route

	1989	1992	1996	2000
Number of Carriers	9	7	7	5
Weekly Seats	42,883	40,189	52,318	68,024
Low cost capacity share	0%	0%	0%	17%
HHI	0.23	0.35	0.28	0.37

Source: OAG.

4.4   Impact of the no-frills sector on traditional charter markets

It is clear that charter operators are particularly vulnerable on the seat only element of their businesses on short sectors of up to 2½ hours flight time. The most successful of the no-frills carriers are concentrating their efforts on this type of route. While the average sectors flown by the vertically integrated charter carriers are around 3½ hours, many of the traditional summer holiday destinations, for example, the Balearic Islands and mainland Spanish resorts, are less than 2½ hours flying time from the main charter traffic generating countries. The greater choice provided by the no-frills airlines in terms of departure time, length of stay and single sector booking, has led to the disappearance of charter flights on many routes of under 2½ hours flight duration. The flexibility offered by the no-frills carriers is proving to be particularly attractive to consumers of short break holidays.

In terms of the charter markets that the low cost scheduled operators have been attracted to enter, it is clear that different strategies are apparent. Three categories of market are evident, namely: intra-European routes with significant levels of business traffic that also have VFR and short break holiday potential, VFR routes with short and long stay holiday potential, and traditional holiday routes. To provide an insight into the impact of the no-frills carriers on these market types, examples of each are cited.

Business, VFR and short / long break holiday routes

Not all routes of around 2-2½ hours flying time with no-frills services though have seen the disappearance of charter traffic. For example, between London and Stockholm there is still a significant demand for charter services. Figure 4.5 shows how charter, no-frills and conventional scheduled traffic has varied between the Swedish capital and London airports during the 1990s. Between 1996 and 2000 overall traffic grew by 62.8%. The impact of Ryanair, which introduced a service to Skavsta[9] in November 1997, is clearly evident. Just under 20% of scheduled service daily capacity is now provided by the low cost airline.[10] Charter traffic on the route has consisted entirely of inbound passengers, most taking a short break holiday in London. In summer 2000, Premiair was operating two flights a week from Arlanda to Stansted, using 379 seat DC-10-10 aircraft, on behalf of its tour operating parent, the Scandinavian Leisure Group (SLG). SLG's costs for transporting city break passengers using this size of aircraft is likely to have been much lower than Ryanair would have been willing to charge to perform the same task.

VFR and short / long break holiday routes

For more than 25 years a large number of Italian destinations have been served from the UK by charter airlines during the summer months, catering both for the VFR market and short and long stay holidaymakers. Over the past three years however, many of these destinations have been subject to the attentions of no-frills airlines and are now no longer served by charter carriers. For example, a route that traditionally has exhibited a significant element of charter traffic is London - Pisa/Florence.[11] The number of passengers carried on charter flights however, has declined considerably since Ryanair began operations between Stansted and Pisa in May 1998, as may be seen from Figure 4.6. In summer 2001, there were only two charter flights per week operating between London's airports and Pisa.[12]

Figure 4.5 London - Stockholm passenger traffic

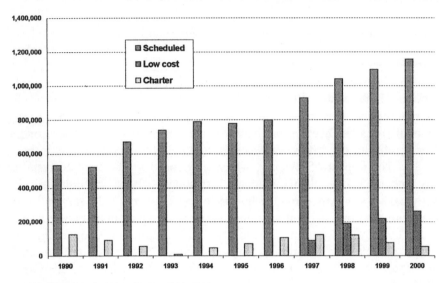

Source: UK Civil Aviation Authority, 1990–2000.

Figure 4.6 London - Florence/Pisa passenger traffic

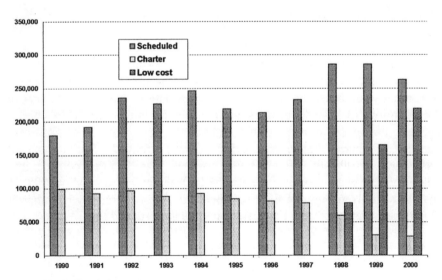

Source: UK Civil Aviation Authority, 1990–2000.

Charter traffic has also all but disappeared on another route of around two hours flight duration, London - Nice.[13] Figure 4.7 shows traffic volumes on the route between 1990 and 2000. Currently, easyJet is operating 38 flights a week from Luton to Nice, compared to BA's 45 and British Midland's 14. In 2000, the no-frills airline accounted for 35.3% of overall demand between London and Nice.

Figure 4.7   London - Nice passenger traffic

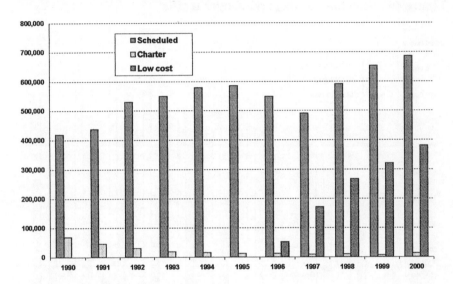

Source: UK Civil Aviation Authority, 1990–2000.

Examples of long stay holiday routes

In 2000, for the first time more passengers travelled by scheduled carrier between London's airports and Malaga than did on charter flights (see Figure 4.8). Around 30% of customers were carried on the scheduled services of low cost operators. Some of these passengers used the scheduled services of charter carriers (Monarch Airlines from Luton and Air 2000 from Gatwick), but the majority travelled with no-frills operators, easyJet and GO. Table 4.19 contrasts the types of services provided from UK airports to Malaga in 1999 and 2000. Whilst scheduled services were provided from only six UK airports in 1999, four of which serve London, as a result of the introduction of scheduled flights to Malaga by charter operator, Air 2000, this had doubled in 2000. By contrast, significant levels of charter traffic, amounting to over 2.21 million passengers in total, were evident at no fewer than 19 UK airports. Close to 65% of this charter traffic was to and from regional airports. This is in marked contrast to the scheduled traffic, of which over 70% was to and from airports serving London.

Figure 4.8   London - Malaga passenger traffic

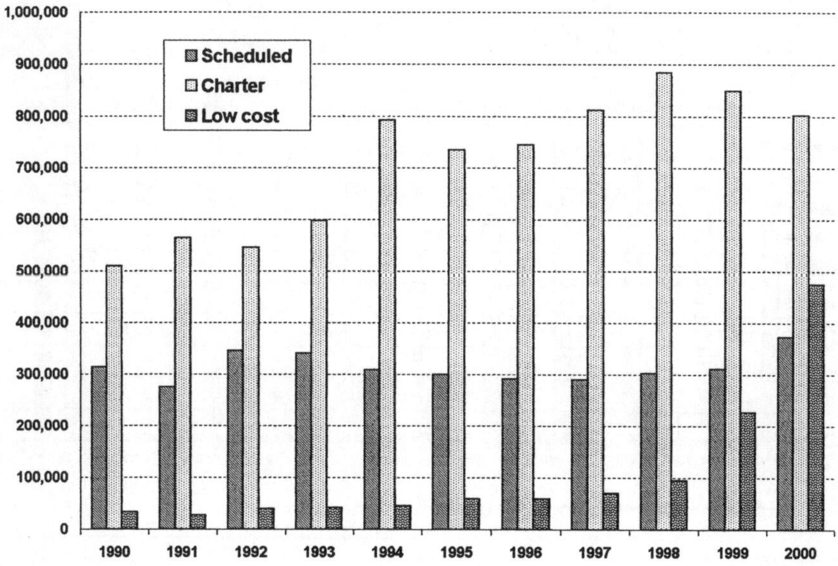

Source: UK Civil Aviation Authority, 1990–2000.

Charter however, continues to dominate on one of the largest holiday routes, namely London - Palma. Figure 4.9 shows the changes in scheduled and charter traffic demand between 1990 and 2000. At the end of this period around 19% of customers were being carried on the scheduled services of low cost operators. As in the case of Malaga, some of these passengers used the scheduled services of charter carriers (Air 2000 and Air Europa from Gatwick), but the majority travelled with no-frills operators, easyJet and GO. Table 4.20 contrasts the types of services provided from UK airports to Palma in 1999 and 2000. Whilst scheduled services were provided from only five UK airports in 1999, four of which serve London, as a result of the introduction of scheduled flights by charter operator, Air 2000, this had increased to eleven in 2000. This increase in scheduled traffic must be set in context, however. Significant levels of charter traffic, amounting to 3.67 million passengers in total, were evident at no fewer than 22 UK airports. Close to 75% of this charter traffic was to and from regional airports. This is in marked contrast to the scheduled traffic, of which over 70% was to and from airports serving London.

Table 4.19   Services from UK airports to Malaga

	With frills scheduled service		No-frills scheduled service		Scheduled service by charter airline		Charter service	
	1999	2000	1999	2000	1999	2000	1999	2000
Gatwick	✈	✈				✈	✈	✈
Heathrow	✈	✈						
Luton				✈	✈	✈	✈	✈
Stansted			✈	✈			✈	✈
Aberdeen							✈	✈
Belfast							✈	✈
Birmingham						✈	✈	✈
Bournemouth							✈	✈
Bristol						✈	✈	✈
Cardiff						✈	✈	✈
East Midlands	✈	✈					✈	✈
Edinburgh							✈	✈
Exeter							✈	✈
Glasgow						✈	✈	✈
Humberside							✈	✈
Leed/Bradford							✈	✈
Liverpool			✈	✈				
Manchester						✈	✈	✈
Newcastle						✈	✈	✈
Norwich							✈	✈
Teesside							✈	✈

Sources: OAG & Airport Timetables UK.

Figure 4.9   London - Palma passenger traffic

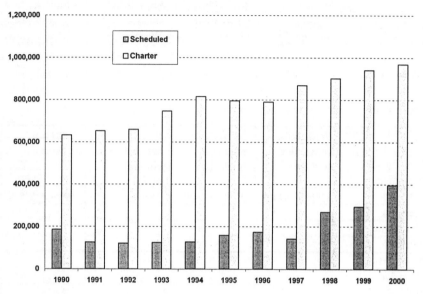

Source: UK Civil Aviation Authority, 1990–2000.

Table 4.20   Services from UK airports to Palma

	With frills scheduled service		No-frills scheduled service		Scheduled service by charter airline		Charter service	
	1999	2000	1999	2000	1999	2000	1999	2000
Gatwick	✈	✈			✈	✈	✈	✈
Heathrow	✈	✈						
Luton			✈	✈			✈	✈
Stansted			✈	✈			✈	✈
Aberdeen							✈	✈
Belfast							✈	✈
Birmingham						✈	✈	✈
Bournemouth							✈	✈
Bristol					✈		✈	✈
Cardiff					✈		✈	✈
East Midlands	✈	✈					✈	✈
Edinburgh							✈	✈

Table 4.20 Continued

	With frills scheduled service		No-frills scheduled service		Scheduled service by charter airline		Charter service	
	1999	2000	1999	2000	1999	2000	1999	2000
Exeter							✈	✈
Glasgow							✈	✈
Humberside							✈	✈
Leeds/Bradford							✈	✈
Liverpool				✈			✈	✈
Manchester						✈	✈	✈
Newcastle						✈	✈	✈
Norwich							✈	✈
Prestwick							✈	✈
Southampton							✈	✈
Teesside							✈	✈

Source: OAG.

4.5 Differences in low cost airlines' operating costs

While no-frills scheduled airlines and charter companies can both legitimately be categorised as low cost airlines, there are substantially differences in the way they each organise and operate their businesses. Table 4.21 provides a summary of the key features of the two respective types of operation. Only in terms of aircraft seating configuration and point-to-point only traffic do the two pursue similar strategies. In all other respects, the two are different.

These dissimilar operating and organisational approaches result in substantially different operating costs. Figure 4.10 compares the unit operating costs achieved in 1997 by a selection of Europe's charter and low cost scheduled carriers. Ryanair, for example, had operating costs per RPK over three times those of charter carrier, Air 2000. In a recent Cranfield Air Transport Group study, the sources of cost advantage integrated charter airlines have over their no frills scheduled counterparts were analysed and these are summarised below in Table 4.22. The combination of larger aircraft, longer sectors, higher load factors, greater labour productivity and considerably lower indirect costs provides charter carriers with a substantial unit cost advantage over their no-frills scheduled counterparts.

Table 4.21 Key features of no-frills operators and charter airlines

Features	no-frills Carriers	Charter Airlines
Direct sell	✓	
Extensive outsourcing	✓	(✓)
High density seating	✓	✓
High public awareness	✓	
No in-flight catering	✓	
Pre-bookable seats		✓
Point to point traffic only	✓	✓
Seat assignment		✓
Secondary airports	✓	(✓)
Short haul focus	✓	
Short turnarounds	✓	
Single aircraft type	✓	
Single class cabin	✓	✓
24 hour operation		✓

Source: Williams, 2001.

Table 4.22   Sources of cost advantage

Characteristic	No frills scheduled	Integrated Charter
Larger aircraft	(✈)	✈
Longer sectors		✈
Higher load factor		✈
Higher aircraft utilisation		✈
Higher labour productivity		✈
Lower distribution costs		✈*
Lower passenger service costs	✈	
Lower landing fees	(✈)	✈
Lower insurance premiums	(✈)	✈
Lower aircraft leasing costs	(✈)	✈
Lower admin & finance costs		✈**

*Arises as a result of being undertaken by tour operators.
**Arises as a result of being partly undertaken by tour operators.
(✈) indicates not all carriers have a cost advantage.

Source: Europe's Low Cost Airlines: an analysis of the economics and operating characteristics of Europe's charter and low cost scheduled airlines, Air Transport Group Research Report 7, College of Aeronautics, Cranfield University, January 2000.

Figure 4.10   Cost comparison of charter and no-frills carriers

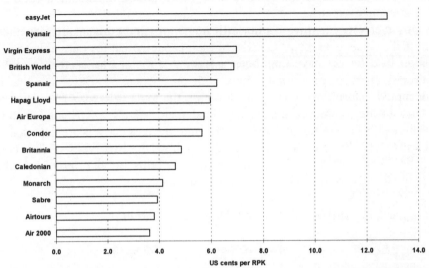

Source: Europe's Low Cost Airlines: an analysis of the economics and operating characteristics of Europe's charter and low cost scheduled airlines, Air Transport Group Research Report 7, College of Aeronautics, Cranfield University, January 2000.

For short and medium haul charter operations the integrated companies mostly use the Airbus 321 (with 220 seats) and Boeing 757 (with 235 seats), whilst for long haul flights the Boeing 767-300 (with 326 seats) and Airbus 330-200 (with 360 seats) predominate. These seating capacities refer to those adopted by UK operators. In most other European countries, the seat pitch is more generous, with, for example, Condor configuring its Boeing 757 aircraft with 25 to 28 fewer seats. Larger capacity aircraft nearly always produce lower direct operating costs per passenger per kilometre.

The integrated charter airlines again have an advantage over the low cost scheduled carriers, as they typically fly sectors of over 2000 kilometres. Figure 4.11 depicts the relationship between sector distance and unit costs for a representative selection of the two types of operator. It is clear that while the integrated charter companies have average sector lengths of approximately 2,500 kilometres, the equivalent figure for the no frills operators varies between 500 and 1,500 kilometres. As a general rule, unit costs (per ATK) for a 2,500 kilometres sector are around one third of those for a 1,000 kilometres routing.[14] The average route length flown by an airline affects its rate of aircraft and crew utilisation, the amount of fuel it uses per block hour, the relative size of its station costs and part of its maintenance expenses.

Another way in which charter airlines derive a cost advantage over their no frills rivals is in the proportion of their capacity that they are able to fill. High load factors have long been a feature of the charter sector. In 1999, aircraft operated by Airtours flew with on average 91.6% of their seats occupied. During the same year, Ryanair, the longest-lived of Europe's no frills airlines, achieved an average load factor of 68%. The load factors achieved by a selection of other charter and low cost carriers are depicted in Figure 4.12. To provide an indication of how the two types of low cost airline compare with a conventional full frills service provider, the equivalent figure for British Airways is included.

Figure 4.11   Influence of sector distance on unit cost

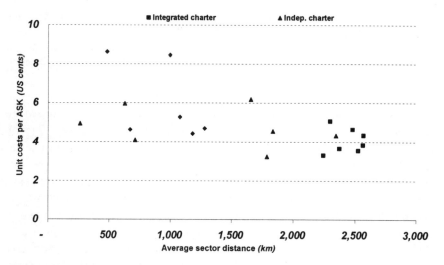

(Diamond shapes indicate no-frills operators.)

Source: Europe's Low Cost Airlines: an analysis of the economics and operating characteristics of Europe's charter and low cost scheduled airlines, Air Transport Group Research Report 7, College of Aeronautics, Cranfield University, January 2000.

Aircraft utilisation for short to medium haul scheduled carriers is with few exceptions lower than that achieved by charter airlines. The shorter turnaround times achieved by the new low cost carriers, however, has reduced the gap that has traditionally existed. Even the best rate of around 10 hours per day achieved by the new breed, though, fails to match the 12 – 13 hours of the charter sector.[15] While short haul scheduled carriers usually are constrained to operating between the hours of 07.00 and 22.00, charter airlines are not so limited. More recently though, some of the low cost scheduled carriers have been following the example of the latter. For example, GO has been operating an overnight service from Stansted to Reykjavik during the summer months and to Tenerife in the winter, and easyJet has been extending their operating day on services to summer holiday destinations.[16] Figure 4.13 contrasts the seasonal variation in utilisation of the Airbus 320 fleets of Air 2000 and British Airways.

Figure 4.12   Variations in load factor (1999)

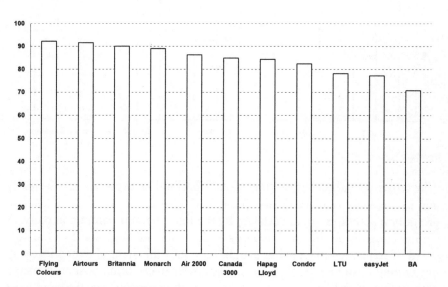

Sources: Airline Business and UK CAA.

The vertically integrated charter airlines typically achieve more than double the labour productivity of the no-frills scheduled operators, as Figure 4.14 reveals. This measure however, is considerably influenced by the extent to which a carrier outsources its activities and by the nature of the product it offers to its customers. While the low cost scheduled and charter airlines share some common features, wide differences are apparent with respect to the degree of outsourcing that occurs. For example, the long established charter operators often undertake their maintenance in-house, whereas the low cost scheduled companies have in the main outsourced this activity.

Figure 4.13   Variations in aircraft utilisation by quarter

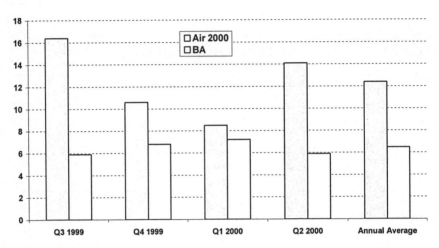

Source: UK Airlines, CAA.

In terms of indirect operating costs, distribution expenses are virtually non-existent for the vertically integrated charter airlines, as sales and promotion activities are undertaken by the tour operator parent company. A similar situation applies with regards to ticketing, although some of the new breed of scheduled players has sought to reduce this item of expenditure by not issuing customers with tickets. The lower distribution costs associated with Internet selling has proved an attractive option for the low cost scheduled carriers.

Administration and Finance expenses are also lower for the integrated charter airlines, as many of the tasks usually included under this category are undertaken by the tour operator parent companies. It would seem likely though that similar sized no-frills scheduled carriers and independent charter airlines would face much the same levels of expenditure on general administration and finance. In terms of passenger service costs, the no frills scheduled carriers have the advantage.

Figure 4.14 Output (in thousands of ASKs) per employee in 1997

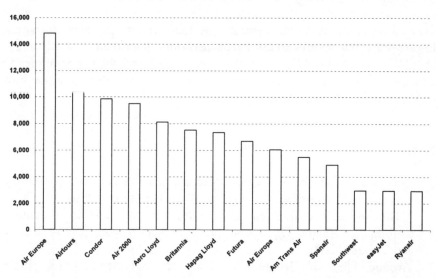

Source: Europe's Low Cost Airlines: an analysis of the economics and operating characteristics of Europe's charter and low cost scheduled airlines, Air Transport Group Research Report 7, College of Aeronautics, Cranfield University, January 2000.

4.6 Concluding comments

The emergence of no-frills scheduled carriers has produced major challenges not only to full service providers but also for charter airlines. The traditional charter product has offered travellers little choice either in respect of the duration of their holidays or in terms of the times that they could fly. The greater choice offered by the no-frills airlines in terms of flight departure times, length of stay and single sector booking has proved attractive to many travellers, particularly those arranging short break holidays. It would seem inevitable that more and more consumers will begin to put together their own holiday packages, leaving charter carriers to face an overall decline in the demand for their traditional product and a dwindling share of the growing seat only market, unless that is they can go some way to matching the flexibility offered by the no-frills airlines.

The ease of making a single reliable transaction with a tour operator using either a local travel agent or the company's web site may continue to be attractive to many people. It is clear though that charter companies can expect to see further encroachment of their traditional short haul markets by the no-frills airlines. The lower operating costs of the charter carriers result primarily from the nature of their business. As long as these companies continue to concentrate on their traditional core activities, namely carrying the clientele of tour operators, then their cost advantage should remain. However, if they were to refocus their operations to concentrate on providing scheduled services, it is difficult to imagine how this cost differential could be sustained.

Notes

1. Gol Transportes Aéreos began operating low fare services connecting seven of the largest cities in Southern Brazil in January 2001.
2. 'Will Europe's charter carriers be replaced by no-frills scheduled airlines?', Williams, G., *Journal of Air Transport Management*, Vol. 7, pp. 277-286, 2001.
3. Around 90% of Britannia's flights are operated for its parent organisation, Preussag.
4. The rivalry between Airtours and Britannia in the UK market makes the carriage of Airtours passengers in Britannia's aircraft and vice versa virtually unthinkable. In Scandinavia however, aircraft capacity is often shared between the two tour operators.
5. A listing of UK charter carriers that have failed or been taken over is provided in 'Best practice benchmarking: a route to competitiveness?' by Francis, Hinton, Holloway & Humphreys in the *Journal of Air Transport Management*, 5 (1999) pp. 105-112.
6. For example, Airtours purchased the Scandinavian Leisure Group and its charter subsidiary, Premiair, in 1994.
7. Sandefjord is located 110 kms to the south of Oslo.
8. For a number of years the company had operated a service to Aarhus from Gatwick, but this was later transferred to Heathrow.
9. Skavsta is located 100 kms to the south of central Stockholm.
10. Ryanair now provides a thrice daily service from Stansted to Skavsta using 189 seat Boeing 737-800 aircraft.
11. As the runway at Florence is relatively short, most jet aircraft serving the region operate into Pisa (one hour away by road or rail).
12. Both services were operated on Saturdays from Gatwick.

13. Charter passengers travelling between London and Nice totalled 12,535 in 2000, representing only 1.2% of overall demand on the route.
14. Source IATA AETF 1998 data.
15. In 1999, easyJet's fleet of Boeing 737-300 achieved a daily utilisation rate of 10.2 hours, some 20% lower than the 12.3 hours Britannia obtained from their Boeing 757s.
16. One of easyJet's services from Palma last summer arrived into Luton at 03.15.

Reference

'Europe's Low Cost Airlines: an analysis of the economics and operating characteristics of Europe's charter and low cost scheduled airlines', Mason K., Whelan C. and Williams G., *Air Transport Group Research Report 7*, College of Aeronautics, Cranfield University, January 2000.

5 Europe – the world's first fully deregulated region

Within continental Europe the effects of airline deregulation have been limited. Many of the densest international city-pair markets in continental Europe remain entirely in the hands of the respective flag carriers. It has been mainly the domestic travellers of continental Europe that have benefited most from liberalisation, as Chapter 3 revealed. Aside from these consumers, those that have never had it quite so good before are the users of Europe's new breed of low cost, mostly no-frills, scheduled carriers. Until very recently, with the exception of services operated from Brussels by Virgin Express, the UK and Ireland was the focus of these companies operations. By way of example, Table 5.1 shows the number of carriers competing on routes to Barcelona from a selection of Europe's major cities in summer 2000. As may be seen, while passengers from London had the choice of four carriers operating direct services, those travelling to the Spanish city from Frankfurt and Paris had only the respective flag carriers.

Table 5.1   Competition on intra-EU routes from Barcelona in 2000

To:	Carriers*	Frequency	Airport(s)	Code-share
Amsterdam	Iberia	2		
	KLM	5		
	Transavia	*1*		
Brussels	Iberia	2		
	Virgin Express	5		Sabena
Frankfurt	Iberia	3		
	Lufthansa	5		Spanair
London	British Airways	5	Heathrow & Gatwick	
	easyJet	4	Luton	
	GO	2	Stansted	
	Iberia	4	Heathrow	
Milan	Alitalia	4	Malpensa	
	Gandalf	2	Bergamo	
	Iberia	2	Malpensa	
Paris	Air France	7	Charles de Gaulle	
	Iberia	6	Orly	

Source: OAG, July 2000. * Lower cost carriers are shown in italics.

By summer 2001, while passengers travelling to Barcelona from Amsterdam, London and Milan had experienced an increase in the number services offered (either from existing low cost operators or from new entrants), those flying from Frankfurt or Paris direct still had only the two flag carriers from which to choose. Table 5.2 lists the carriers currently operating services to Barcelona from a selection of Europe's major cities. Passengers travelling from London now have five carriers from which to choose and those from Milan four. While services to Barcelona from Brussels, Frankfurt and Paris continue to feature two operating airlines, there are very wide differences in the levels of fares charged. The presence of no-frills carrier Virgin Express on the Brussels - Barcelona route has provided consumers with an alternative to paying the high fares normally experienced on services provided by national airlines. For example,

Table 5.2 Competition on intra-EU routes from Barcelona in 2001

To:	Carriers*	Frequency	Airport(s)	Code-share
Amsterdam	Iberia	3		
	KLM	5		
	Transavia	2		
Brussels	Iberia	3		
	Virgin Express	5		Sabena
Frankfurt	Iberia	3		
	Lufthansa	5		Spanair
London	British Airways	7	Heathrow & Gatwick	
	British Midland	2	Heathrow	
	easyJet	4	Luton	
	GO	2	Stansted	
	Iberia	4	Heathrow	
Milan	Alitalia	4	Malpensa	
	Gandalf	3	Bergamo	Air France
	Iberia	3	Linate & Malpensa	
	Meridiana	1	Linate	
Paris	Air France	8	Charles de Gaulle	
	Iberia	6	Orly	

Source: OAG, August 2001. * Lower cost carriers are shown in italics.

Significant changes however, are now occurring in continental Europe as a result of the entry of established low cost companies, easyJet and Ryanair. In 2001, easyJet began operating from a new base at Amsterdam, as did Ryanair from Charleroi (advertised as Brussels South). A listing of the routes operated in continental Europe by low cost airlines is shown in Table 5.3.

Of course, it can also be argued that even with only the two respective flag carriers operating an international route, consumers have some degree of choice. Aside from the considerably lower fares available to those travellers willing to return the following week, price competition has also been evident between national airlines for those passengers willing to travel via an intermediate point. The lower fares that can be obtained in exchange for the longer journey times are commonly available for both economy and business class travel. An added incentive to attract the regular traveller is the enhanced frequent flyer points that can be obtained from indirect routings.

For example, it was possible in July 2001 to fly from Birmingham to Madrid via Brussels with Sabena in business class for a return fare of under £400. This offer it should be pointed out did not require the traveller to stay a Saturday night in Madrid. The same journey in economy class using the only direct flight between the two cities (provided by British Airways) was priced at over £650. Undoubtedly, in this instance a choice did exist, but hardly much of a one! For those customers willing to undertake the same journey via Basel using the services of Crossair, quadruple Qualiflyer frequent flyer points await.

Table 5.3 Routes operated in continental Europe by no-frills airlines

Airline	Routes
Basiq Air	Amsterdam - Barcelona
	Amsterdam - Nice
	Rotterdam - Barcelona
	Rotterdam - Nice
EasyJet	Amsterdam - Barcelona
	Amsterdam - Geneva
	Amsterdam - Nice
	Geneva - Barcelona
	Geneva - Nice
Ryanair	Charleroi - Carcassonne
	Charleroi - Pisa
	Charleroi - Treviso (Venice)
Virgin Express	Brussels - Barcelona
	Brussels - Copenhagen
	Brussels - Madrid
	Brussels - Malaga
	Brussels - Milan
	Brussels - Nice
	Brussels - Rome

Source: OAG.

To provide some idea of the range of choice available to travellers, examples are given below of three intra-European journeys. Each example involves a weekday trip undertaken in mid-September 2001, with for the purposes of simplicity, the return element of each excluded. Table 5.4 provides a summary of the options available to consumers in each case. In the case of Oslo - Zurich, three direct services were offered, all flown by Swissair. The OAG for the day in question lists no fewer than 59 possible connecting flight combinations. Of these, because of code-sharing the number of actual connecting options is only 37.

Direct flights are shown with an elapsed time of 2 hours 20 minutes, while the two shortest connecting options take 3 hours 40 minutes. One of these connections is online with SAS involving a change of aircraft at Copenhagen, whilst the other via Hamburg with 40 minutes on the ground combines a Lufthansa flight with one operated by Swissair. Connections are shown as being possible at 13 airports (Amsterdam, Basel, Brussels, Copenhagen, Dusseldorf, Frankfurt, Gothenburg, Hamburg, Milan, Munich, Paris, Prague and Stockholm). The distances flown vary from 872 miles in the case of Frankfurt to 1,172 miles for a journey via Stockholm. None of the flights shown involves the services of a low cost carrier.

Table 5.4   Examples of intra-EU travel options

Route & Distance	Direct flights (& flight time)	Connecting options	Connecting cities	Distances (miles)	Journey time
Oslo - Zurich	3 (2h 20m)	37	13	872 - 1172	3h 40m -
Glasgow - Frankfurt	2* (1h 55m - 3h 25m)	37	9	667 - 1069	3h 10m - 4h 55m
Paris - Lisbon	10 (2h 20m)	46	16	920 - 1471	3h 30m - 5h 15m

*One of the two through flights operates via Southampton.

The Glasgow - Frankfurt route differs from Oslo - Zurich, in that a low cost carrier operates one of the two through services on offer. The other service is provided by British Airways subsidiary, Brymon Airways. It involves an intermediate stop at Southampton. No fewer than 83 possible connecting flight combinations are shown by the OAG. Of these, because of extensive code-sharing the number of actual connecting options is only 37.

The shortest direct flight is shown to have with an elapsed time of 1 hour 55 minutes, while the two fastest connecting options take 3 hours 10 minutes with a distance flown of 805 miles. Both of these connections are online with British Airways involving a change of aircraft at Birmingham.

Connections are shown as being possible at nine airports (Amsterdam, Birmingham, Bristol, Brussels, Copenhagen, East Midlands, London [City and Heathrow] and Manchester). The distances flown vary from 691 miles in the case of Brussels to 1,069 miles for a journey via Copenhagen. Both direct flights leave Glasgow in the middle of the day. Given the close proximity of Edinburgh and the provision of two better-timed direct flights a day to Frankfurt with British Midland however, many business travellers may well prefer this routing.

In the case of Paris - Lisbon, ten direct services were offered, flown by Air France (from Charles de Gaulle) and TAP (from Orly). The OAG for the day in question lists no fewer than 72 possible connecting flight combinations. Of these, because of code-sharing the number of actual connecting options is only 46.

Direct flights are shown with an elapsed time of 2 hours 20 minutes, while the shortest connecting option takes 3 hours 30 minutes. This connection involves travelling via Bordeaux using an Air France flight for the first leg of the journey and thence with Regional Airlines. Time on the ground is only 25 minutes in this instance. Connections are shown as being possible at 16 airports (Amsterdam, Barcelona, Basel, Bordeaux, Brussels, Frankfurt, Geneva, London, Lyons, Madrid, Marseilles, Nice, Porto, Toulouse, Valencia and Zurich). The distances flown vary from 920 miles in the case of Bordeaux to 1,471 miles for a journey via Frankfurt. None of the flights shown involves the services of a no-frills carrier.

5.1 Fare competition

To provide an insight into the impact of low cost carriers (and occasionally other airlines) upon the fares available to travellers when undertaking journeys in continental Europe, a selection of routes to Barcelona, and from Madrid and Paris have been analysed. In each case two journeys undertaken in September 2001 have been priced, one involving a mid-week trip (out Tuesday, returning Thursday) and the other over a weekend (out Friday and back the following Monday). The routes involved are shown in Table 5.5.

Figure 5.1 shows the lowest fares available for a mid-week return journey from the selected destinations to Barcelona. With the exception of Frankfurt and Milan, the fares are under £125. The fare from Amsterdam is available with easyJet, that from Brussels with Virgin Express, from Frankfurt with both Iberia and Lufthansa, from London with easyJet, and from Milan with Air France flying with Gandalf out of Bergamo. Figure

5.2 shows the lowest fares available for a mid-week return journey to the selected destinations from Madrid. With the exception of Frankfurt and London, the fares are over £575. The fare to Amsterdam is available with Iberia, that to Brussels with Sabena, to Frankfurt with Lan Chile (only one flight per day),[1] to London with easyJet, and to Milan with Alitalia and Iberia. Figure 5.3 shows the lowest fares available for a mid-week return journey to the selected destinations from Paris. With the exception of London, the fares are over £375. The fare to Barcelona is available with Air France, that to Frankfurt with Lufthansa, to London with British Midland,[2] to Madrid with Spanair, and to Milan with either Air France flying with Gandalf to Bergamo or Air France (and also Alitalia) to Linate.

Table 5.5   Routes analysed

Barcelona from	Madrid to	Paris to
Amsterdam (1239)	Amsterdam (1460)	Barcelona (858)
Brussels (1082)	Brussels (1315)	Frankfurt (448)
Frankfurt (1090)	Frankfurt (1420)	London (346)
London (1146)	London (1246)	Madrid (1065)
Milan (742)	Milan (1181)	Milan (644)

Figures in brackets indicate distance in kilometres.

Figure 5.1   Mid-week fares to Barcelona

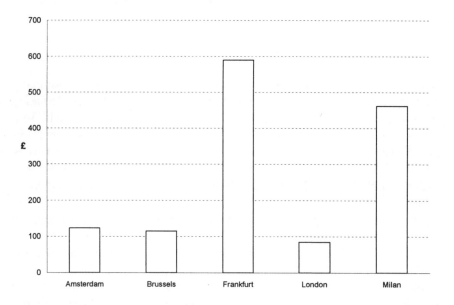

Figure 5.2   Mid-week fares from Madrid

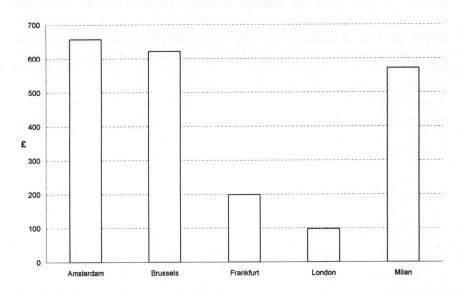

Figure 5.3   Mid-week fares from Paris

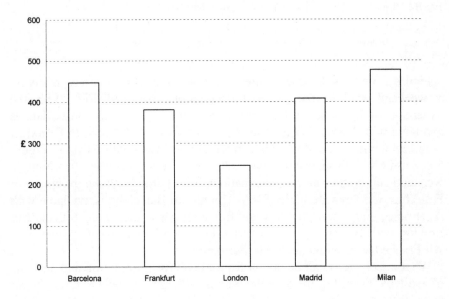

Figure 5.4 shows the lowest fares available for a return journey involving a weekend stay from the selected destinations to Barcelona. With the exception of Frankfurt, the fares are under £135. With the exception of the fare from London, which is available from Lufthansa using the services of bmi British Midland, those to all other cities are with Iberia.

Figure 5.4   Weekend fares to Barcelona

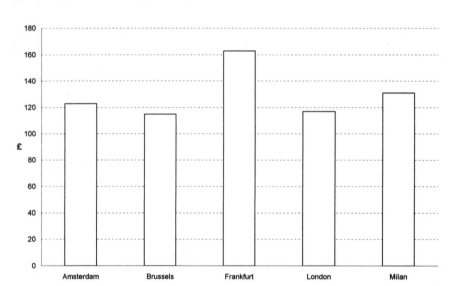

Figure 5.5 shows the lowest fares available for a return journey involving a weekend stay to the selected destinations from Madrid. With the exception of London, the fares are over £100. The fare to Amsterdam is available with Iberia, that to Brussels with Sabena and Iberia, to Frankfurt with Lan Chile, to London with easyJet, and to Milan with Alitalia. Figure 5.6 shows the lowest fares available for a return journey involving a weekend stay to the selected destinations from Paris. With the exception of Frankfurt, the fares are under £160. The fare to Barcelona is available with Air France and Iberia, that to Frankfurt with Air France and Lufthansa, to London with British Airways, to Madrid with Spanair, and to Milan with Air France flying with Gandalf to Bergamo.

What conclusions can be drawn from the above information and analysis of available fares. For the traveller who is willing to spend a Saturday night away from home there are low fares on offer, apart from at peak holiday times, to nearly all destinations in Europe. The less time sensitive these consumers are the greater the likelihood of them being able to obtain a low fare, even at busy travel periods. By accepting an indirect routing with a flag carrier, it is often possible to get a lower fare than would be available from a low cost carrier. This is particularly the case during peak travel periods.

For those unwilling to extend their trips to include a Saturday night, the options for cheap air travel are considerably fewer. The prospect of a three to four hours journey, instead of less than 2 hours non-stop, deters many from taking a cheaper indirect routing. A key question is whether or not it is reasonable that time sensitive passengers should typically have to pay £500 to £750 for a return trip within Europe, especially given that few sectors exceed 1,000 miles.

Figure 5.5   Weekend fares from Madrid

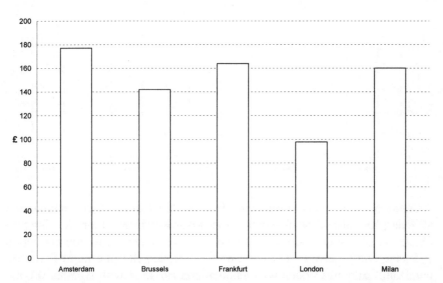

In order to provide an answer to this thorny question, the operating costs of a typical 150-seat jet aircraft for an intra-European sector with a block time of one hour have been estimated. Large variations are apparent, of course, in the costs operating such an aircraft over different routes, as a result of different airport handling and ATC en-route charges, meaning that it is only possible to come up with a very broad ballpark figure. The UK CAA undertook a similar calculation when it sought to analyse the per passenger cost difference between full service airlines and no-frills carriers.[3] In the CAA's analysis, the cost to British Airways of carrying a passenger for one hour was estimated to be around £80. This was assuming a load factor of 70% on an aircraft equipped with 135 seats. The equivalent figures for British Midland and Ryanair were respectively £62 and £38. The CAA's calculations indicated that in 1997 it cost British Airways of the order of £7,500 to operate the one-hour flight.

Figure 5.6   Weekend fares from Paris

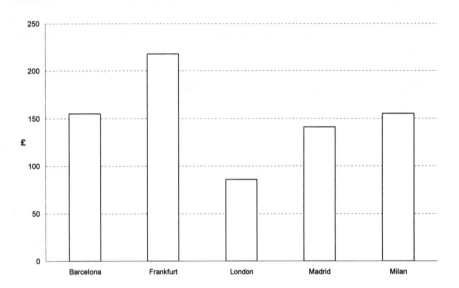

Based on these calculations and data available from other sources, and allowing for some cost inflation, let us assume that the figure has risen to £8,000. It is further assumed that load factors (on an aircraft equipped with 135 seats) vary between 60% and 85%. Table 5.6 shows a number of fare level and passenger demand combinations, in an attempt to reflect the variation that exists in the traffic carried on a short haul flight. At the busiest times, the airline is shown to be making a profit of £18,500, whereas when demand is at its lowest a loss of £3,300 is incurred. In reality however, these revenue projections probably underestimate the revenue generated during periods of peak demand and considerably overestimate revenue extracted at off-peak times. Many fares will be lower than those indicated as a result of pro-rating for connecting passengers.

One answer to the question of whether current fully flexible economy and business class fares are justifiable or not is that if customers are willing to pay them then by default they are justified. If they were overpriced travellers would seek other means to reach their destinations, or not travel at all. This begs the question that an alternative exists. This may not always be the case however. The practice of yield management, or price discrimination as it more honestly is called, is now so widely used that it is almost impossible to link the unit cost of providing an airline seat with *the* price that should reasonably be charged for it. Excluding taxes, the marginal cost of carrying an additional passenger between London and Glasgow on a Boeing 757 already loaded with 150 passengers is likely to under £10. With 150 seats filled, using the data contained in the above example, an average fare of £54 would need to be charged for the airline to cover its costs. The highest single fare is in fact £167, more than three times this level. The large majority of passengers would however, be paying considerably less than this amount. Given that competition is thriving on the London - Glasgow route with many options available to air travellers, one would be hard pressed to provide a convincing case that consumers are being exploited.

Table 5.6 Possible fare and passenger demand combinations

Return Fare	Christmas	Monday am	Monday pm	Wednesday midday in February
£100			20	35
£150	10	18	25	25
£200	20	20	10	11
£250	25	20		
£300			15	5
£350	25	20	15	5
£400	35	30	10	
Revenue (£)	34,500	30,700	21,500	12,700
Profit (£)	18,500	14,700	5,500	-3,300
Load Factor	85%	80%	70%	60%

Notes

1. The fare with Iberia and Lufthansa is £743.
2. No-frills carrier Buzz also offers low fares between Charles de Gaulle and Stansted airports.
3. The Single European Aviation Market: the first five years, UK CAA, CAP 685, 1998, pp.140-145.

6 Air transport provision in remoter regions

One of the consequences of deregulation has been the elimination of cross-subsidy from loss-making domestic services and its replacement with direct subvention. In the past, in exchange for monopoly route rights, a flag carrier, or a subsidiary company, covered the losses on its lightly trafficked routes with the profits earned on the busier parts of its route network. With liberalisation other carriers have entered the domestic markets and brought about the demise of this practice. This is not to say that cross-subsidisation has altogether disappeared. Airlines continue to cross-subsidise their loss-making (often short haul) operations with the profits they earn on other parts of their networks (mostly long haul routes). The arrangement whereby a single carrier supplied a nation's domestic routes without the need for state support though has. To ensure the continuation of air services on non-commercially viable routes, the European Council of Ministers have enacted legislation permitting the provision of direct subsidies.

6.1 The PSO system

The ability of an EU state to impose a Public Service Obligation (PSO) on any route, or group of routes, requiring subvention arises from Article 4 of the 1992 Council Regulation on access for community air services to intra-community routes. In situations where the maintenance of regular air services are considered vital for the economic development of a region and a commercially viable operation is not possible, a PSO is justified. In preparing PSOs, Member States are required to issue a public invitation to tender that is published in the *Official Journal of the European Communities*. The invitation to tender is open to all air carriers registered in the European Economic Area (EEA) and can be made in relation to a single route or a group of routes. The deadline for submitting tenders is one month following the date of publication.

PSO tenders, which cover a period of three years, usually specify minimum service levels in terms of capacity and frequency, and often stipulate the schedule that the selected airline would need to provide. Maximum fare levels also feature in most PSOs. The take-up of PSOs by the Member States has been subject to wide variation. Reynolds-Feighan (1999) showed that of the 161 PSO routes imposed in EU/EEA states between 1994 and 1997, 78 of these were in respect of France and 58 of Norway. Since then the total number of PSO routes has fallen to 146. Greece is in the process of imposing PSO routes, following the deregulation of their domestic market in 1999. Sweden to date has had only one PSO route, but a further ten are being given PSO status.

The original intention for the PSO system was to ensure the maintenance of essential air services to remote and peripheral regions. Such services invariably were loss making and for them to survive required the provision of subvention in one guise or another. As Reynolds-Feighan (1999) makes clear, unlike the US Essential Air Services Program there is no consistency in the provision of subsidy for PSO routes. While there is a common approach that has to be adopted by each Member State in the process of nominating a PSO route and the subsequent tendering approach, it is at the discretion of each government to determine the level of service to be provided and the fares to be charged. Wide differences are therefore apparent in the amounts of subvention that have been provided for routes carrying similar volumes of passenger traffic.

Besides imposing the largest number of PSO routes, France has the widest variation in the types of sector with direct subvention provided. One unusual group is the large number of cross-border routes that feature. Of the 78 French PSO routes referred to above, 14 involve operations to other EU states. All but two of these are to ensure the provision of direct air services to Strasbourg from each of the EU States for Members of the European Parliament. Other than these special exceptions, there are very few examples of cross-border PSO routes. Also unique to France are the large number of PSOs that involve the capital city. No fewer than twenty routes from Paris Orly have a PSO imposed upon them. With such status, the possibility of slots being transferred to other more lucrative destinations is avoided.

Routes serving peripheral or development regions can have *their* slots protected at congested European airports. The argument being that peripheral and development regions require regular, convenient and affordable air services to major economic, administrative and political decision making centres in order to maintain social cohesion, sustain economic activity and help promote much needed inward investment. Article 4, of Regulation 95/93, grants powers to Member States to reserve slots for services where PSOs have been imposed or for domestic air services that are considered vital on socio-economic grounds but which do not have PSO designated status. In the case of non-PSO commercial air services however, protection can be withdrawn if a second carrier enters the route. The Regulation also states that slots can only be reserved for a route (which is not airport specific) that had been operating before 1995.

Given the common EU-wide tendering system for PSO routes, it is perhaps a little surprising that so few examples exist of carriers from other countries operating such services. Table 6.1, for example, lists the carriers serving the currently operated Irish PSO routes. Similar information is provided in Tables 6.2, 6.3, 6.4 and 6.5 for the Scottish, Norwegian, French and German PSOs respectively. The only example of a PSO route from these three countries that is not operated by a local carrier is Dublin-Derry, which is served by the Scottish airline Loganair. As may be seen, frequency varies from one to four daily services. Of the cases cited, with the exception of services to Corsica, the seating capacity of aircraft employed varies from nine seats up to 50.

Table 6.1   Current Irish PSO routes and their operating carriers

Route	Carrier	Daily Frequency	Aircraft type
Dublin-Donegal	Aer Arann	1	ATR 42
Dublin-Derry	Loganair	2	Saab 340
Dublin-Galway	Aer Arann	5	ATR 42
Dublin-Kerry	Aer Arann	4	ATR 42
Dublin-Knock	Aer Arann	1	ATR 42
Dublin-Sligo	Aer Arann	2	ATR 42

Source: OAG.

Table 6.2   Current Scottish PSO routes and their operating carriers

Route	Carrier	Daily Frequency	Aircraft type
Glasgow-Barra	Loganair	1	Twin Otter
Glasgow-Campbeltown	Loganair	2	Twin Otter
Glasgow-Tiree	Loganair	1	Twin Otter
Kirkwall-North Ronaldsay	Loganair	2	BN Islander
Kirkwall-Papa Westray	Loganair	2	BN Islander
Lerwick-Fair Isle	Loganair	2	BN Islander

Source: OAG.

Table 6.3 Current Norwegian PSO routes and their operating carriers

Route	Carrier	Daily Frequency	Aircraft type
Andenes-Bodø	Widerøe	3	Dash 8-100
Andenes-Tromsø	Widerøe	2	Dash 8-100
Brønnøysund-Bodø	Widerøe	4	Dash 8-100
Brønnøysund-Trondheim	Widerøe	5	Dash 8-100
Fagernes-Oslo	Guardair	3	Dornier 228
Florø-Bergen	Coast Air	6	ATR 42
Florø-Oslo	Coast Air	3	ATR 42
Førde-Bergen	Widerøe	2	Dash 8-100
Førde-Oslo	Widerøe	4	Dash 8-100
Hasvik-Hammerfest	Widerøe	1	Dash 8-100
Hasvik-Tromsø	Widerøe	1	Dash 8-100
Lakselv-Tromsø	SAS	4	Fokker 50
Leknes-Bodø	Widerøe	7	Dash 8-100
Mo i Rana-Bodø	Widerøe	4	Dash 8-100
Mo i Rana-Trondheim	Widerøe	5	Dash 8-100
Mosjøen-Bodø	Widerøe	4	Dash 8-100
Mosjøen-Trondheim	Widerøe	5	Dash 8-100
Namsos-Trondheim	Widerøe	3	Dash 8-100
Narvik-Bodø	Widerøe	3	Dash 8-100
Ørsta-Volda-Oslo	Widerøe	3	Dash 8-100
Røst-Bodø	Guardair	2	Dornier 228
Sandane-Bergen	Widerøe	2	Dash 8-100
Sandane-Oslo	Widerøe	1	Dash 8-100
Sandnessjøn-Bodø	Widerøe	5	Dash 8-100
Sandnessjøn-Trondheim	Widerøe	4	Dash 8-100
Sogndal-Bergen	Widerøe	2	Dash 8-100
Sogndal-Oslo	Widerøe	5	Dash 8-100
Svolvær-Bodø	Widerøe	7	Dash 8-100
Vadsø-Båtsfjord-Berlevåg-Mehamn-Honningsvåg-Hammerfest-Kirkenes	Widerøe	2	Dash 8-100
Vardø-Kirkenes	Guardair	3	Dornier 228
Værøy-Bodø	Helikopter Service	2	S 61N

Source: OAG.

Maps of the routes referred to in Tables 6.1, 6.2, 6.3 and 6.5 are contained in Figures 6.1, 6.2, 6.3 and 6.4.

Table 6.4   Current French PSO routes and their operating carriers

Route	Carrier	Daily Frequency	Aircraft type
Agen-Paris (Orly)	Air France	3	ATR 42
Aurillac-Paris (Orly)	Air France (Proteus)	2	Brasilia
Bergerac-Paris (Orly)	Air France	3	Beech 1900
Castres-Paris (Orly)	Air France (Proteus)	2	Brasilia
Castres-Rodez-Lyon	Hex Air	2	Beechcraft
Epinal-Paris (Orly)	Air France	2	Beech 1900
Le Puy-Paris (Orly)	Hex Air	2	Beechcraft
Lorient-Lyon	Air France (Proteus)	3	Brasilia
Pau-Nantes	Air France	2	Beech 1900
Périgueux-Paris (Orly)	Air France (Proteus)	3	Brasilia
Roanne-Paris (Orly)	Air France	2	Beech 1900
Rodez-Paris (Orly)	Air Lib	3	ATR 42
Saint Brieuc-Paris (Orly)	Air Bretagne	2	Beechcraft
Strasbourg-Copenhagen	Air France (Proteus)	2	Embraer RJ145
Strasbourg-Milan	Air France (Proteus)	2	Brasilia
Strasbourg-Vienna	Tyrolean	2	CRJ
Strasbourg-Madrid	Iberia (Air Nostrum)	2	CRJ
Ajaccio-Paris (Orly)	Air France	3	Airbus 319
Bastia-Paris (Orly)	Air France	3	Fokker 100
Figari-Paris (Orly)	Air Lib	1	MD-80
Lyons-Ajaccio	Corse Mediterranee	1	ATR 72
Lyons-Calvi	Corse Mediterranee	1	ATR 72
Marseille-Ajaccio	Corse Mediterranee	4	Fokker 100
Marseille-Bastia	Corse Mediterranee	4	Fokker 100
Marseille-Calvi	Air Littoral	2	ATR 42
Marseille-Figari	Air Littoral	3	ATR 42
Montpellier-Ajaccio	Air Littoral	1	ATR 42
Montpellier-Bastia	Air Littoral	1	ATR 42
Nice-Ajaccio	Corse Mediterranee	3	ATR 72
Nice-Bastia	Corse Mediterranee	3	ATR 72
Nice-Calvi	Air Littoral	1	ATR 42
Nice-Figari	Air Littoral	1	CRJ

Source: OAG.

Table 6.5   Current German PSO routes and their operating carriers

Route	Carrier	Daily Frequency	Aircraft type
Erfurt-Berlin/Tempelhof	Walter	2	Dornier 228
Erfurt-Hamburg	Walter	2	Dornier 228
Erfurt-Cologne	Walter	2	Dornier 228
Erfurt-Munich	OLT	3	Saab 340

Source: OAG.

Figure 6.1   Map of Irish PSO routes

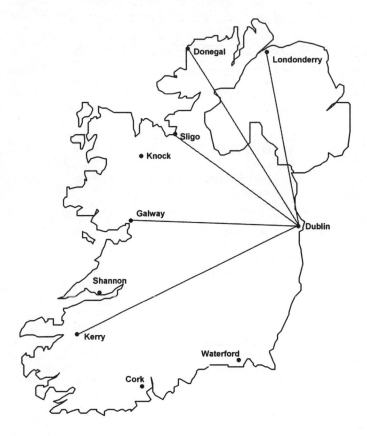

Figure 6.2   Map of Scottish PSO routes

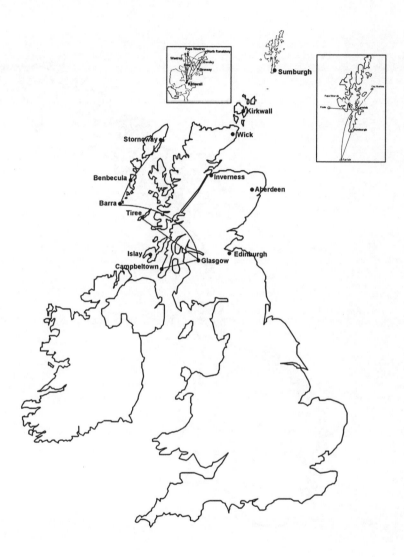

Figure 6.3   Map of Norwegian PSO routes

Figure 6.4   Map of German PSO routes

6.2 Deciding an appropriate dividing line for subvention

A number of factors influence the amount of subvention that will be required to operate a given PSO service. The costs of operating a route will be strongly affected by the size and type of aircraft to be used. An older, unpressurised machine, such as a Shorts 360, will invariably be less expensive to run than a regional jet, for example. The route length, available airport infrastructure, the volume and seasonal nature of the traffic, and the type of route will determine the choice of aircraft to be employed. Operations to small islands such as those in the west of Ireland are really only feasible with small aircraft seating fewer than ten passengers. In other circumstances, a trade off will exist between service frequency and aircraft size. On a given route, for example, using a 19 seat aircraft it may be possible to offer three flights per day, whereas use of a more sophisticated 50 seater may restrict operations to once daily. The nature of the route will also affect the schedule to be provided. It may be that the service links an outlying island with a regional centre, in which case the traffic will be mostly point-to-point. In other instances, the service will be providing feeder traffic to connect with other regional operations.

To demonstrate the strange mix that is apparent between EU countries two routes are contrasted below. Information about the two operations is contained in Table 6.5. It is interesting to note that it is the more heavily trafficked route between Dublin and Donegal (Carrickfinn) that has the higher subsidy. The Scottish route from Glasgow to the Hebridean island of Tiree with around half the traffic of the Irish example requires 45% less subvention. Both routes have a service once a day during the week, with load factors in the low 40s. The Donegal service was operated by Aer Arann until recently with a Shorts 360 aircraft, equipped with 36 seats. This has subsequently been upgraded to a 50 seat ATR 42 machine, providing a more comfortable journey for passengers. A much smaller and less sophisticated aircraft, the unpressurised De Havilland Twin Otter, equipped with 19 seats, provides the service to Tiree. The use of this aircraft by operators Loganair is to a large extent influenced by their PSO operation to the island of Barra. The airstrip at Barra is the cockleshell beach at Castlebay, to which the Twin Otter is ideally suited. Attempts to use a larger, heavier aircraft on this service have not proved successful. Hence, the Tiree operation remains in the hands of the Twin Otter.

Table 6.6   Contrasting routes: PSO versus non-PSO

	Dublin - Donegal	Glasgow - Tiree
Sector length (kms)	222	174
Service frequency	Daily	Daily except Sunday
Pax traffic in 1999	10753	5030
Daily capacity	36 seats	19 seats
Load factor in 1999	42%	43%
Return fares	£65 - £74	£96 - £144
Route subsidy	£450,000	£250,000
Subsidy per single trip	£43	£50
% of costs subsidised	38%	31%
Break even load factor	90%	70%

Source: Williams, 2001.

Fare levels are also of key significance in explaining the differing levels of subvention. On the Dublin-Donegal route, the maximum return fare was set at £74, whilst the equivalent price for the Glasgow-Tiree service was close to double this level at £144. In terms of subsidy per single passenger journey, the Tiree operation was a little more expensive. Without the higher fares however, the level of subvention would have been much higher. Overall though, it is clear that the Irish Government is more generous in providing subsidies for essential air services than is the UK Government.

Subsidy may not always be required to maintain an air service however, even when traffic volumes are low. For example, the route between Inverness and Kirkwall (Orkney islands) is not subsidised despite the fact that traffic volumes were only 7,900 in 1999. The service, with a sector length of 168 kms, is operated on a twice-daily basis by Loganair using Saab 340 aircraft. With the low passenger demand if all this capacity were devoted solely to the sector, load factor would be of the order of 20%. The aircraft however, are operating multi-sectors, one routing being Glasgow-Inverness-Kirkwall-Shetland and the other Edinburgh-Inverness-Kirkwall. As a result, the actual average load factor achieved between Inverness and Kirkwall was around 50% in 1999.

6.3   Access to slots at congested airports

At Europe's busiest airports, as a result of "grandfather rights", it is airlines that allocate takeoff and landing slots. For example, at Heathrow virtually all of the slots are "grandfathered". Subject to the availability of appropriate terminal facilities, an airline can choose which destinations it wishes to serve with its slots. For example, if airline X has had a 10.15 departure slot at Heathrow for a number of years and been using it for a service to Jersey, it is a commercial decision for the carrier alone whether it continues to use the slot for this purpose. If the airline in question has gained additional route rights for a service to Johannesburg, for example, transferring the slot to the long haul operation would without doubt improve the company's profitability. It is therefore not in the least surprising that the number of domestic destinations served from Heathrow has fallen considerably over the last fifteen years.

For many of the towns and cities in the UK that have lost their links with Heathrow, travel by surface mode is not too unreasonable an alternative. The same however, cannot be said for Inverness. By rail the journey takes eight hours. Whereas, many of the destinations no longer served from Heathrow have direct connections with at least one major hub airport, thereby providing access to a wide range of medium and long haul destinations, the capital of the Highlands has for the most part not been so provided.

Although many UK towns and cities continue to have air connections with London, several of the operations were transferred from Heathrow to Gatwick. Heathrow's position as the world's busiest international airport provided those travelling to and from the regional airports with an enormous choice of long, medium and short haul destinations. Although the number of points served by scheduled services from Gatwick is now greater than is the case at Heathrow, the main long haul business destinations are served best from the latter. While it is true that it is possible to fly from Gatwick to New York, the choice currently is restricted to four flights per day whereas at Heathrow there are 25 daily services on offer.

To help overcome this problem, several countries have reserved slots at their major airports for their PSO routes. Around 30% of the available slots at Paris Orly, for example, are ring fenced for domestic operations involving both PSO and non-PSO routes. The German, Italian, Norwegian and Swedish authorities either already have a similar attitude to the safeguarding of slots for these essential services, or have it mind for the future. At present, it is up to the discretion of individual Member States as to whether or not to ring fence slots for essential services. For the purposes of achieving a common policy with respect to the wellbeing of remote regions, it would not seem unreasonable to argue that all such essential air services should have their slots at congested airports reserved as a matter of EC wide policy.

References

Subsidisation Policies in the Provision of Air services to small Communities: European and US Approaches, Reynolds-Feighan, A., First Forum on Air Transport in Europe's Remote Regions, Nairn, June 1999.

Deciding an Appropriate Dividing Line between Subsidised and Non-subsidised Air Services, Williams, G., Second Forum on Air Transport in Europe's Remote Regions, Jersey, April 2001.

7 Competition on the North Atlantic

Despite the greater opportunities afforded to carriers based in countries that have established "Open Skies" deals with the US, the UK continues to account for around 40% of the passenger traffic between the two continents. While overall traffic has grown by 60% between the US and European countries during the 1990s, certain states have experienced a decline. Table 7.1 shows the percentage change in the numbers of passengers travelling between the US and individual EU countries in 1990, 1994 and 1998. While most have experienced some growth in traffic, Denmark and Sweden have experienced a fall in the number of passengers travelling direct. The largest percentage growth in direct traffic has occurred between the US and the Netherlands.

Table 7.1 Passenger traffic between the US and EU countries

	1990	1994		1998	
	Passengers	Passengers	% change	Passengers	% change
Austria	128,128	147,446	15	329,727	136
Belgium	807,947	707,614	-12	1,171,105	66
Denmark	613,532	512,007	-17	504,842	-1
Finland	235,105	278,523	19	235,129	-16
France	3,381,689	3,884,908	15	4,661,776	20
Germany	4,847,279	5,630,824	16	6,631,475	18
Greece	259,553	384,060	48	376,660	-2
Ireland	729,565	1,008,278	38	1,152,884	14
Italy	1,514,267	1,858,373	23	2,167,848	17
Luxembourg	16,088	6,485	-60	34,258	428
Netherlands	1,605,547	2,720,928	70	4,095,052	51
Portugal	308,165	319,123	4	359,463	13
Spain	1,084,096	1,126,599	4	1,346,003	19
Sweden	428,039	278,114	-35	303,281	9
UK	9,997,883	11,923,421	19	15,915,774	33
Total	25,956,883	30,786,703	19	39,285,277	28

Source: Air Services Agreements Between the United Kingdom and the United States, 18th Report of the House of Commons Environment, Transport and Regional Affairs Committee, July 2000.

Air services between the UK and US remain subject to the terms agreed in the 1977 Bermuda II bilateral. While this agreement was less liberal than its 1946 predecessor, a number of subsequent amendments have enabled new routes and extra frequencies to be added over time. A major bone of contention however, has been that only two carriers from each country are allowed to operate services from Heathrow. The advantages of Heathrow over Gatwick are apparent from the scramble by airlines to switch services between the two whenever the opportunity arises. The considerably larger volumes of business traffic at Heathrow compared to those at Gatwick are reflected in the substantially higher yields that carriers obtain on routes from the bigger airport. The limiting of airlines designated to operate services to the US from Heathrow has proved most beneficial to the two UK nominated carriers, British Airways (BA) and Virgin Atlantic (Virgin). A key aim of the US Administration has been therefore to prise open Heathrow.

7.1 Impact of "Open Skies"

A significant difference can be observed between the way routes and traffic develops with and without an "Open Skies" agreement. "Open Skies" removed restrictions on capacity, fares, routings and the number of airlines each country could designate. It also provided access to all points in each country and unconstrained code-sharing. The Netherlands was the first country in the world to sign such a bilateral with the US. Of key concern to KLM was to have the ability to collude with its partner Northwest. For this to be possible however, the two carriers had to be granted anti-trust immunity by the US Department of Transportation. The US Government was willing to agree to this in exchange for the signing of an "Open Skies" agreement. From 1992 it became possible for the two airlines to make joint decisions on capacity, scheduling and pricing. The agreement marked the start of the formation of global alliances.

The KLM-Northwest alliance has had a major impact on the numbers of passengers travelling between Amsterdam and US cities. As is shown in Table 7.2, 41 out the 64 weekly flights in 1988 were operated to Chicago, New York and Los Angeles, whilst by 1998 of the 107 weekly services 49 were to Atlanta, Detroit and Minneapolis. Prior to the "Open Skies" agreement, there were no direct flights from Amsterdam to either Detroit or Minneapolis. Aside from the doubling of frequency between 1988 and

2001, a considerable rerouting of traffic via the hubs of Northwest and Delta has occurred. The impact of the KLM-Northwest alliance in particular has been profound. The routing of substantial amounts of traffic through Northwest's hub at Detroit is clearly apparent from the five daily services operated to there from Amsterdam in summer 2001. Point to point traffic between the two cities would probably only be sufficient for one flight per week.

Table 7.2   Weekly service frequencies to the US from Amsterdam

	1988	1992	1996	2001
Atlanta	5	13	11	14
Baltimore	0	4	0	0
Boston	4	7	7	7
Chicago	10	8	11	16
Denver	0	0	1	0
Detroit	0	7	14	35
Houston	7	7	7	7
Los Angeles	8	7	10	11
Memphis	0	0	6	7
Miami	0	0	4	12
Minneapolis	0	3	14	14
New York	30	36	34	39
Oakland	0	0	2	0
Orlando	0	3	4	3
Philadelphia	0	0	0	7
San Francisco	0	0	3	7
Seattle	0	0	2	7
Tampa	0	0	1	0
Washington	0	0	14	14
Destinations	6	10	17	15
Frequencies	64	95	145	200

Source: OAG.

The contrast with route and traffic developments in the UK - US market could not be greater. In the absence of an immunised alliance between British Airways and a major US carrier, traffic continues to be concentrated on routes to the major centres of population rather than to the major hubs of airlines as Table 7.3 reveals. Of the 759 weekly frequencies between the UK and US operated in summer 2001, 440 were to the cities of Boston, Chicago, Los Angeles, New York and San Francisco.

Table 7.3 Weekly service frequencies to the US from London

	1992	1996	1998	2001
Anchorage	2	0	0	0
Atlanta	21	21	21	28
Baltimore	7	7	7	7
Boston	35	35	42	56
Charlotte	7	7	14	14
Chicago	34	49	56	80
Cincinnati	7	7	7	7
Cleveland	0	0	0	7
Dallas	21	21	21	21
Denver	4	0	7	7
Detroit	7	14	21	21
Houston	14	17	21	24
Las Vegas	0	0	0	3
Los Angeles	45	40	55	56
Miami	33	26	35	28
Minneapolis	7	7	7	7
New York	143	166	200	206
Orlando	10	11	13	21
Philadelphia	14	14	21	28
Phoenix	0	0	7	7
Pittsburgh	0	7	7	7
Raleigh - Durham	0	7	7	7
St Louis	7	7	7	7
San Diego		7	7	7
San Francisco	15	34	35	46
Seattle	11	7	10	7
Tampa	0	2	5	3
Washington	35	35	42	47
Destinations	21	23	25	27
Frequencies	479	548	675	759

Source: Air Services Agreements Between the United Kingdom and the United States, 18th Report of the House of Commons Environment, Transport and Regional Affairs Committee, July 2000.

The proportion of UK-US passenger traffic accounted for by British Airways (BA) and Virgin Atlantic (Virgin) is significantly higher than that of the six US carriers providing transatlantic services. Table 7.4 shows the numbers of passengers carried by each of the operating carriers in 1999. While BA and Virgin carried 57.7% of the overall number of passengers travelling between the two countries, on scheduled routes from Heathrow to the US their share was 64%. At Gatwick the passenger traffic was much more evenly distributed, with US airlines accounting for 44% of the scheduled passenger traffic. Interestingly, it is the US carriers that account for the lion's share of passengers travelling direct to the US from UK regional airports.

Table 7.4 UK - US scheduled passenger traffic by carrier in 1999

Airline	Passengers (000s)	% share
British Airways	6,886	40.7
Virgin Atlantic	2,996	17.7
UK carriers Total	*9,882*	*58.4*
American	2,380	14.1
United	2,070	12.2
Continental	1,023	6.1
Delta	741	4.4
Northwest	378	2.2
US Airways	286	1.7
TWA	146	0.9
US carriers Total	*7,024*	*41.6*
Grand Total	16,906	

Source: Air Services Agreements Between the United Kingdom and the United States, 18th Report of the House of Commons Environment, Transport and Regional Affairs Committee, July 2000.

The contrast between the proportions of traffic carried by UK carriers and by US airlines between the UK and US that is point-to-point is of particular interest. In 1998, 90% of the 6½ million passengers carried by British Airways from the UK to the US did not interline. In the opposite direction the equivalent figure was 51%. The respective figures for the other UK carrier operating scheduled services between the two countries, Virgin Atlantic, were 91% and 86%. The corresponding statistics for individual US carriers are shown in Table 7.5, but the overall equivalent figures were respectively 53% and 75%. The US carriers' ability to provide online domestic connections in the US but not in Europe is clearly shown, whilst the opposite is evident for the British carriers. The main reason why British Airways wishes to gain regulatory approval for a full alliance with American Airlines are apparent from these figures.

Table 7.5 Shares of connecting and terminating traffic by carrier

	Passengers	% terminating in UK	% terminating in US	% connecting in UK	% connecting in US
British Airways	6,499,887	51	90	49	10
Virgin Atlantic	2,557,472	86	91	14	9
UK carriers	9,057,360	61	90	39	10
American	2,018,446	69	61	31	39
Continental	557,820	78	45	22	55
Delta	454,421	91	29	9	71
Northwest	338,502	86	45	14	55
TWA	159,169	89	39	11	61
United	1,741,696	74	58	26	42
US Airways	101,324	88	26	12	74
US carriers	5,371,377	75	53	25	47

Source: Air Services Agreements Between the United Kingdom and the United States, 18th Report of the House of Commons Environment, Transport and Regional Affairs Committee, July 2000.

The disadvantage of this arrangement for airlines is clearly apparent in terms of their inability to provide online connections at destination gateways. For example, while the vast majority of KLM's passengers on their five daily flights from Amsterdam to Detroit would be travelling on to other domestic points using alliance partner Northwest's services, 90% of BA's passengers to the US in 1998 terminated their air travel at gateway airports. In the opposite direction, 75% of passengers travelling with US airlines terminated their travel at UK gateways. The only means currently available by which a non-US airline can provide online connections within the US is by establishing an alliance with a locally based carrier. Without immunity from anti-trust legislation in the US however, the alliance partners would not be able to engage in any form of collusive activity. The benefits of being able to provide joint services, agree common pricing strategies and give passengers seamless service over a considerably larger route network than would otherwise be possible, have been apparent in the additional traffic that immunised alliances have been able to attract.

With UK airlines accounting for nearly 60% of the scheduled passenger traffic between the two countries, the incentive to radically alter the terms of the bilateral from the British perspective has not been overwhelming. While most US carriers have much to gain from a more liberal agreement, particularly in respect of access to Heathrow, without the ability to operate in the US domestic market the same cannot be said of British Airways and Virgin Atlantic. The views of bmi (formerly known as British Midland) however, which is keen to establish transatlantic services from Heathrow, are more akin to those of the aspiring US carriers, such as Continental and Delta.

Even with an "Open Skies" agreement though, UK airlines would not have cabotage rights in the US. An immunised alliance with American Airlines (AA) would allow British Airways (BA) to circumvent this restriction. The UK flag carrier would be able to apply its flight code to AA domestic flights and so provide online connections to a much larger number of destinations in the US than it is currently able to serve. The immunity from antitrust legislation would enable it to fully coordinate its services with those of American, in effect providing jointly priced and operated services. Regulators are likely however, to preclude fare collusion on routes on which the two carriers were heavily dominant.

7.2   Transatlantic air fares

In US Department of Transportation (DoT) report published in October 2000 transatlantic airfares were shown to have fallen considerably as a result of "Open Skies". A number of different types of market were considered, including: behind gateway to beyond gateway (BB), behind gateway to gateway (BG), gateway to beyond gateway (GB) and gateway to gateway (GG), where a gateway is defined as a major hub airport in the respective country. It is clear from Table 7.6, which provides a summary of the DoT findings, that "Open Skies" agreements have proved beneficial to all travellers. Those gaining the most in terms of lower fares have been passengers travelling from a US gateway city to beyond a European gateway city, such as those flying with KLM/Northwest from Detroit to Vienna via Amsterdam.

Table 7.6   Changes in average airfares (%) between 1996 and 1999

	BB	BG	GB	GG	All
"Open Skies"	-23.9	-19.9	-24.8	-17.0	-20.1
Non "Open Skies"	-13.2	-14.6	-15.8	-5.1	-10.3

Source: US Department of Transport, October 2000.

Even without "Open Skies", traffic between the UK and US has grown strongly in recent years. Despite the large increases in capacity offered between the two countries however, business class airfares are significantly higher when compared to those offered for journeys to the US from other European hub airports. To illustrate this point, some evidence prepared for the House of Commons (House of Commons Environment, Transport and Regional Affairs Committee, 2000) is shown in Table 7.7. As may be seen, business class return fares are shown for flights to New York from four European hub airports. Comparisons are given in both UK pounds and US dollars, the latter calculated by converting the fares in local currencies using Purchasing Power Parity (PPP) exchange rates, in order to alleviate differences in price levels between the various countries.

Table 7.7 Lowest business class return fares to New York - June 2000

From	UK£	US$
London	3,394	5,111
Amsterdam	1,785	3,184
Frankfurt	1,779	2,900
Paris	2,382	3,916

Sources: Travelocity.co.uk and OECD.

The fare from London to New York in UK pounds is shown to be 42.5% more than an equivalent journey from Paris. In terms of US dollars (using PPPs) while the difference is reduced it is still 30.5% higher. In response to this evidence, Virgin Atlantic claimed that... "published business class fares may appear relatively high, but very few passengers actually pay them. Discounting is particularly prevalent in the UK market, almost certainly more so than in most other European countries".[1] Unfortunately, data is not readily available in the UK and EU to discover how much passengers actually pay for their tickets on such routes.

Note

1. Evidence provided by Virgin Atlantic Airways in "Air Service Agreements Between the United Kingdom and the United States", 18th Report of the House of Commons Environment, Transport and Regional Affairs Committee, 26 July 2000 p.151.

References

International Aviation Developments Second Report, Transatlantic Deregulation – The Alliance Network Effect, U.S. Department of Transport, Office of Secretary, October 2000.

Air Service Agreements Between the United Kingdom and the United States, 18th Report of the House of Commons Environment, Transport and Regional Affairs Committee, 26 July 2000.

8 Prospects for global deregulation

Most international air transport services continue to be subject to the terms of bilateral air services agreements between countries. Only in relatively few areas of the world have these individual arrangements between pairs of states been superseded by multilateral regimes. In Europe, the driving force behind this radical transformation was the desire to establish a common market in which goods and services could be freely traded between and within the member countries. Without this fundamental objective it is extremely unlikely that the ability to exercise all eight freedoms of the air could ever have been realised. Elsewhere, this common trading objective with the important legally binding set of rules underpinning it does not exist. As a result, bilateralism remains the way by which most countries trade their air services. Easing the restrictions contained in the myriad of such agreements has been the way in which air transport liberalisation has been realised. Widely differing attitudes have been apparent though between countries in terms of how far each has been prepared to go in liberalising their international air transport services.

The US has been at the forefront of this drive to liberalise. After being the first country to deregulate its domestic market, it has persuaded more than 50 of its bilateral partners to date to agree "Open Skies" deals. (Table 8.1 lists the countries that have signed "Open Skies" agreements with the US.) This description of these new bilateral arrangements however, is misleading. The words convey the impression that a free market in air transport services now exists. Though more liberal than earlier air services agreements, these "Open Skies" deals contain significant restrictions. While all eight freedoms of the air can be exercised by EU registered carriers within the Community, seventh and eighth freedoms are excluded in "Open Skies" agreements. Designated airlines must also be substantially owned and managed by nationals of the two respective countries. So while Lufthansa can exercise seventh and eighth freedom rights within the EU, for example by flying if it wished between Amsterdam and Madrid, and between Milan and Rome, even with an "Open Skies" agreement it cannot

159

carry traffic within the US or between the US and other countries, including those in the EU.

Table 8.1 Countries with US "Open Skies" bilateral agreements

Europe		Africa		Latin America	
Country	Date	Country	Date	Country	Date
Netherlands	1992	Ghana	2000	Panama	1997
Luxembourg	1995	Namibia	2000	Costa Rica	1997
Finland	1995	Gambia	2000	El Salvador	1997
Austria	1995	Burkina Faso	2000	Guatemala	1997
Iceland	1995	Tanzania	2000	Honduras	1997
Switzerland	1995	Nigeria	2000	Nicaragua	1997
Denmark	1995	Morocco	2000	Aruba	1997
Norway	1995	Rwanda	2000	N. Antilles	1998
Sweden	1995	Benin	2000	Peru	1998
Belgium	1995	Senegal	2000	Chile	1999
Germany	1996			Argentina	1999
Czech Rep.	1996	**Asia-Pacific**		Dominican Rep.	1999
Romania	1998	Singapore	1997		
Italy	1999	New Zealand	1997	**Middle East**	
Slovakia	2000	Brunei	1997	Jordan	1996
Turkey	2000	Malaysia	1997	UAE	1999
Portugal	2000	Taiwan	1998	Bahrain	1999
Malta	2000	South Korea	1998	Qatar	1999
France	2001				
Other regions					
Uzbekistan	1996	Pakistan	1999		

Source: Chang and Williams, 2001.

Eleven EU states have so far signed "Open Skies" bilateral agreements with the US. Each of these agreements contains a requirement that the carriers designated by the two countries be substantially owned and operated by nationals of the respective state. (While there are exceptions to this restriction, the restriction applies in the vast majority of bilateral air services agreements.) The discrimination against *foreign* airlines from other EU countries lies at the heart of the European Commission's aim that future bilateral negotiations with third countries should be undertaken at Community level and not by individual EU states. To this end in 1995 it sought to obtain a mandate from the European Council of Ministers to undertake negotiations with the US Administration with regards to establishing an EU - US bilateral agreement.

As the Council were only prepared to grant the Commission a mandate to negotiate *soft* rights, in 1998 the Commission referred nine EU states (Austria, Belgium, Denmark, Finland, Germany, Luxembourg, Netherlands, Sweden and the UK) to the European Court of Justice. At the heart of the matter is the question of Community competence. In the Commission's view the achievement of the single aviation market gives the Community exclusive competence to negotiate *hard* traffic rights with third countries. All but one of the cases involve "Open Skies" agreements, which permit US carriers to exercise fifth freedom rights within Europe, but preclude eighth freedom rights for EU airlines in the US. The UK with its more restrictive bilateral was also the subject of legal referral. It is widely anticipated that the Court, which is expected to reach a decision by the end of February 2002, will find in favour of the Commission.

8.1 The experience with partial ownership of foreign airlines

One of the most obvious ways for an airline to overcome the limitations of the bilateral system would be to acquire full control of carriers in other countries. This option however, is only a possibility in a very few areas of the world. Within the EU, Community based carriers are able to acquire full ownership of airlines based in other EU states. Elsewhere, in nearly all instances majority ownership is not permitted. Table 8.2 shows the current state of play with regards to the restrictions placed on airline ownership in a selection of countries. Interestingly, Australia and New Zealand allow airlines operating domestic services to be fully owned by foreigners. New Zealand adopted this policy in 1988, but Australia only amended its laws in 1999. The attempts to get a locally owned third domestic operator established in Australia following deregulation had proved fruitless, hence the change. Removal of the ownership limit on domestic airlines allowed Air New Zealand to take full control of Ansett Australia and permitted Richard Branson to set up low cost, no-frills carrier, Virgin Blue. New Zealand's earlier change in its airline ownership rules had allowed Ansett to establish a domestic carrier (Ansett Australia) in the country.

Recent developments in the region have been particularly dramatic, with Ansett Australia closing down due to financial difficulties in September 2001. Earlier in the year, Qantas New Zealand, which operated under a franchise agreement with the Australian flag carrier, went into receivership. Qantas New Zealand was a rebranded Ansett New Zealand, following its acquisition by New Zealand-based Tasman Pacific Airways. Following the collapse of Ansett Australia, Singapore Airlines has increased its shareholding in Air New Zealand from 25% to 34%.

Table 8.2 Airline foreign ownership restrictions

Country	Foreign ownership restrictions
Australia	49% for international airlines 100% for domestic airlines
Canada	25% of voting equity
China	35%
Chile	No limit. Designation as a Chilean carrier (domestic or international) requires only that the company's principal place of business be in Chile
Indonesia	Requires airlines designated under bilateral agreements to be substantially owned and effectively controlled by the other Party
Japan	33.3%
Korea	50%
Malaysia	45%
New Zealand	49% for international airlines 100% for domestic airlines
Philippines	Requires substantial ownership and effective control
Singapore	27.51%
Taiwan	33.3%
Thailand	30%
United States	25% of voting equity

Source: Changing the rules – amending the nationality clauses in air services agreements, Yu-Chun Chang & George Williams, Journal of Air Transport Management, Vol.7, July 2001, pp. 207-216.

Many other examples exist of airlines that have acquired shareholdings in carriers based in other countries, but very few have proved to be worthwhile investments. Even under the multilateral regime of the EU, the experience has been poor. Table 8.3 provides details of these transactions. Two carriers in particular, have been keen to acquire subsidiaries in the EU. The large French and German domestic markets were the focus of British Airways' attentions, while the Swiss flag carrier being located outside the Community set its sights on acquiring interests in a mix of EU airlines, beginning with the troubled Belgian carrier, Sabena.

British Airways (BA), one of only three airlines allowed to operate services to Berlin until the late 1980s, purchased a 49% shareholding in Delta Air, a German regional carrier, in 1992. The company was renamed Deutsche BA and competed mainly in the German domestic market. BA acquired full ownership of the airline in 1997. The same year it purchased its German subsidiary, BA bought a 49.9% shareholding in TAT, a French regional operator. As with Deutsche BA, the UK flag carrier acquired full control of TAT in 1996. During the same year it purchased the bankrupt Air Liberté. It absorbed TAT into Air Liberté in 1998. Faced with aggressive competition from Air France and Lufthansa in their respective markets, BA's subsidiaries were mostly loss making. In 2000, BA decided to abandon the French domestic market and sold Air Liberté to AOM, an airline owned by the Swissair Group. After breaking even for the first time in 1999, Deutsche BA contributed 3 million DM to BA's half-year results in 2000. The company however, is once again unprofitable and its future as a BA subsidiary is currently under review.

Table 8.3   EU airlines cross-border equity stakes

Airline stakeholder	Subsidiary	1985	1990	1995	2000
Aer Lingus	Futura (Spain)	0.0	25.0	85.0	85.0
Air France	Austrian	0.0	1.5	1.5	1.5
	Sabena	0.0	0.0	37.5	0.0
Alitalia	Air Europe (Italy)	0.0	0.0	27.5	0.0
British Airways	Deutsche BA	0.0	0.0	49.0	100.0
	GB Airways	49.0	49.0	49.0	0.0
	Air Liberté (TAT)	0.0	0.0	49.0	0.0
KLM	KLM uk (Air UK)	15.0	14.9	45.0	100.0
Lauda Air	Lauda Air SpA (Italy)	0.0	0.0	33.0	33.0
LTU	LTE (Spain)	0.0	25.0	100.0	100.0
Lufthansa	Business Air	0.0	0.0	38.0	0.0
	Cargolux	24.5	24.5	24.5	0.0
	Lauda Air	0.0	0.0	39.7	20.0
	Luxair	0.0	0.0	13.0	13.0
	British Midland	0.0	0.0	0.0	20.0
Luxair	Cargolux	24.5	24.5	24.5	34.9
Maersk Air	Maersk Air (UK)/BEA	40.0	40.0	100.0	100.0
SAS	British Midland	0.0	24.9	40.0	20.0
	Spanair	49.0	49.0	49.0	49.0

Source: Chang and Williams, 2000.

In 1995, Swissair concluded an agreement with the Belgian Government to acquire 49.5% of Sabena's share capital. A further agreement reached between the two parties in 2000 anticipated Swissair's shareholding in Sabena increasing to 85%, subject to the successful completion of the Swiss–EU bilateral treaty. Being outside of the EU, it had not been surprising that Swissair would wish to have a presence within the Community. This strategy however, was pursued with increased vigour after 1997, with the company acquiring substantial shareholdings in a further six EU passenger carriers. In 1998, Swissair purchased 49.9% of Air Europe (an Italian long-haul charter carrier), 44% of Air Littoral (a French regional airline), 49.9% of LTU (a large German charter company), and 34% of Volare (a recently established Italian regional operator). The following year the airline acquired 49% of the share capital of AOM and had intended to purchase 34% of TAP, the Portuguese flag carrier.

The strategy of acquiring carriers based in the EU has not proved to be a success for the Swissair Group, however. In July 2001, faced with mounting losses at Sabena, Swissair reached an agreement with the Belgian Government to end its commitment to increase its shareholding in the ailing carrier to 85%. In return for this agreement, Swissair agreed to inject 260 million euros into Sabena. Earlier in the year, the company also undertook to provide financial support to its two French subsidiaries, AOM-Air Liberté and Air Littoral, during the course of its sale of both airlines to local interests. Since then however, Swissair itself has faced overwhelming financial difficulties, which caused it to cease trading in October 2001. In Europe, it would appear that very few airlines have been able to successfully establish operations away from their countries of origin.

8.2 Circumventing the airline ownership rules

The main means by which airlines have sought to overcome the ownership restrictions contained in nearly all bilateral air services agreements is through the formation of strategic alliances with other carriers based in other countries. The process had its origins in 1989 when KLM acquired a minority shareholding in Northwest Airlines. Crucial to the development of the alliance however was the signing of the "Open Skies" deal between the Netherlands and US Governments in 1992. In return for agreeing to liberalise its air services in this way, the Dutch flag carrier was granted anti-trust immunity by the US Department of Transportation for its proposed alliance with Northwest Airlines. It now became possible for the two carriers not only to operate joint services between their two countries, but also to extend *their* individual route networks to destinations that had previously been denied them. The arrangement between the two carriers, often unofficially referred to as the Wings Alliance, was expanded in July 2001 to include Malaysian Airlines. As yet however, and despite being the first strategic partnership to be established, the alliance has not developed much beyond the link up between KLM and Northwest.

In all there are five alliance groupings in existence, including KLM-Northwest. The most developed of these groupings is the Star Alliance, which was established in 1997 by Lufthansa, United, Air Canada, SAS and Thai Airways. Since then Star has expanded to include twelve member airlines. The membership of each of the five alliance groupings is shown in Table 8.4. As may be seen, not all can be regarded as global alliances. Even though some of its members have sizeable international route networks, Qualiflyer is really only a regional alliance as all of its members are based in Europe. In addition, SkyTeam and *Wings* do not yet have members from each region of the world. Only Star and oneworld therefore can be regarded as truly global strategic alliances. The prospect of further consolidation of the various airline groupings would seem very likely, particularly in the

Table 8.4 Membership of alliance groupings

Star Airline	Date	oneworld Airline	Date	Qualiflyer Airline	Date
United	1997	American	1998	Swissair	1998
Lufthansa	1997	British Airways	1998	Sabena	1998
Air Canada	1997	Cathay Pacific	1998	Crossair	1998
SAS	1997	Qantas	1998	Turkish	1998
Thai	1997	Iberia	1999	AOM-Air Liberté	1998
Varig	1997	Finnair	1999	TAP	1998
Air New Zealand	1999	Lan Chile	2000	Volare	1999
Mexicana	1999	Aer Lingus	2000	LOT	2000
All Nippon	1999			Air Littoral	2000
Austrian	2000	**SkyTeam**		Portugalia	2000
Singapore	2000	Delta	1999		
bmi	2000	Air France	1999	**Wings**	
		AeroMexico	1999	KLM	1989
		Korean	2000	Northwest	1989
		CSA	2001	Malaysia	2001

Source: Airline Business, July 2001.

light of the demise of Swissair and the possibility of British Airways acquiring a shareholding in KLM. In the medium term it is probable that only three globally aligned airline groupings will remain.

8.3 Concluding comments

As the air transport sector becomes increasingly a global industry, further consolidation of airlines is inevitable. Changes in the way international air transport is regulated will eventually permit the industry to merge and consolidate as other sectors have done. This is not to say that the process will be speedy; national interests will continue to take precedence over other concerns as has been recently evident in Canada. The tortuous route through alliance formation by which carriers have sought to circumvent the current regulatory constraints will be superseded by more normal market behaviour. This will in certain regards make the task of the regulator easier to accomplish, but not entirely. It will depend to a large extent on a common set of rules that determine what is acceptable competitive behaviour being adopted and implemented by governments across the world.

References

'Strategies for Airlines in the Asia-Pacific Region', European Transport Conference, Yu-Chun Chang and George Williams, Homerton College Cambridge, September 2001.

'Prospects for Change in Europe's and the United States' Airline Ownership Rules', Yu-Chun Chang and George Williams, 42nd Transportation Research Forum, Annapolis, November 2000.

9 A new role for regulators

Use of the word deregulation has been misleading; liberalisation better describes the process that has actually taken place in the airline industry. The sector will continue to remain highly regulated in all manner of ways; it would be naïve to expect anything different given safe travel is the desired outcome. The notion that sustainable, strongly competitive markets can be achieved universally without any form of economic regulatory control is utopian and in the light of experience unrealistic. Undoubtedly, there are numerous examples of city-pairs across the world on which market forces have produced a level of competition that has benefited consumers over the longer term, both in terms of fare levels and product choice. Others exist however, where competition has been very short-lived and clearly unsustainable.

It can hardly have come as a surprise that incumbent carriers would do all in their powers to defend their markets from interlopers. Sometimes though, the new entrants themselves have done all in their powers to ensure that their existence has been little more than fleeting through poor judgement. There are many examples however, where flag carriers have used all their might to stymie the efforts of those seeking to establish themselves in previously monopolistic (or near monopolistic) markets. Where the result is in effect a return to what existed before but without the limits on fares that regulators could previously impose, a choice exists as to whether a government accepts this as an inevitable outcome of the *free* market or decides to intervene in order to redress the problem.

To rely entirely on market forces without having recourse to direct intervention when situations arise which clearly are not in the interest of consumers seems curious. The prospects for sustainable competition in the domestic air transport markets of France, Germany and Norway would not appear to be too high. In Norway, the coexistence of Braathens and SAS was ensured for over three decades by regulators limiting the routes each could serve and dictating how much capacity each could provide. With all economic controls removed, the more powerful carrier, SAS, has been able to attract more and more of the higher yielding traffic. Color Air's short existence exacerbated an already over supplied market, making Braathen's plight even more precarious. The latter's attempts to become a supplier of

167

air services to Scandinavia also failed in part because of the flag carrier's highly effective frequent flier program. In summer 2001, Braathens threw in the towel and agreed a deal with SAS for it to be taken over. The argument that Braathens' financial situation was so dire that there was little other option was not initially accepted by Norway's competition authority. The prospect of SAS being the sole supplier of nearly all of Scandinavia's internal air transport is not one that is proving attractive to the governments of Norway and Sweden.

The very use of the word intervention may be a problem. It is an emotive term, for it carries with it the connotation of action being undertaken that is uncalled for. One is in effect interfering with a process that is believed to operate much more effectively and efficiently if left to its own devices. What if this belief is correct though and unbridled market forces because of the particular economic characteristics of airlines lead to a situation of monopoly supply in certain instances, such as in Norway's domestic market. Would intervention in these circumstances be a reasonable response, given the outcome is neither that which was anticipated nor desired? If the Norwegian Government were to impose measures on SAS designed to ensure the wellbeing of a second carrier, its intervention would be to counter an outcome that was not in the best interests of Norwegian consumers. In these circumstances, it would perhaps be better to regard this intrusion in the more benign manner in which other regulations pertaining to the sector are viewed. For example, airline pilots are strictly limited in terms of the number of hours that they are permitted to fly. This clearly is an intervention, but few would regard it as unwarranted for obvious reasons.

Where market forces have been shown to produce sustainable competitive conditions, regulatory intervention would be clearly counterproductive and as such should be rightly regarded as interference. When situations arise however, in which consumers are faced with high fares and little or no choice, then regulatory intervention should be viewed as being likely to be of benefit in much the same way as technical regulations and those governing the flying hours of flight crew are regarded. The precise form that such intervention would take would depend on the particular circumstances, but should be such as to minimise any possible knock on effects in other markets that are exhibiting strong and healthy competition. Prior to deregulation it was possible to believe that unconstrained market forces would produce the desired effects under nearly all circumstances. There is now a wealth of evidence available that clearly shows that this is not proving to be the case. Moving the regulatory pendulum back a little from its totally free market stop point would seem to be justified.

It is also apparent that there needs to be different layers of regulatory control. To be able to regulate the behaviour of global alliances, it would seem necessary to apply as consistent a set of rules as possible across as many countries of the world as can be persuaded. Individual countries or regions would continue to be able to intervene locally where and whenever circumstances dictated. The overriding aim should be to ensure that competition thrives and that innovation is not prevented. Intervention must be realistic though. Simply freeing up slots at congested airports for new entrants, as the European Commission did in the case of routes between Germany and Scandinavia following the alliance between Lufthansa and SAS, was not. In certain situations it would have been sufficient, but not in this case with two such dominant and aggressive carriers.

Concluding comments

Nearly a quarter of a century after the US Government deregulated its domestic air transport market, it seems at times bizarre that with all of the lessons this event produced the airline sector continues to be so volatile. Many would of course argue that this results from the lack of commercial freedom which airlines have in acquiring carriers based in other countries, that if permitted would allow the industry to consolidate globally. Even where such freedom exists however, the propensity for poor judgement has been high. The industry in its unconstrained natural state would appear to be forever hell bent on generating excess capacity. Unless the supply of seats on even the busiest routes is constrained however, the financial results are not surprisingly poor. Incumbent airlines constantly seek ways to control this tendency to over-supply, but few have been consistently successful in this regard. City pair markets on which the numbers of seats supplied have for long periods of time matched the level of demand at fare levels that generate comparable profits to those earned in other sectors, in fully deregulated markets are relatively few.

Low cost, no-frills airlines have revolutionised short haul air travel in the US and Europe. Such carriers now account for around 25% of demand in the world's largest air transport market. The spectacular growth and financial performance of Southwest has set an important standard for the rest of the industry. Its simple philosophy from which it has not faltered has been copied by other carriers in both the US and Europe. The traditional bearers of the low cost airline mantle in the latter have been the charter sector. Europe is unusual in that a sizeable proportion of passenger traffic is carried on charter flights. Carriers that are owned by vertically integrated tour operating companies perform the vast majority of these operations, which also incorporate travel agencies, hotels and ground transportation companies. Considerable consolidation of both a horizontal and vertical nature occurred in this sector during the 1990s, but it too has been feeling the effects of the new breed of low cost airlines.

While many of the tactics and strategies adopted by US carriers in the aftermath of deregulation have been emulated by European airlines, a full replication has not occurred. The continent-wide route networks built up by the larger US airlines as yet do not feature in Europe. Those carriers, such

171

as British Airways, that have tried to gain access to the local (domestic and regional) markets of other EU states have not met with great success. As a consequence, the networks of routes operated by Europe's major players have not altered in the same radical manner as those of their US counterparts. To extend their spheres of influence across Europe, many carriers have sought to have their flight codes added to services operated by other airlines. These moves have been designed both to keep at bay those seeking to gain access to "their" routes and to enhance hub feeder traffic.

The most dramatic changes experienced in the US are only now beginning to occur in Europe, the very recent failures of Swissair and Sabena being prime examples. National markets continue to be dominated by national carriers, recent events in France and Scandinavia appearing to reinforce this point. This is not to say that considerable upheaval has not taken place in several European countries. Liberalisation of the domestic markets of several Southern European states, for example, has transformed the range of services offered to consumers. The national carriers of these countries have experienced strong competition from more efficient new entrants, many of which were established charter operators. On intra-European routes however, the level of competition experienced by incumbents has been mild by comparison. Only in those city-pair markets that have witnessed the arrival of no-frills operators can competition be said to be strong.

Apart from within Europe, international air services remain subject to the terms of mostly restrictive bilateral agreements, which in nearly all cases require the designated carriers to be owned and managed by nationals of the designating state. The effect of this regulatory straightjacket has resulted in the industry being unable to reorganise its activities on a global scale. Attempts to overcome this limitation through the formation of alliances are often fraught with difficulties and produce only a small fraction of the efficiency gains that would result if global consolidation became possible.

The annual analysis produced by IATA of first, business and economy class travel has consistently revealed the business cabin to be the segment that is most profitable. It is unsurprising therefore airlines have been keen to maintain high business class fares. Competition between carriers for passengers using such services is high, with improvements and enhancements to the product both in-flight and on the ground evident. The recent introduction by British Airways of seats in business class, which convert into beds, is a good example of this type of rivalry.

In the US domestic market, on short haul routes (100 – 750 miles) the highest 5% of fare payers accounted for only 8% of airline revenues in 1992. In 1998 however, the equivalent figure for those paying the highest fares was 18% (Special Report 255: Entry and Competition in the US Airline Industry, TRB, 1999). At the other end of the price range, the 25% of travellers paying the lowest fares in 1998 provided only 10% of the industry's passenger revenues compared to 14% in 1992. Airlines have developed and honed their ability to manage yield. Business travellers on short haul routes, on which there is little competition, have experienced large increases in fares. This experience has been repeated in Europe where passengers travelling on business are usually unwilling to spend Saturday night away from their homes.

Future choice for consumers in short haul markets is likely to be between low cost, no-frills (but not necessarily low fares) airlines and full service providers. The choice though of a £650 economy class return fare with frills (quite why anybody regards reasonable leg room and a meal or refreshments as *frills* is perplexing) or £150 with no-frills may seem to many consumers as rather limiting. For longer journeys, a less direct routing will remain the primary trade off for a lower fare.

Nearly all of the above has been written before the tragic events of 11th September occurred. The resulting large downturn in demand coming on top of an economic slowdown has plunged many airlines into profound financial difficulties. It is clear that some will not survive the turmoil, giving those remaining the opportunity to consolidate their positions. Whether the sector will rationalise along the lines of other industries remains to be seen, but given the strong link between national interests and flag carriers this would seem still to be a long way off. Change will undoubtedly occur, but the neat consolidation of the sector into a few global airlines that many predict is doubtful.

Index